JESSICA HUGHES AND CONTRIBUTORS

Radical Self-Love

How To Ignite Your Light Through Creativity

ILLUMINATED PRESS
BOOK PUBLISHING

First edition

ISBN: 9798858927891

This book was professionally typeset on Reedsy.
Find out more at reedsy.com

Contents

Foreword   vii

Preface   x

I   — Inspire and Ignite —

1   JO DAVIS - Radical Self-Love is Badass   3

2   SUSAYE GREENE - Supremextreme is Maxin' the Millennium   8

3   EKATERINA POPOVA - Surrendering to the Flow   13

4   DAWN BOVA - The Dream: A Message of Radical Self-Love   18

5   LINDA SAMUELS - Forgiveness = Freedom   22

6   IRENE VIVANCO - Replace Selfless Service with This   28

7   SHARON GOODENOUGH - Are We Good Enough Though? We Certainly...   33

8   TAYLER AVA FRIAR - Unlocking the Magic Within: Insights from...   38

9   JENNY SCHUSTER - What If Radical Self-Love Actually Looks...   43

10   TONIA MAJORS - I Choose Joy   48

11   MARIA TEDJAMULIA - Motherhood, Leadership, Love   52

12   RACHEL BUSH - Know and No Love, Radical Self-Acceptance and...   57

13   DIANE HUNT - Deep Connections Through Painting   59

14   LINDA DAMGAARD - Radical Self-Love/Care   64

15 JOANNE ENDERS - Finding the Way to Me   69

16 JANE BELLANTE - Stop, Listen, and Breathe   74

17 DR. ZERRI (DR. Z) GROSS - Pay Me First! With Love   79

18 THERESA ALLEN - Radical Self-love When You are Functioning...   84

19 COURTNEY BARNARD - Our Success Lies Within   89

20 DANIEL COHEN - Loving Who You Are   94

21 KATHY FREDERICK - Self Love Through Scripture   99

22 ANGIE NORDSTRUM - Quitting My Job as an Act of
    Self Care   104

23 ARIELLA COHEN - You are Enough   108

24 CATE RAPHAEL - The Joyful Soul Journey — How I
    Found Radical...   113

25 ESTHER JOY MARUANI - Embracing Self-Care, Setting... 118

26 PRISSY ELROD - How Embracing Loss Created a
    Mosaic of Art...   123

27 KRISTEN HOARD - Sculpting Self-Love: Embracing
    Creativity to...   130

28 KYLE HOLLINGSWORTH - COURAGE: The Key to
    Radical Self-Love &...   136

29 SUSAN PEPLER - Create A Life That ROCKS!   141

30 TAMARA MULKEY - Embrace the Moment and Move   146

31 TINA MARIE ROMERO - Cultivating Self-awareness
    as a Path To...   150

32 JOANN RENNER - Turning Adversity into Positive Life Changes   155

33 LAURIE KORALEWSKI - My Favorite Things   160

34 KAREN STEPHENSON - Creativity Can Ease Your Grief   163

35 SHANNON HEAP - Power of Positivity and Perspective   168

36 WENDY DREWS - Put Your Oxygen Mask on First   174

37 COLLEEN BROWN - Awakening the Financially Empowered Creative...   181

38 CAREY KIRKELLA - The L.E.N.S. Method™ & Connecting with Your...   187

39 REBECCA ROSAS - Radical Self Love Is Listening To Your Heart   193

40 REE FREEMAN, GRIGSBY FREEMAN & WALKER FREEMAN - Reclaim your...   199

41 KELLY CLARK - Unveiling the Menu of Intention   206

42 MAGGIE O'HARA - Artful Affirmations   210

43 ELIZABETH KING - The Dance of Self-love and Fertility 216

44 KIM BRUNSON - Chasing to B Seen   221

45 TRACEY BOWDEN - Finding Your Inner Creative Flow Through...   226

46 DIANA STELIN - Self-Love isn't Selfishness. It's a return to...   231

47 JESSICA HUGHES - Activating Creative Healing and Expression...   236

48 BONNIE McVEE - Soulful Living in Technicolor Grace   241

49 KAT BREEDLOVE - Create a Zine for Your Inner Child   246

50 ANNETTE WALTERS - Finding Me In the Chaos   251

51 MICHAELENE SHANNON - Yes to Love   257

52 EMILY ROSE - What Does Radical Self-Love Mean?   262

53 AMBER PRICE - Finding Focus and Self-Compassion Through...   267

54 PHYLLIS ABBOT - Radical Self Love By Giving Your Body Your...   272

55 MISTY FULGENCIO - Transformation Through Forgiveness of Self...   277

56 DIANA KNEZEVICI - What Happened When I Meditated For 365...   281

57 CAROL ARSCOTT - Living Your Purpose   287

58 JOAN FULLERTON - Radical Self-Discovery   292

59 JENNIFER WATSON - Radical Self Love For Your Heart   298

60 WENDY COOPER - Re-Parenting Your Child Self   303

61 ANNE ALMEIDA - 8 Ways to Love Yourself More   308

About the Author   314

Also by Jessica Hughes and Contributors   316

Foreword

By Christy Whitman

There is a profound connection between your level of love you have for yourself and your power as a creator. And by creator, I'm not only referring to the ability to create great works of art. You are creating – or manifesting – in every situation and relationship you find yourself. And how much you love yourself determines how much you will love what manifests in your life.

Within the personal development space, the term self-love has become something of a cliché. At worst, it's incredibly vague, and at best, it means something different to nearly everyone who writes about it. But self-love is distinct from self-care. It goes far beyond getting a weekly massage or taking a trip to the nail salon. Self-love is a vibration. In fact, it's one of the highest vibrations in all of the universe.

When you're in a state of genuine love and appreciation for yourself, you're in a vibration of spaciousness, worthiness, allowance and flow that puts you in perfect alignment to rendezvous with everything that your life has caused you to ask for. And while it's true that we can sometimes stumble into this heightened state of consciousness by chance, it's wise to learn to cultivate self-love at will and on purpose – not just as a notion, but as a lived and felt experience at all five dimensions of our being.

As human beings, our consciousness exists in five distinct spheres or modes of expressions. It's made up of 1) the perspectives that we hold, 2) the emotions that we feel, 3) the thoughts we think, 4) the words we speak, and 5) the actions we take. *Radical Self-Love: How to Ignite Your Life Through Creativity* will help you to define what it actually means to love yourself in each one of these important layers of your experience.

Self-love is about cultivating a firm belief in our own goodness, as well as faith in the benevolence of this universe in which we were born. It's about listening to, decoding, and acting on the wisdom that our emotions hold for us. Sometimes self-love calls us to say no, to establish rigorous boundaries, or to give ourselves permission to ask for something we need. Ultimately, self-love is about acknowledging that we are, above all else, energetic and vibrational beings, and making a daily commitment to tend to our vibration with the same level of care we extend to our physical bodies.

Imagine getting sixty-three extremely gifted artists, entrepreneurs, transformational coaches and New Thought luminaries together in one place to share what they have found to be the most important actions or principles that you need in order to manifest your heart's desires. That's what Jessica Hughes has done here, in a format that's fun to read and with takeaways that are instantly applicable.

The experts that Jessica has assembled here each offer their unique wisdom as it relates to the many aspects of self-love, and on these pages you'll find tool after tool for releasing the past, transforming your wounds into wisdom, and opening yourself to receive the abundance of life that is your birthright.

The external experiences that we manifest at every moment of our lives always reflect our internal state of consciousness. With the help of the wisdom you'll find on these pages, you'll learn the art of cultivating self-love, which is the key to manifesting any outcome you desire to create.

Christy Whitman

Scottsdale, Arizona

Summer 2023

Preface

As you flip through this book, "Radical Self-Love: How To Ignite Your Light Through Creativity," understand that you're holding in your hands not just pages and ink, but a living tapestry woven with dreams, struggles, triumphs, and most of all, love.

This book is the embodiment of a journey—a journey that sixty-three unique souls, including myself, have embarked upon, to help light the way for you.

We live in a world that often nudges us toward uniformity, even invisibility.

Yet, in our hearts, lies an ever-present ember, a yearning to blaze brilliantly and authentically.

The question is: how can we fan this spark into a roaring flame?

The answer: through creativity.

When 63 visionaries—wellness maestros, groundbreaking artists, impassioned creatives, and innovative business leaders—come together, what transpires is nothing short of alchemy.

This book is a testament to that magic.

Each page is infused with personal tales of transformation, heartfelt testimonies of challenges turned into opportunities, and, most crucially, a treasure trove of actionable guidance designed to inspire and equip you.

It's been said that stories are the most powerful tool we possess, and within these chapters, you'll discover a spectrum of stories that resonate. They are mirrors, windows, and doors. Mirrors that reflect parts of your journey, windows offering glimpses into other worlds, and doors beckoning you toward newfound expanses of self-expression and love.

The essence of creativity is not just to craft art but to sculpt a life that rings true to one's soul. Through our collective experiences, we aim to show that each brushstroke, each note, each word penned, is a step closer to recognizing and celebrating the radiant being that you are.

"Radical Self-Love" is an invitation—a call to immerse yourself in the world of creation, to dance on the edges of your comfort zone, and in doing so, to kindle the luminescent light within.

To love oneself radically is to embrace life fully expressed, with all its chaos, beauty, and infinite potential.

When we engage with our innate creativity, we awaken parts of ourselves that have been dormant. We cast off the shackles of convention, and step into a world where possibilities are endless. It's in these moments that self-love thrives. By immersing ourselves in the act of creation, we allow self-love to emerge, unburdened by judgments or preconceived notions.

However, the journey to radical self-love isn't always linear. It is fraught with detours, speed bumps, and sometimes, roadblocks. But that's where the beauty lies—in the imperfect process, the raw vulnerability, and the unrelenting will to seek one's own truth.

This book is an invitation.

To dare. To dream. To create.

But most importantly, to love oneself with a fierce intensity that illuminates not just our lives, but also the world around us. As you turn the pages, let the words be more than mere words. Let them be catalysts, igniting your light and guiding you towards a life imbued with purpose, passion, and profound self-love.

Join me on this odyssey, not as a passive reader, but as an active participant. Let's embark on a transformative journey together. May this book be your compass, guiding you toward a life where your light doesn't just shine—it dazzles.

Here's to the journey ahead, where creativity and radical self-love intertwine in a way that lights up YOUR soul.

Jessica Hughes & 62 Brilliant Co-Authors

I

— Inspire and Ignite —

Get ready to embark on a daring journey of self-discovery and unlock the awe-inspiring power of radical self-love! These authors share a kaleidoscope of perspectives where boundaries are shattered, and norms are redefined so that you can elevate your relationship... with your amazing self!

1

JO DAVIS - Radical Self-Love is Badass

How to navigate in a world that does not want you to change: the things I wish I had known when I began my radical self-love (RSL) journey.

Yes! You've finally done it! You have made the conscious choice to love yourself madly. You have decided to honor your sacred space, mind, body, and soul with choices that heal and energize you. You have gathered all the great ideas in this book and are ready to launch this rocket called radical self-love (RSL). Congratulations!

Let me stop by saying that this book should have come with a warning label on the front...

Why? Because when you put yourself first and honor your sacred space, some of the people closest to you are going to lose their shit. It's going to get rocky! Stay strong! The payoff for exercising RSL is 100% worth disappointing people who do not deserve your awesome sauce!

Not to be dramatic, but many take this journey because it is "Life or death." Self-preservation is a common theme in this book. I remember the moment I decided that healing myself was more important than being helpful, available, or the world seeing me as a "good person." People pleasing my way through relationships, my soul was aching for authenticity in myself and others. My body was paying the price for years of trying to prove my worth and the cost was full-blown adrenal fatigue. I had poured myself into others for so long that I had completely lost myself. Convinced I must be dying, I took out a third life insurance policy and began sorting through my earthly possessions. Like many of the stories in this book, it took a life-altering event to finally put my health, happiness, and soul work ahead of my ego and insatiable need to be liked and accepted.

Be warned, your personal growth is inconvenient to some and they may not support this badass new you. They like how you put them and their needs ahead of your own. They count on your lifelong commitment to proving you are a "good person." It makes you ripe for asking for favors, borrowing time, money, and self-sacrifice. So when you start exercising that new RSL muscle, it will thin the herd quickly. RSL is the ultimate truth serum. It will show you who on your team wants to see you happy, healthy, and thriving. And it will show you the consumers, opportunists, and everyone showing up for purely self-serving reasons. The more toxic the relationship, the more upset they will get when you deny their wishes. Don't be distracted by the fallout.

When you begin the RSL journey, it looks awkward and messy. You feel unsteady. You are a hot mess. Trust the process. Show up. Own your time and your space. Put on your blinders. Be present for yourself.

Feel into what brings you joy.

When we were children, we understood joy. We sought out joy-filled experiences that fed our souls. We quickly pushed through our fear of rejection and the response of others was none of our business.

Imagine your first middle school dance. (Insert traumatic eighth-grade flashback here.) You start by mustering enough courage to get dressed and walk out your front door. You decide to do a new thing for YOURSELF. Pushing through the sheer terror of getting onto the dance floor, it feels strange to do this new thing, but you take action. You begin timidly moving your body, offbeat, and primarily focused on not injuring anyone around you. Maybe in that moment, you would have given anything for the earth to open under your feet and swallow you whole. But you keep going. After a few minutes, you begin to own your space. You close your eyes and become fully present in the moment. You keep moving.

This process is beautiful and brutal but also essential to your happiness, just like the journey of RSL. Someone in the room will declare, "Who do you think you are??" They will be upset because you dare to take up the space they wanted on the dance floor. They may think you should be on the sidelines serving punch instead of living your best life. Someone is waiting to be offended by this new courageous you. And someone in the room will likely even be jealous. Yes, jealous. Because as you move your body and start having the time of your life? Your face begins to soften. Your body begins to find its rhythm. Your heart opens BIG! You are filled with pure joy. And most importantly, YOU STOP CARING WHO IS WATCHING. This is the dance of RSL.

Be the Rebel. Dig deep.

The words "Radical Self-Love" stir up images of rebellion. We see the exhausted mom setting fire to piles of dirty laundry in the front yard and driving away to get a mani-pedi. All the while, the girl power music is booming in the background. Or maybe you imagine the guy telling his boss to shove it, packing up his red stapler, and moving to a generic beach town. The closing scene shows him drinking a fruity drink as the credits roll. But if only real life worked that way?...

In real life, this process isn't glamorous. It's gritty and it takes a rebel to say no when you mean no. To opt out of events and gatherings that are draining and not fulfilling, to speak your feelings, set boundaries, and take back your weekends to recharge instead of fulfilling the wants of others. Stay consistent, be kind, and operate from a space of integrity. People will be ready to test your tenacity. They will call you selfish, guilt you, and tempt your inner people-pleaser to cave into old habits. Dig Deep. Imagine that your life depends on this because it does.

Keep it simple.

Make this your new mantra. **"Does this moment honor my sacred space and serve my highest good?"** Ask yourself this in every conversation, social media interaction, the food you eat, and how you spend your time. If it doesn't fill your heart, heal you, or bring you joy? Walk away.

"If I only had five years left to live? Would I waste one more second doing THIS? Would I remain here in this moment?" If the answer is "HELL NO!" the words will hang there in the room. The feeling will be inescapable. You might feel tightness in your shoulders and neck, a dull headache, or even an upset stomach. When I ask myself this question, the answer comes back black or white. I either feel warmth in my heart and gratitude for the moment. Or, I want to claw my way out. Pay attention. Your body is always talking to you.

The people that love you for you will celebrate this new season of your life. The people who have only shown up to meet THEIR needs will get frustrated with you and eventually move on. Let them go! Make room for more incredible people and new epic experiences. You have one life to live. It is your responsibility to take good care of it. Doing so will attract other badass souls who respect and care about you without unrealistic expectations.

Jo Davis is a #1 International Best-Selling author, speaker, gifted intuitive, adventure addict, and the Founder of Lift A Sister Up – an organization driven by the belief that our highest calling is to support and inspire other women to chase their dreams both personally and professionally. Jo is a highly gifted intuitive with over 150,000 followers and students. Believing that everyone has these powerful gifts, she shows ordinary people how to tap into their intuitive superpower through her one-on-one sessions and her course, "Big Mess to Big Magic." Her clients include world thought leaders, best-selling authors, and Grammy Award Winning Artists.

She is also a world-renowned artist and owner of Sky Soul Photography, Sky Soul Art, and Jo Davis Art, showcasing over a thousand pieces of work with clients worldwide.

2

SUSAYE GREENE - Supremextreme is Maxin' the Millennium

Who knew, when I was a little girl, that one day I would become the last member of the Supremes, to sign to Motown Records?!

Make no mistake; it's not easy being Supreme. There's all that big hair to be responsible for, and of course, there is the great expectation to shine. Even on rainy days, when one wishes to curl up in a big chair and binge-watch something inconsequential, there are interviews, rehearsals, meetings, or travel to distant lands. Once a Supreme, always a Supreme, they say. Regardless of my continued dreams and path in life, that is a running theme of my destiny, and it continues to inspire me in many ways.

One of the greatest blessings in my life has always been inspiration. As a child, my mother would sit me down, put a canvas and a paintbrush in my hand, and I was ready to go. She knew where to find me for the next several hours. Or, she'd take me to the library, where I was allowed to read anything. Unencumbered by restrictions, I wandered through the halls of my imagination and the skill of great storytelling and reference books.

As a creative, I've always been affected by things that have inspired me wholly: weather, color, sunshine, large bodies of water, flowers, trees, animals, children, faces, air, sky, and challenges. I immerse myself in any activities that ignite my passion and urge to create. That is why I've never been lost, looking for a key to open my own imagination.

From time to time, imagination has flooded through me with such surety and velocity, that it has astonished me. I have a huge capacity to give. Now that I'm older and more experienced, I'm delighted to find the spark inside me still – one that lights up my life, and hopefully the lives of others,(because I do love to inspire others). It comes from a deep desire to take extremely good care of my soul and spirit.

As the sixth child in America diagnosed with Lupus, my sister Jade died at 12. I realized two things then: a child's viewpoint is largely ignored during times of great distress, and that we all have only one life to live. Because of that, I began to push my limits of creativity to the furthest degree possible. As a child who lost her best friend and hero to Lupus, I dug deeply into my own self-care at 6 years old by digging into what I was most confident in – my creativity.

I have had extraordinary blessings in my life, and I've never been without the simple things that bring me peace, in spite of troubled times. I'm a great believer in faith, knowing that creativity and the outpouring of that are what have made my life so joyous and full.

Opportunity has fallen into my path time and again. I haven't been afraid to try new things. That is how I wound up singing with such wonderful artists as Ray Charles, Stevie Wonder, The Rolling Stones, Quincy Jones, and The Supremes, and writing hit songs for the likes of Michael Jackson, Deniece Williams, and many other brilliant creative people.

At this point in my life, I believe I need to push even more deeply because there are so many outside influences, and so many tides of change; since not all of them are joyful, I dig deeper. I look for things I haven't done before and I look for a new way to do things I have done, in a new way.

I feel blessed to have been born in this remarkable time, when art and artists who have never had much opportunity have found many, because of technology. There are new universes to explore: Web3, Blockchain, Cryptocurrency, NFTs, Artificial Intelligence, and the Metaverse, all of which are serious passions of mine now.

I am intent upon leaning solidly into the future, enjoining these new realms, with my imagination and digital 3D art and animation. The tools have finally met up with our present creative landscape. The artistic Renaissance is once again a blissful playground for any creative brave enough to jump in.

For my own sake, my own humanistic healing, and my own spiritual self-care and growth, I leap forward! I was told as a young artist, that I could never be able to compete with the Disneys of the world. Because of Artificial Intelligence many of us will outpace what was and is the status quo of the creative arts. We can do things that were never possible before.

It's given me a chance, as a person who has always reached for the highest criterion of creativity in the healing space in front of me. The fire I have been able to stoke in myself has led to million-selling projects, paintings from my fantasy, inclusion in films, concerts, and other continued projects and opportunities. Which creative person wouldn't dream of doing that, all in an entirely new way? Who wouldn't put a hand or a foot out, daring to jump into this future? Who wouldn't fly now, given the inspiration and support?

Creativity has been the key always; lighting a fire under my world, and there are so many things to come. There are many mountains to climb, paintings to paint, photos to take, and music to construct. New films, new ways to make them, new ways to function. At the core, and in spite of how all these things will help all of us, I will continue to create for myself – for my own personal joy, and self-care.

I suggest to all creative people to go firmly into the future, and quickly. Many older people stagnate because they do not have enough that interests them and challenges them, passionately.

I am sure many people do not recognize the importance of their destiny. I believe you must recognize your destiny, and pin it to the top of your life to-do list because recognizing your place in destiny gives you the confidence of spirit, direction, purpose, determination, and the courage to move forward with your passion.

Knowing you are a part of destiny gives you the freedom to move on your instinctual path! You were meant to do this – to shine from your wildest heart and fly as a leader of creativity. In essence, you must trust yourself. Trusting in your intuitive guide will take you where you deserve and are meant to go.

Now is the time – as if a portal had opened in the sky of everything you ever reached for, presented as a life gift. If you can reach inward and find courage now, there is no reason to fear anything and you can gain everything you have dreamed of.

We will continue to move forward, snatching up opportunities that surely build our spirits and the soul of creativity. We are the newest creators of the newest age of humanity, steering our own ships into a future of exploration, dreams accomplished, and destiny fulfilled. Trusting our path is our greatest legacy.

Susaye Greene is the last member of the Supremes signed to Motown Records. She is an accomplished song writer, singer, story teller and tech entrepreneur. Susaye was honored by the Motown Museum as an innovator and influencer.

Susaye has traveled the world with Ray Charles and as Stevie Wonder's featured soloist. Of her many accomplishments, she wrote Michael Jackson's hit song "Can't Help It" with Stevie Wonder. She is also featured in Spike Lee's "Michael Jackson's Journey From Motown to Off The Wall."

She is the co-Founder of Capital Code, a tech and media company, and President of Dollface Records and Dollface Music International.

Susaye is passionate about spending time with her grandchildren, supporting STEM, Space Science, Tech, and is an AI VR enthusiast. She is also developing games and animated 3D films for Web3 and building in the Metaverse.

3

EKATERINA POPOVA - Surrendering to the Flow

Sometimes we feel like we're going backward to leap forwards.

Sometimes, it feels like we're moving backward before experiencing a massive shift in life, art, or business. Have you ever noticed this? Suddenly, everything you've worked so hard for seems to be washed away. You watch as the shores of your life recede, perhaps desperately trying to cling to what appears to be moving further and further away. The harder you try to grasp it and hold on, the more painful it becomes.

A radical act of self-love may be the willingness to let go and surrender to the season of change. When I embarked on my art and entrepreneurship journey in 2013, I was obsessed with growth, progress, and checking off boxes. While I believe in expanding and reaching our fullest potential, I have also learned to recognize that, like nature, we have our seasons and cycles.

Art show after art show, I began to manifest dream opportunities, achieve business milestones, attract events, clients, and followers. The problem was that I was happy when I saw these results, but I quickly got down on myself when things weren't happening fast enough. Progress sometimes slows down because we have outgrown our current chapter, and it's time to move on. This can feel scary and uncomfortable, but it's necessary.

If you're ready for the next level (and you are, since you're reading this), maybe the only thing standing in your way is the anchor you're clinging onto. Anchors can take different forms, from relationships to habits or behaviors. In some cases, we are ready for bigger opportunities, but we're forcing the old ways to work when they have simply expired. In my case, it has often been the fear of disappointing someone and people-pleasing.

When we stand in front of a sandy shore and watch the waves flow in and out, we don't worry about their return. We trust and know that they will. Sometimes they come back with greater force, delightfully splashing us with cool water or even sweeping us off our feet. Those moments at the beach are joyful, like playing tag with nature.

However, cultivating this level of trust is sometimes challenging in our daily lives. We worry when things are being "taken away" that we did something wrong or "manifested" trouble upon ourselves.

Here's what I know to be true: I understand that the Universe, God, is good. And yes, we can make mistakes, self-sabotage, and even manifest undesirable things, but it's all happening for us. When I reflect on my life and all the incredible opportunities I have experienced, many of them followed a season of disappointment or even crushing defeats.

Allow the waves of life in this season to carry away what is heavy, not aligned, or expired. Allow these shimmering waters to wash away what's no longer yours and make room for new creations, ideas, and growth. It's simply too much to hold on so tightly, so go ahead and allow your hands to relax, release, and watch as everything is carried away for the highest good of all.

Have you been saying yes to projects that feel draining?

Have you allowed people, situations, and patterns to rob you of your joy and freedom?

Have you felt trapped by how things are, not letting go to bring necessary changes to your life?

What personal expenses (financial or energetic) have you allowed to continue that are not producing the desired outcomes?

What projects have you agreed to that are not a full-body "hell yes"?

Can you donate clothes or items to make space in your life?

Imagine yourself standing on the golden shores, reflecting on this season. Picture yourself letting go of the clutter. Take each of the things that weigh you down and imagine them as smooth sea rocks you can throw into the water. They belong there; it's safe to let them go. Decide to fulfill outstanding commitments, as you always act with integrity, and then let it all go.

Call in what your soul is craving as you feel lighter and lighter. More time to write, paint, sing, dance, cook—whatever brings you ultimate bliss. Perhaps it's a day trip to a local town where you can discover new inspiration for your art or meet an old friend for a hike.

Know that the Universe is supporting you because it created you. It knows what you deeply desire and wants to give it to you as soon as you let go.

Once you have a clear image of the new season, it's time to put it down on paper. In a journal or on a new page, write down the new ideas, projects, and art you will create. You can make a collage or a Pinterest board with the latest chapter. Create a juicy playlist that puts you in the mood to dream and do.

Know that whatever you desire is possible for you. Know that it's already done. The metaphorical shore is always here for you, ready to bring you blessings and take the burden off your back when the load has gotten too heavy. Let this next part of your journey be light and playful.

Ekaterina Popova is an award-winning artist, entrepreneur, master coach, and advocate for women in the arts. As the founder and editor-in-chief of Create! Magazine, Ekaterina has created a platform that showcases emerging and established artists, providing them with a platform to share their work and stories.

Her dedication to promoting women artists and creative entrepreneurs led her to establish the Art Queens Society, a coaching service and community that aims to uplift and support women in the arts.

Popova's art has been exhibited internationally at galleries such as Cohle Gallery in Paris, Menorca, Art Miami Fairs, James Oliver Gallery in Philadelphia, and more. Her paintings explore themes of home, identity, vulnerability, and the human experience. In addition, her work has been featured in various blogs and publications, including Colossal, Beautiful Bizarre, American Art Collector, The Jealous Curator, DPI Magazine, Friend of The Artist, Iceview, and The Philadelphia Inquirer.

Ekaterina is a co-author of The Complete Smartist Guide and The Creative Business Handbook. Drawing on her own experiences and expertise, she helps artists and creatives navigate the complexities of the art world and develop strategies for success.

4

DAWN BOVA - The Dream: A Message of Radical Self-Love

Have you ever had a dream that's so powerful it stays with you for years to come? Six years ago, in the fall of 2016, I lay awake in bed, my heart heavy with grief. I was searching for anything that could connect me with my son, Brad, who had tragically passed away. It was during this time of deep sorrow that I received a message, not an ordinary message, but one from one of my son's friends, a young woman who received a gift she knew she needed to share with me.

As I spoke to this beautiful soul, she shared with me a dream or vision that had left an indelible mark on her heart. In her dream, she described a hazy, dark, and rainy day on the otherwise sunny coast of Florida. Everything was shrouded in shades of grey, and the air was cold and damp. But amidst the gloom, she noticed a faint light in the distance. Intrigued, she began walking towards it, step by step, drawn to its ethereal glow.

As she approached, the light appeared brighter, and she saw a magnificent array of rainbow colors shining down in a single beam, illuminating a solitary spot in the sand. As she moved closer, there, in the midst of the radiant light, she saw the figure of a young man. It was Brad. A huge beaming smile spread across his face, the glowing lights danced around him, he was glowing. As he turned towards her he simply said, "It's beautiful here. Tell everyone I love ya, and I'll see you soon."

As she described this vision or dream, I could picture every detail. The weight of grief that had consumed me every waking moment began to lift. The dream, with its vivid imagery and Brad's loving message, brought me comfort and solace. It became a beacon of hope, a reminder that love transcends the boundaries of life and death.

This dream, with its profound impact, became a turning point in my healing journey. I realized that my life could not be squandered on feelings of loss, lack, and loneliness. I made a conscious decision to embrace radical self-love, to nurture and care for myself in ways I had neglected before.

One of the ways I began expressing myself was through painting. I have discovered that when I allow myself to be fully immersed in artistic endeavors, the light inside me begins to glow. It grows bigger and brighter with each stroke of the brush, each word penned on paper. Through art, I've found a channel for my emotions, a means to process my grief and transform it into something beautiful.

But radical self-love isn't just about creativity; it encompasses all aspects of my life. It demands self-care, giving myself permission to take time for stillness and reflection. Meditating, finding solace in the quiet moments of introspection, listening to music that stirs my soul, allowing the melodies to uplift and inspire me are all important aspects of my radical self-love journey. I love long walks in nature, connecting with the world around me and finding peace in its beauty. Creativity helps me light the internal fire and my desire for radical self-love.

Radical self-love also means embracing new experiences and forming deep, rooted connections with people. I honor the relationships I had with those

I knew and loved, cherishing every moment spent together. But I also open myself up to new connections, meeting people who enrich my life in unexpected ways. Each day is an opportunity to forge new bonds, to learn from others, and to grow as an individual.

In this journey of radical self-love, I am discovering the importance of gratitude. I realize that every day, every moment is a gift. I appreciate simple joys, laughter shared with loved ones, the warmth of the sun on my skin, and the beauty that surrounds me. Gratitude has become a guiding force, reminding me to live life to the fullest, to seize every opportunity, and to embrace the present moment with open arms.

So, I invite you to join me on the path of radical self-love. Gift yourself the love and care you deserve. Embrace your creativity, your passions, and your unique voice. Take time for self-reflection, for stillness, and for nurturing your soul. Form deep connections with those you love, and be open to the magic of new connections. And above all, cultivate gratitude for the gift of life and the beauty that exists within and around you.

Because, my friend, "It's beautiful here" and I know with all my heart, that "I'll see ya soon."

Dawn Bova is a multi-talented artist, best-selling author, and healer whose

work has touched the lives of thousands. Rooted in faith, she brings a unique perspective to her intuitive paintings, illuminating the depths of her soul with every stroke. Her dedication to helping those impacted by substance use and grief is a testament to her strength and compassion, and her own experiences with recovery and loss have given her a profound understanding of the healing power of art.

5

LINDA SAMUELS - Forgiveness = Freedom

I'm going to start this by saying that I've survived two long term relation-ships, both ending atrociously, but still managed to stay out of prison. So, there's that.

I often get looks (you know the ones where they squint their eyes, give their head a little shake) when I tell them that I'm very close to my ex-husband's wife. Or more recently when I say that I'm still friends with my ex-boyfriend of 10 years.

I'm not going to get into the psychology of forgiveness or talk about scientific mindset. You have Google for that. This chapter isn't meant to air my dirty laundry, or to make anyone close to me uncomfortable. It's meant to explain how I was able to move past the pain of betrayal and create healthy and loving relationships with all parties involved. But bombs are gonna drop, there's just no way around it.

Let's begin with my ex-husband. We were married for twenty years; our marriage had what I'd call a bipolar quality to it. We couldn't get on the same page, at the same time. We did get two gorgeous daughters from this marriage, and subsequently three adorable grandbabies. When he told me he was leaving, my reaction was sheer disbelief. Even though we were rocky at best, we were forever, right? Wrong. I realized that he wanted out, and the reason why didn't matter. He wanted out and I wanted in. Marriage is not a life sentence, and sometimes, it just doesn't work. We divvied up our assets and went our separate ways.

When I found out he had a girlfriend, I watched my ego, self-esteem and self-worth go swirling around the vortex down the toilet. (Insert crying emoji here) To say it was gut wrenching having to drop off our daughter at what used to be our home, is putting it mildly. His girlfriend's car would be parked in the driveway and the thought of slashing her tires did not escape me, not gonna lie. Fast forward several months, and I'm waiting in my car for our daughter to come out and I see her car. As I sat there, staring at it, I thought "Huh. I don't feel the urge to smash into the side of her car today." And just like that, the anger, the bitterness, and resentment were released.

How I got to this point took time and a lot of inner work. In fact, I went through a phase where I feel I earned a spot in the Guinness Book of World Records for repeating the same curse word. I'd love to share that with you here, but it would likely get the book banned, so you'll have to fill in the blank with your word of choice. Make it count.

Truth is, I lost him to another woman. I didn't lose him to an accident, or a disease. He was still here, healthy, and a great dad to our kids. That thought floated in and out of my mind constantly. Life happens. Shit happens. Nobody wakes up one morning and decides that's the day they're going to end their marriage. It builds up and it takes two. It takes two to make it work and it takes two to break it down. Let that sink in for a sec.

Our daughter was planning her wedding and at this point, I had not met his beloved. In fact, I did everything I could to avoid them. I shopped at stores I knew they would never go to. The last thing I wanted was to turn my cart into the next aisle and be faced with them and be like…"Oh hey!"…Awkward AF.

We wanted to throw our daughter an engagement party and I thought, she's only having one wedding so she's only having one engagement party. With that mindset, I reached out to my ex and arranged a meeting. I may have consumed a few glasses of wine prior. Don't judge. I wanted to put our differences aside and make this party a success for her. And that's what I did.

While at family events, we would always find our way next to each other. It wasn't long before I realized that I really f'kn liked her! I got to know her as a real person, rather than an illusion of her that I had conjured up in my mind. She makes him happy and is great with our girls, what else matters?

I was judged on how I handled our breakup. And not in a good way. Most couldn't understand why I chose to handle it the way I did. It's easy. We had kids. Kids who didn't ask for any of this. People will think and say what they want and that's okay. You do you, and I'll do me. Honestly, the only thing I had in my arsenal was a positive mindset. Your mindset is the number one tool that will get you through **anything** life throws at you. At the end of that year, my daughter sent me a text. It read, "You have come through this year with class, and your dignity intact. For this, I am proud to call you my mother". Wow!

We are now an imperfectly perfectly blended family, and I can say that I love him, and I love his wife. If anything, other than keeping my sanity, how I decided to handle this, taught my daughters the importance of forgiveness.

My ten-year relationship is a different story. This was a complete blindsided hit. It knocked me straight into another time zone, let alone another week. But just because this wasn't a marriage, or that we didn't share children together, didn't mean that I would wash my hands of him. I'm either a f'kn idiot or I truly like having peace in my life.

This happened five months to the day of the start of this chapter, so the wound is still gaping. Because no two scenarios are the same, I couldn't apply the exact same thought process as before. So, I turned my frequency dial to positive and let my mindset do the rest.

What I was able to do was separate myself from the situation to try and understand what he was feeling. (I'll explain later). I focused on helping him heal and tried my best to listen. What happened didn't change how I felt about him, it changed how I felt about our relationship.

I came up with an analogy for those who have been cheated on. Let's say your partner wants to go to the casino. Being a non-gambler (if they are chronic gamblers, this analogy won't work, so move onto the next paragraph) They decide on an amount of money that they are prepared to lose. Let's say, $100. You've now become that $100. When they decided to cheat, you were a risk that was worth taking. Don't ever settle to be someone's hundred bucks.

Alone on New Year's Eve, I made a vow to myself. Not what will 2023 bring me, but **what will I bring to 2023**. Writing this chapter is part of that. I also booked a women's healing retreat in Scotland and will spend another full week on my own, exploring the countryside and doing some serious whiskey tasting. All by my beautiful self. ♥

As an artist, I am only able to create when my soul is in receiving mode, which is another reason why being able to forgive is so important to me. Otherwise, y'all would be looking at blank canvases!

It's important to know that this is not linear, in that it's not a straight line from point A to point B. It takes time, patience and practice. A huge help in getting there is through meditation. A simple morning and night meditation helps keep you grounded and acts as a reminder of what's truly important in life.

One thing I know for sure, is that my spirit is set free with forgiveness. People come and go your entire life. You are your only constant. Treat yourself with kindness and allow yourself forgiveness.

I know I said I wouldn't become all scientific and stuff, but a fellow artist/author friend of mine, Nishah Dennison, shared a presentation she did on Mirror Neurons. She wrote: *"... mirror neurons are brain cells that help us understand what someone else is feeling. They assist us to recognize a feeling and relate to it..."* She continues to say: *"Interestingly, reminded by creative's, highly sensitive people often have mirror neurons that are more active than usual, so have greater empathy: greater ability to absorb the feelings in others."* And there you have it, boys and girls, my main component in forgiveness.

I sleep better at night because of this and know that I'm out there living my best life.

I wake up each morning feeling as fresh as a daisy, as opposed to a pissed-on dandelion.

Be free, my queens. x

Canadian abstract figurative artist Linda Samuels' passion for boldness and color characterizes her work. A native of Montreal QC, she now resides in Kingston, ON, where she works out of her home studio.

Linda is an award-winning, self-taught artist, who started her abstract journey in 2018. Her ability to mesh figuration with abstraction is evident in her series of paintings, a compelling collection titled Empowerment. Her collection shows the many emotional challenges facing women. Linda has the capability to transfer the emotion from the subject onto the canvas, allowing the viewer a glimpse into the subject's world.

Linda Samuels is a co-author of the internationally #1 bestselling "The Creative Life Book". In 2021, Linda's Empowerment work was exhibited at the Florence Biennale, which was followed by a digital exhibition at M.A.D.S. Gallery in Milan. Subsequently, part of this collection was featured in House & Garden UK.

6

IRENE VIVANCO - Replace Selfless Service with This

I've become a radical. I walked away from my belief in selfless service. Since the age of 5, I had wanted to be a teacher. After earning my teaching credential, Masters in Education, and teaching in multiple schools, I found myself depleted, depressed, heartbroken, and confused. I had the best intentions, and yet playing the part of a selfless servant wasn't working. I had to find a better way to serve.

I once heard, When you squeeze an orange, you get orange juice, and when you squeeze an apple, you get apple juice. When we are operating from a place of feeling selfless and perhaps even an undertone of unworthiness, what squeezes out of us for others? And once we are squeezed, what is left? Is that truly of service to humanity? I want to be filled with so much love and compassion and desire and joy, for myself, that whenever someone is in my presence, I am oozing with self-love. And when I get squeezed, either in a warm embrace or in a moment of tension, what kind of juice do I want to flow out of me and onto the other? For me, it is the juice of love, which will only come from that radical self-love of SELF-FUL service.

I am now leading a revolution—to end the era of selfless service and step into

SELF-FUL service. We can serve with greater impact and longer influence from a place of **FUL**fillment. It is not selfish or self-centered to love yourself. It is the most abundant and loving thing you can do for yourself and for humanity. I will share 2 Buddhist teachings that helped me to learn to embrace myself at the heart of LOVE.

When I am trying to love others out of selfless service, I am less for myself to make more for others. It is transactional, and in the process, I deplete my reserves. There is a more effective way. It is the way of **interdependent co-arising**. We are dependent on each other to rise together. The more I am filled, the more I fill others. Together, we rise.

How do we make this shift? By focusing on **the 4 immeasurables: love, compassion, joy, and equanimity.** When we practice the 4 immeasurables, begin with an inward focus, on self first. Remember that, with interdependent co-arising, what I do for one, I do for all, so I will start with myself, knowing that it will impact all.

The beauty of the 4 immeasurables is captured in the very name— they are non-measurable, non-quantifiable, the realm of abundance. When we remember this, we see the folly of selfless service. We were using transactional service to try to achieve an immeasurable result.

And I know, we do it with the best intentions. I was a true believer in selfless service: "I will have less so others may have more. I will give to others instead of giving to myself. I will prioritize others' needs before my own. I will think about myself less, about myself even last..." People-pleasing and performing in service of others. It takes a while before we realize the error in this way of functioning. At first, it feels noble and successful and people admire you and come to you for help. It feels good and honorable. But it is like gliding through the air when you think you are flying. Eventually, when you need extra lift, you realize you can't. You are depleted, and you start free-falling. In that fall, you realize you don't have the skills to lift yourself

29

up, and perhaps, in a way, it was an illusion that you were serving others as well as you had thought. You were offering a counterfeit version of love, one that was transactional instead of immeasurable, and one that did not see the interdependence of humanity's rising.

After this fall, you rebuild yourself, this time, with the engine of love, compassion, joy and equanimity. You build the engine of SELF-FUL service, of honoring your energies and your desires and all that is good in you. You fill your tank, and this time, you soar. You bring love inward. This creates systemic change that will not only bring you up in love but will fuel those around you with love. It creates the radical transformation you seek.

So how do we practice SELF-FUL service with the 4 immeasurables? Here are some suggestions to begin filling yourself with, and transforming yourself through, radical self-love:

Self Love:

- **Offer yourself loving touch**. For me, this has looked like touching my throat, my arms, or my heart space when I feel agitated.
- **Honor your journey** by owning your life story. Remember the strengths of each of your past stages in life and honor your past self/inner child. Look at pictures of yourself from the past and write letters to your younger or future self.
- **Move your body** and honor what it needs. Hiking in nature, yoga, dancing, swimming, wiggling your toes, shaking your arms out, etc. Feed yourself delicious and healthy food.

Self Compassion:

- **Acknowledge your emotions** and process them. Find an Emotions Wheel online and download it. Learn the names of emotions and how they feel. Give yourself time and permission to cry or scream and journal and move in safe spaces. Many of the things you feel guilty or ashamed of come from conditioning outside of you. Release the blame and offer yourself loving words of compassion and understanding, like you would for a friend. Forgive.

· **Allow time for rest**, calm, silence, and even playfulness and creativity. It's easy to get sucked into your roles in your family and career and other obligations, but also give yourself ample time for boredom, quiet, and peace. The beauty of music comes from the interplay between sounds and silences.

Self Joy:

· **Admit that you have desires** and things you want. Keep a list of ALL the things you want and the things you have already. Make it a big, juicy, extravagant list, and keep adding to it over time. Express gratitude for these desires in you, they are good.
· **Give yourself permission** to use time and space and money to invest in things that light you up. You are worth it.

Self Equanimity:

· **Breathe deeply** to give yourself space and calmness.
· **Honor the present moment**. Rather than focusing on the past and feeling depression, or focusing on the future and feeling anxiety, build awareness about what IS in this present moment.

Dig into yourself with curiosity and love. Learn practices to honor your energy as you evolve. Bringing love into yourself is the revolutionary and radical catalyst for the kind of love that we all truly desire. To better serve the world, simply begin practicing the 4 immeasurables with an inward focus of radical self-love.

Want to dig into the 4 Immeasurables and other Self Love Practices? Let's

VIVA YOUR VISION.

Irene Vivanco is a best-selling author, public speaker and the founder of Viva Your Vision. As an online course coach, she guides impassioned entrepreneurs to create custom programs that impact the world with their wisdom. She does this by combining her curriculum design skills from her Masters Degree in Education with her deep sense of compassion, stemming from her own journey of self discovery. Through her coursework, coaching, books, and involvement with the DFW Women's Club, she empowers women to honor their energy and their personal story to tap into their feminine gifts.

7

SHARON GOODENOUGH - Are We Good Enough Though? We Certainly Are!

Would you do it? You know, that thing you're passionate about, that thing you have talked about for so long but put off?

You have that knowing inside you, what would it mean if you could take that leap of faith and do it anyway?

What if your life depended on it, would you do it then? Well, it does......

So, there he was, a giant standing right in front of me, I don't think I had ever seen anyone this huge before. We were on a break, and this was our opportunity to get a copy of his book signed. "Awaken the Giant Within," had been launched the year before and I was on a four-day seminar led by this incredible, transformative coach. The weekend included a guided meditation, a firewalk, and a lot of deep soul-searching, this was day two and for me, at 23 years old, it was absolutely life-changing. Grieving the loss of the family unit I craved so much, following my parents' divorce six years previous, that weekend brought me back into the light and Tony Robbins gave us all the strategies and beliefs that we can overcome anything if we put our minds to it. His message was "Live life with Passion".

Fast forward to my early forties. My son was at school and I had some time back to fulfill my passion and get creative. My mind and body, however, had been hijacked and perimenopause had moved in. I didn't understand what was happening to me; there was a gradual decline in my energy coupled with low mood and although I felt I had absolutely nothing to feel sad about, hopelessness and despair emerged. My husband was and still is my rock but even he was wondering where his happy wife had gone. My doctor's solution was antidepressants. I knew I wasn't depressed, so I refused them and stumbled through the next few years trying every homeopathic remedy, cream, gel, and supplement, while still gaining weight and feeling defeated. The anxiety and night sweats kicked in, and then came the palpitations. Not knowing anyone else who was experiencing this, I felt exhausted, overweight, despondent, and alone.

Initially help arrived in the form of HRT for me and once my energy levels were restored, I was slowly able to start moving forward again. The other symptoms reduced and eventually eased off completely. My mood lifted back up to its optimistic self and my creativity returned. My confidence, however, had taken a massive knock and the thought of showing any of my artwork filled me with dread. Was it good enough? I cringed at the thought of people judging it. My husband and close friends urged me to exhibit and were convinced I had an audience for it. Remaining doubtful, I enrolled in several art courses – again convincing myself it was essential to improve my skills first. In reality, I was procrastinating in perfectionism and paralyzed by fear of rejection.

It was time to get a coach. I couldn't navigate all these changes to my body alone. I was determined to lose weight and get fit; however, nothing worked the same as it used to. The solution presented itself to me, Claire & James Davies from "The Midlife Mentors". Over the coming months, they held my hand through some massive personal challenges, I lost weight through precise exercise and nutrition for my midlife body and I felt strong. However, the weight loss wasn't the overriding triumph – the biggest transformation for me was my mindset. New neural pathways were formed, allowing me to maintain healthy habits along with the clarity and acceptance of myself I needed to continue healing during this chrysalis phase. As I continued the work - healing the inner child, being kind to myself, and letting go of perfectionism, an amazing ripple effect touched every other aspect of my life, and everything began to flow.

Painting became a portal for allowing my vulnerability to flow through me and onto the canvas. I felt a sense of freedom about my work and while I now accepted that not everyone would like it, I knew that with a little faith, my people would come. Releasing my paintings into the world and remaining detached from the outcome was incredibly liberating. I asked myself more helpful questions about my artwork and if I was still unsure, I practiced gratitude for the freedom and support I had been given to create. Realizing that the objective wasn't to make art, it was to be in a beautiful state first that makes art inevitable.

Opportunities started presenting themselves to me, collectors wanted to buy my work, and I knew that to move further forward I had to really move outside my comfort zone and into growth.

But first, how do we move forward creatively if we are feeling stuck or paralyzed by fear?

If we can at least accept who we are with our self-doubt and fears, we somehow change the energy of it, and it has less power over us. Have you ever thought how it would feel if you never created anything again? If that makes you happy then it's entirely your decision because "*our desire to create must be greater than our fear of it.*"

So, do you still wish to create? Fantastic!

1. BREAK IT DOWN: Let's break it down into small pieces and lower the expectations for a start. This is the beginning, and it doesn't define us. For example: a simple drawing, a small canvas, a short poem/story, or a few lines.

2. MOVE ON: Complete this first project and move on to the next one. This next piece is a stepping stone to the following work. As we continue along this path it's helpful to view what we're working on as an exploration.

3. PLAY: Whatever the outcome is, we will learn something that will be useful which will benefit the next piece. There are no expectations and this is a time for play and with a playful spirit, it's easier to create from a beautiful state.

4. KEEP IT FLOWING: Challenge yourself to create something small every day for a week and then keep going. You'll notice the difference in the work when you frame it this way too. With a playful heart and an open mind everything that you want to achieve in life is available to you — it's already here. Keep practicing and it will evolve naturally.

We are all brave, we can overcome hard things but moving outside of what's comfortable can be nerve-wracking. How incredible is that feeling though, that feeling when you have achieved something you never thought possible, something that was incredibly important to you, you experienced some discomfort and you pushed yourself through it and into GROWTH. It's these wonderful moments when we gift ourselves that radical self-love and find the magic waiting for us with open arms on the other side...hold that feeling and repeat it again and again, WARNING: it becomes addictive!

From these magic moments, like the cocooned chrysalis **we've transformed, we've grown and it's our time to fly**. Good Luck.

Sharon Goodenough is a British fine artist specialising in marine artwork, her seascapes with expansive skies are inspired by nature and touched by light.

In Sharon's early career, she worked as a makeup artist for celebrities and emerging musicians where her work appeared in the national press and on album covers. More recently Sharon's paintings have been represented by a gallery in Madrid, she has exhibited internationally and has been published in several articles around her journey to becoming a full-time artist, inspiring others along the way to follow their passion. Sharon's most recent article can be found in Artist & Illustrators Magazine, Summer Edition where she appears as a guest columnist sharing tips on "How she makes it work," as a full-time artist.

8

TAYLER AVA FRIAR - Unlocking the Magic Within: Insights from an Art Historian

Sometimes people ask me questions about how I've built the life I have now. While it's not practically perfect in every way (and what life is?), what I can tell you is that it is filled to the brim with what can only be described as abundant magic.

I'm not kidding.

Over the last decade, I've built a beautiful life gathering a community of friends across Europe, Asia, and Africa - and now find myself curating a vision of home between Mexico and Paris. Over the years I've found ways to live in gorgeous flats with skyline views, private countryside estates with yoga studios, usually with cute animal companions included, and more often than not it hasn't cost me a penny. If you were to take a snapshot of my day-to-day life, you'll probably find me tucked in the corner of a quaint cafe somewhere having an almond cappuccino and writing. At dinner parties, I've been known to respond to ordinary questions about myself with: "Well, I sat next to a woman at the nail shop and by the time we finished our pedicures, she invited me to Vienna", or "I met a guy out salsa dancing... turns out he was a prince!"

I can't make this stuff up.

By the way, before we go any further, here is a list of things that I'm not: an Instagram model, an actual model, a trust-funder, manipulator, over-the-top extrovert, show-off, delusional, or Rihanna. All of these are fine things to be - quite possibly great to be if you are Rihanna - but, I just don't qualify.

So what am I? I'm an art historian. Simple.

Having a job dedicated to investigating great creatives past and present has added light to my life like I've never imagined. However, the biggest revelation that attracts magic into my space is grounded in realizing that we are not so different from the artists we admire. So okay, I'll never paint like Monet or produce soulful poetry like Maya Angelou. But when I'm out living life, facing challenges, or having moments of uncertainty, I remind myself: Monet wasn't always *the* Monet. And Angelou wasn't always *the* Doctor Maya Angelou. Like us, they had *moments* of magic that they seized, that helped shape their creative journey - and most of those moments involved connecting with others.

For a while now, I've made it my business to build heaps of knowledge on these important junctures of choice. And when it matters, I draw from artists' stories to help me persist on my own. Keeping in mind that this is all very personal and subjective, here are three tips I apply in my own life that you can use to infuse more magic into yours.

Tip 1: Say hello
Since leaving home in 2013, I've arrived in countless countries without knowing a single person. Yet, I often find and create beautiful friendships and opportunities. Recently, a chance encounter with a lady I met in town led to an invitation to lecture at the leading university in Mexico, and eventually, the offer to curate on behalf of Mexico for an Italian exhibition. WOW, right? All these encounters have one thing in common: It starts with hello.

There will always be moments when you see something that makes your ears perk up. Often we just let those moments pass by. Some call that minding your business, but sometimes, that's a missed opportunity. In 1944, author James Baldwin had a moment just like this, when he crossed paths with Richard Wright in Brooklyn. With Wright's assistance, Baldwin eventually secured funding for his first novel and permanent relocation to Paris. Without that magic moment of hello, we might not know of Baldwin. I often think about these examples, particularly when I'm feeling introverted or intimidated. Love, friendship, and life opportunities can all be at your doorstep. So experiment! Make eye contact, say hello, and see how the world opens up to you.

Tip 2: Remember, you aren't alone: Creating is hard

When I was in the final stages of my thesis and my PhD was within reach, I reacted by having a massive emotional meltdown (several, actually). I would spend hours in front of my screen doing edits and get nowhere. Luckily for me, around that time I discovered the blog of writer Bernadine Evaristo OBE. Her content is a fun collection of travels, Black academia, and insights into her writing process. In reflecting on her 2021 autobiography, "Manifesto", she talked candidly about how even after 40 years of writing, editing her manuscript was a terrible ordeal. Later that same day, I found a quote from Charles Darwin, who surprisingly was a *painter* as well as a naturalist. In an 1861 letter, he wrote "But I am very poorly today and very stupid and hate everybody and everything." I felt so *seen*. The point is: Everybody, even the best creatives, stumble within their process. Whatever it is you are building, step away and make a cup of tea, then return. Evaristo and Darwin charged forward and made masterpieces. So did I. So can you. When we are faced with doing hard things, remember: you are in great company.

Step 3: Speak up and look for the helpers

A few years ago, I created a short film which celebrated the cultural and spiritual presence of Africa in Mexico. After it was featured in a handful of festivals, I was tapped to be a TEDx speaker on the subject. WOW, I thought.

Magic moment loading! But pretty quickly, the initial excitement was replaced with dread. "I'm not a public speaker," I thought. As I rehearsed, imposter syndrome reared its ugly head. But then, I remembered someone: Mr. Rodgers. Random, but true. Amid my panic, I recall this 1960's interview he did discussing hardship. He said: "When I was a boy I would see scary news and my mother would say 'Look for the helpers. You will always find people who are helping.'"

There are always going to be moments in life when you feel isolated or alone. The key to moving out of them is by voicing *what you need*. Once I began speaking out loud my needs: behold! The helpers popped up like daisies – at lunch at a Lebanese restaurant, at a women's retreat, and at another cafe, my army of helpers showed themselves and were ready to work. Together, we rewrote and refined and soon I had a speech I was confident in. Magic comes in many forms to those who call for it. You are never without help.

If you're ever in Bristol, on Lower Lamb Street you'll find some early work of the elusive British street artist, Banksy. Spray painted on the brick, it says: "You don't need planning permission to build castles in the sky." I think he (or she?) is right about this. We all have permission to be the architects of our own lives. Whether you are in your hometown or across the world, the choice to cultivate magic is a daily practice that can paint your world with possibilities. This must be done intentionally, with a courageous heart. So get going.

Tayler Ava Friar PhD is the founder of ART|unknown LLC, a global multidisciplinary creative agency exploring the intersection of art, black voices, and the Sustainable Development Goals. Tayler is a TEDx speaker and has held various positions with the United Nations, the World Bank, and Google. As a writer, she is a contributor at Business Insider and has been featured in publications like Vogue Magazine speaking on black consciousness. Her bespoke exhibition FLOW of Change (2022-2024) was the largest climate-inspired installation in Mexico City marking the opening of the UN Climate Conferences. As a creative entrepreneur, she is credited with bringing the first West African art installation to Burning Man. She hopes that her bold curatorial vision will inspire individuals and organizations to uplift unconventional art in unconventional spaces to amplify diasporic voices.

She has been featured in Travel Noire, Yahoo News, World Bank publications, UNDP publications, The Miami Herald, Burning Man Journal, and Vogue Magazine.

9

JENNY SCHUSTER - What If Radical Self-Love Actually Looks Like Loving Others...What If?

Allow if you will, to entertain the thought that you were placed on this earth to be different. I mean really different. Imagine that you are here to bring such a positive change to this world that it will radically turn it upside down and on its axis. And that you...yes, you....were meant to bring goodness into even the darkest of places. To bring change and hope to those that have so very little. And that just by being open to this, it will blow your heart, your mind, and your world so far open that you will never be the same. Your willingness to do this will give you the beautiful opportunity to experience the greatest love of all. Because, when you reach out to others whose hands can barely lift for themselves, your real journey of radical self-love begins.

I'm going to ask you to be open to the concept that loving yourself and true radical self-love actually look different than how others define it. It's the idea of your eyes being turned outward instead of inward. And in a world where inner-healing is so popular and obviously so good and important... what does it even look like to focus on loving outward? How do you even begin? And how will that in the end, help you love yourself even more than you could've ever imagined?

Since the very moment life was breathed into you, your purpose was for more. For something bigger. You weren't meant to just show up. There is something else. And once you know it, you can't unknow it. It's the undeniable realization that the very reason you are here on this earth is for so much more. More than you dreamed possible. And that by helping bring in the light, the love, the hope, and all the good things, everything changes...even you.

It goes against the grain to put others first. It goes against almost everything you're hearing and being shown. How truly radical would it be to believe that maybe you are here to just help others? What if that is your soul's purpose? To be a witness to light entering the world through others and to help usher that precious light into the darkness. And in return, what if the love you receive is everything you've been searching for?

Connection, real connection, is the most beautiful, basic part of being on this earth. I think most of us know it. Deep down, we've always known it. But in the midst of the chaos and the day-to-day grind, time constraints, work demands, and clock ticking, we just sometimes forget to remember. So, I want you to start with the small step of stopping in your tracks, closing your eyes, breathing, and pushing the noise and chaos out of your mind. Listen to what your heart and mind are saying. Push all the clutter away and remember why you are here. Keep breathing. Be willing to see outside of yourself and to understand that although we are all so very different, we are all so very much alike. We come from different backgrounds, life experiences, cultures, and upbringings. The list goes on and on. We are different, you and I. But yet, we are all so truly connected by the same thing. The need for love, hope, purpose, identity, and connection. We crave the same things. Whether it's subconscious or not, we all crave them.

We aren't so different you and I, are we? We never have been and we never will be.

I can say that during the darkest hours of my life, I was so 100% focused on myself and focused inward that I couldn't see anything or anyone else. I was so focused on what I wasn't receiving, what I wasn't getting, and what I was lacking, that it became a never-ending cycle that caused the exact thing I feared would happen. I received less for wanting all those things, just for myself. But when I started to turn my heart outwards, the most beautiful thing started happening. I started to receive more than I ever could've imagined and my journey of personal healing began. My radical self-love started showing up by just turning to those that needed so much more than I did and by realizing that maybe... just maybe if I'm here on this earth for just one other person to experience hope, love, purpose, and connection...maybe that is enough? Maybe that is why I'm here.

It's radical and it's not the norm, but it's about taking this idea of taking your eyes off of yourself for a moment and looking outwards to help turn the tide of chaos and confusion in not just yourself, but in this world. Can you imagine collectively, if we all just took this chance, how it would push this world upside down and eventually right side up? It's not trending and it's certainly not popular, but let me tell you what that simple act does when you turn outward. You heal. You help heal others. And when you start showing up for others...everything changes. It's literally the most beautiful thing to experience and witness. Because the light shows up. And self-love? It shows up like you've never seen it before.

It shows up in the smallest acts of kindness. In the acts of service for another that seem like they have no importance.

It shows up in the phone call checking in on someone. Even if they didn't check in on you.

It shows up in driving someone to an appointment so they aren't alone when the news is delivered – even if they can't do the same for you.

It shows up in giving to someone who can never give back.

It shows up in listening to someone who is at the end of their rope but who cannot be there for you when you need it most.

It shows up in helping others that you may never meet. With far-reaching effects that you may never see.

It just keeps showing up.

Radical self-love shows up in the world when you are willing to love outward. And the light and love it brings...it just makes the darkness disappear. Dare I say, maybe that is why we are here? And maybe learning to love ourselves shows up in the midst of loving others. And maybe learning to radically love ourselves flows from one to another in the light we share with those who need it most. When we give of ourselves to those in need, to those less fortunate, to those who can never repay us, we receive so much more. So much more. It IS radical to show love to a world that appears so unlovable. We are here to bring change into this world, you and I.

My promise to you....if you start to love outward you will experience the greatest, most radical self-love you've ever known. If you are willing to try, you will never regret it. Ever.

Jenny Schuster is a writer, powerhouse communicator, public speaker, and community builder. She co-founded the non-profit "Matthew's Voice Project – MVP" which has served countless high school students experiencing homelessness by filling critical and emergency needs. She has successfully worked in the Real Estate Industry for over 25 years and is currently in the top 1.5% of real estate agents in the U.S.

Jenny is a wife and mother of two. She is an enthusiastic, energetic business owner driven by human connection, humor, and a focus on positive results for all she encounters. Her biggest hope is to encourage others to do big things, practice self-care, take action despite their fears, and shine their light brightly.

10

TONIA MAJORS - I Choose Joy

What is the purest form of joy?

The purest form of joy comes to us in ordinary moments, and those moments can happen in any place where gratitude is alive. Lunch with a parent or partner. The sweet embrace of a grandchild's arms squeezing your neck.

I was once so miserable. Young and working full time. I was constantly being tugged in every direction. I put pressure on myself to do my best work. As a wife, Mom, and a person with health conditions of my own, I was tired, I was exhausted, with no energy. Looking back, I felt mean, miserable, unkind, and sarcastic. I am honestly so sorry I didn't learn earlier in life to take care of myself. I made the changes that I could. Such as dropping hours to work part time. I learned to take the time to refill my cup before caring for others. You can not help others if your tank is empty.

"The root of joy is gratefulness." - David Steindl-Rast
Becoming thankful doesn't "just" make you a happier person; it boosts your immune system, lowers blood pressure, decreases depression, improves your love life, and gives you more patience in enduring times.

Choose Joy. We only get one chance to live this life. You can only control how you act or react to events in your life. Choose Joy no matter what life puts you through. Choose Joy in this instant to create a happy, grateful heart and a future full of hope. Don't wait for life to get easier or less complicated. Do not deny yourself Joy waiting on perfect timing. Search out and find an activity to bring you joy today. Each positive moment builds joyous momentum refreshed each day. Life will always have complications. Do not wait until every aspect of your life is perfect. Do not approach your life with constant worry, fear, or a victim mentality. Choose to be Joyful each day. Time is too precious. Use the fine crystal glasses and fancy plates each day. You are worth it, there is no need to save them for someone special-that's You! Otherwise, you may run out of time.

Not everyone can choose joy. The disease that people are unable to feel joy is called Anhedonia, or the inability to derive joy or happiness from anything around us, and is a common indication of an underlying mental health issue such as depression, post-traumatic stress disorder, or anxiety, being detached from people, experiencing conflict in relationships, eating disorders, addiction, lack of social support, relationship issues, or not getting needs met. When these external circumstances are addressed, people can begin to feel happier. The good news is that, in most cases, anhedonia will go away with treatment. For cases in which addiction is the leading cause, anhedonia may go away with sobriety. Generally, treating the accompanying condition will lessen anhedonia because it doesn't typically happen independently.

I am a woman, wife, sister, friend, artist, photographer, mother, grand-mother, nurse, United States Army veteran, a thirty-four-year Multiple Sclerosis Warrior, and caregiver. I cared for my Mother for over ten years, the last three with her living in my home. Each role gave me different life lessons. Learn from your experiences. I have learned:

1. Always have your equipment clean and packed. Sleep when you can. Eat a balanced and healthy diet.

2. Enjoy the sights and sounds of nature.
3. Nurturing others takes patience and a full cup to pour from.
4. Experience gave me a master problem solver attitude. Not much surprises me after all these years.

While I was caring for my Mom in 2017, I spread out a newspaper on the kitchen table. I watched a couple Youtube videos and then put paint on a canvas board. I felt as though I had completed a masterpiece! That confidence burst Joy into my heart. It was a boost that I didn't even realize I needed. Through abstract mixed media art, I found a peaceful, calm, and accomplished feeling.

It isn't realistic for me to paint and create on days when I have other commitments. Develop a routine you can complete at the start of your day to bring you Joy. Drink your favorite flavored or specialty coffee from that big mug you like. Read your bible. Meditate. Do deep breathing exercises. Complete a workout. Dance while you are brushing your teeth. Spend a few minutes writing or drawing in the journal to get rid of negative feelings. Loudly listen to the music you like while doing your morning routine. Read a good book. Snuggle into a warm bed on a rainy day. Light a scented candle such as: fresh linen, newly cut grass, sugar cookie, or cinnamon spice.

Laugh by reading funny dad jokes, comics, or punny jokes. Recite three reasons to be Grateful. Give more of your time—volunteer at church or a food bank. Be kind to everyone; many are struggling with troubles that are not visible. Smile at everyone and make eye contact. Wear your favorite color of blouse or shirt. Watch and listen to the morning chatter of the birds. Close your eyes and visualize your favorite place on earth with the sun or wind on your face. Most snooze buttons give you nine more minutes in bed, you could have used your time to enjoy the sunrise.

Does God want us to live in joy?
Psalm 32:11, "Be glad in the LORD and rejoice, you righteous; And shout

for joy, all you upright in heart!" When you read these verses, you quickly realize that joy is not a suggestion for the believer but a command. It is one of the most repeated commands in the Bible.

It's Your Choice. Choose Joy. Go forward into the day with that one positive thought, a moment that brings you a smile, a pleasant warm place in your heart to carry you through your day. Day after day, say yes to feeling Joy in your heart every day! When you choose Joy each day, eventually, Joy will reside within you to shine your light brightly with each step.

Tonia Majors is a creative soul with a passion for mixed media abstract art and photography. As a U.S. Army veteran, Tonia earned her instructor status and completed the Primary Leadership Development Course as a noncommissioned officer in less than 1 year. With 37 years of experience as a nurse, Tonia has a natural ability to transform spaces and create a vibe that speaks to the heart. Tonia's work is a reflection of her vibrant spirit and her unwavering commitment to inspiring others to live their best lives.

11

MARIA TEDJAMULIA - Motherhood, Leadership, Love

I was twenty-nine years old, and it would appear I had everything I ever wanted. My tall, dark, handsome husband of five years supported me like bedrock. We lived in a beautiful home in the San Francisco Bay Area, where nearly every day felt like spring. My husband had a great job in Silicon Valley. I had exited the corporate rat race, gone back to school, earned my MBA, and quit full-time work to finally live my desired dream: full-time motherhood. I was grateful to be at home with my kids all day. I had just given birth to a perfect little girl, my second child. We had the kids, the home, the credentials, the life.

So why was I so miserable?

Behind the polished exterior, my reality was in stark contrast. Feelings of depression were my uninvited guest, hovering like a gloomy shadow. Unruly dishes seemed to have a life of their own, multiplying faster than I could control. Mounting laundry piles threatened to take over our home. Unanswered texts and stacks of mail nagged at the back of my mind, yet remained neglected. Paralyzed by this chaos, even a simple shower seemed like a mammoth task.

One day, I was eating the leftover mac and cheese off my toddler's plate for lunch when my phone buzzed. It was my mom. Something in her mother's intuition told her that I was in trouble, and she reached out to me with a lifeline to rescue me from the fog.

"Maria," she said, "What's one thing you can do right now to apply your MBA at home?"

I almost choked. What on earth was she suggesting? Wasn't it evident that I was just barely getting by? But her unusual question ignited a spark within me.

I had always been business-minded, but how could that relate to motherhood? As my mother continued to prod, I began to see parallels. I realized my home was not just a home; it was an enterprise, and I was its CEO.

As I tried on this new way of thinking, I discovered my feelings of suffocation came from viewing myself as the maid in my home, trapped in a vortex of unending diaper changes, meals to be prepared, and messes to be cleaned. But as I began to adopt a CEO's mindset, my vision broadened, and I rediscovered joy. Suddenly, the day-to-day chores seemed less formidable; life was no longer just about survival—it was about creation.

Adopting the mindset of a CEO, or as I prefer to dub it, stepping into the shoes of the Chief Home Officer (CHO), enabled me to lead my household and my life more strategically, proactively, and balanced. I started asking myself questions like, "What life do I wish to shape for my children and me?" "How do I want my home to be?" "What values do we want to live by?" "Are there simpler methods to handle house chores?" "How can my husband and I work together and enlist the support of others to achieve our short- and long-term family objectives?"

Such thought-invoking inquiries led me to establish systems that stream-

lined routine tasks like dishwashing, laundry, meal preparation, bill payments, and scheduling, thereby making them less daunting. It allowed me
to think bigger and set up systems for those parts of my life that were less
urgent, yet vital to create the kind of life I wanted, including systems for
my long-term legacy, finances, and experiences. I also realized that for
leadership to be effective, I had to be at my best, which put self-care and
personal development high on my list of daily priorities.

As these systems took effect, I noticed a shift towards more balance and
fulfillment in my life as a mother; I was rediscovering myself. Activities that
ignited my passion made a comeback, enhancing my sense of accomplishment. Even amid expanding my family and nurturing babies, I managed
to carve out space and energy to follow my divine calling. I became a co-
founder of a nonprofit dedicated to improving women's lives, launched a
consulting firm that organized events at remarkable locations, including
the United States Capitol, and played a part in the birth of a tech company
that's reached millions. I now guide and coach moms on designing their
personal Home Operating Systems as Chief Home Officers. The CHO mindset
has enabled me to accomplish all this while still making time for activities
like taking my toddler to the park and chaperoning school field trips.

Recently, I found myself unexpectedly in the hospital with my youngest
son as he battled for his life. It was terrifying and completely absorbed my
attention. However, during this critical period at the hospital, I had faith
that things at home were running smoothly. With a Home Operating System
in place, I was confident that my older children would attend their sports
practices, that my bills were being handled, and that my home would not
require weeks to restore order when I returned. That's a level of peace that
money cannot buy.

If your feelings align with most moms I engage with, you deeply cherish
being a mother, yet there's a calling you can't overlook. You yearn to
contribute to the world (and possibly to your family's financial well-being

as well!), but you're exhausted from trying to manage it all and feeling like you're falling short. You're weighed down by guilt, not wanting to miss out on the priceless moments of raising your children, but there's something missing, a deep-seated void within you.

Embracing the CHO leadership mindset can help mend these gaps, letting you evolve as a leader and regain the freedom, motivation, and energy you desire. By transitioning from a maid's role to leading your most significant organization—your home—and integrating systems like the Mom MBA Home Operating System, you're taking a momentous step towards self-love—becoming the leader of your own life.

My philosophy is uncomplicated yet profound: Every woman, every mother, is a leader. By accepting this leadership role within our homes, we can pave the way for a life of freedom and joy, revealing deeper love and fulfillment. This change, I am convinced, can transform the commonplace into the extraordinary.

Are you ready to be the CEO of your life? Grab my free gift for you now at https://m ommba.com/book-gift and own your journey. xo, Maria

Maria Tedjamulia is a 4-time business founder, creator of the Mom MBA, and mom of 5 who is dedicated to inspiring purpose-driven mompreneurs

to embrace leadership in all aspects of their lives, helping them find greater freedom and balance with their time, money, and energy through her proprietary Home Operating System. She's been seen on CNN, featured in business trade publications, received various national and international marketing awards, and can be found playing with her kids at the park Fridays at noon.

12

RACHEL BUSH - Know and No Love, Radical Self-Acceptance and Care

I just want you to practice saying the word "No." "No" is a complete sentence made up of only two letters that will dramatically improve your life. Try it. It is a powerful tool that immediately puts you back in the driver's seat. Breathe; you are taking control of your life. You are the author of your own life, and you can write a much better story. You deserve the opportunity to take care of yourself; you need to prioritize your own needs.

In the beginning, this will feel uncomfortable; remind yourself that you are brave and strong. This is your chance to stop pleasing other people. You are not walking yourself to the back of the line.

Take care of your body, and your body will take care of you. It is simple; tune into your breath and see what your body is telling you. Are you thirsty? Is it time to rest? Maybe it is time for lunch. Nourish yourself like you are a warrior.

As your tank refuels, you might notice that you are feeling less stressed and more relaxed. Take yourself and walk. Shift your mindset and think about three things you are grateful for right here, right now.

We all have a special inner voice that guides us and knows the truth. Our intuition is a precious gift that will guide us on our own journey toward bettering the health of the body, mind, and spirit. We need to make good choices and be gracefully disappointing when it is time to say, "I am sorry, but that won't work for me!"

You are the person who has the ability to establish relationship boundaries for yourself. You do not have to sit and stay at any table where respect is not being served. It is your obligation to model radical self-love. Lead with your big heart. I believe in karma and that you get what you give. Do everything you can to generously teach radical self-care to your children or other young people in your life. Learn to love and respect your intuition and bring your light and love with you. I genuinely believe that the best moments of your life haven't happened yet. The world needs balance and inspiration. I think that learning to say no makes room for inspiration, creativity, and joy.

My name is Dr. Rachel Bush. I am a survivor, clinical psychologist, trauma-informed 500-hour yoga instructor, bestselling author, nature photographer, and intuitive multi-media artist. I help everyone who is brave enough to ask me for my help on their mental health and wellness journey. I help people of all ages heal, grow and trust their choices in order to live with vitality, creativity, gratitude, beauty, laughter, and health to make the world a better place.

13

DIANE HUNT - Deep Connections Through Painting

We are all on our own paths in this life, but we can learn and help each other on our journey. Sharing our stories and the things we've learned from our own experiences can help to guide others so that they can avoid missteps and benefit from our journey. It's all about connections. Connections to ourselves, to art, to each other, and the bigger world around us.

The use of art can play a big role in connecting our innermost thoughts and feelings to the world and people around us. Bringing our unique voice not just into the world but connecting us to it in a deep way. Creating art allows us to express ourselves when we find words to be too difficult or painful to voice. There are many examples in my life where I've used art to help me. For example, when I was a little girl, I was able to use art to communicate my thoughts and feelings when the words were outside my grasp. As an adult, I was able to use painting to express my feelings about a place and time as well as to heal from traumas. Painting helped me to work through the emotions I was feeling and come out on the other side with a better understanding of the situation and myself. The meditative process of painting can interrupt our minds. It can give our mind the space and time it needs to see things more clearly, preventing us from spiraling out of control. We can immerse ourselves into the creative process and take a step out of our crazy busy lives. Giving us a respite from the constant noise and things in our lives that are pulling us in a million different directions.

Before you say I'm not an artist or I can't do that, everyone has creative energy that resides within them. We are all born with it. Creativity is one thing that separates us from other animals on this planet. From the time you can hold a pencil or crayon in your hand, we have all shown that we are born with the need to create. The only difference is that some of us have continued to create into adulthood and have practiced more than others. But we all have a need to find our creative voice and when we do, it can bring us great joy.

If you don't worry about becoming an instant Michelangelo and creating a masterpiece whenever you pick up a brush, you can really benefit from the creative process. Truth be told, there are no artists that create masterpieces every time they paint and few create paintings worthy of being hung in a museum. Don't worry about painting without mistakes and making everything perfect. There is no such thing. Get comfortable with learning from the mistakes and moving forward. I make mistakes and learn things every time I paint, and I have been painting for years. That is how you get better. Take that pressure off yourself and just enjoy being creative and making paintings you love. If you would like to go further in your painting journey you can always take classes, join painting groups in your area and on Facebook, watch YouTube videos, or find a mentor to teach you more. Connecting with others that are also painting can make learning much more enjoyable and bring new people and experiences into your life.

But the important thing is to just start. Don't put unrealistic expectations on yourself. Just remember we are all on our own journey, so don't get stuck by comparing your paintings to someone else's paintings that have been painting longer than you. We were all beginners at some point. If you continue to practice, you will get better.

Setting aside a specific place and time each week to paint is the best thing you can do. You can work painting time into your schedule, whether it's a few minutes each day or one day a week. You don't need to complete a painting in one sitting. You would be surprised how much you can accomplish if you are consistent and work for even just a few minutes at a time. The time you spend should be considered sacred and protected. It is something that you need to do for not only your own well-being but for all those around you. It is important. You are important.

For me, creating paintings of the natural world around me helps me in more ways than I can count, but there are two main ways. First, it helps me to connect with nature. Painting outside immersed in nature creates a connection with God, the universe – whatever you want to call it. That connection reminds us that we are all a part of something bigger than just ourselves and we do matter in this world. Our unique voice can and does make a difference. There is something in knowing this that gives us a sense of peace. The second thing is creating a painting of a place and time is a way of recording that memory in a deeper more meaningful way than just snapping a picture. When you slow down and study a location, spending hours there painting it, those memories get embedded in your soul. They become a part of you. You can see that painting years later and instantly be transported back to that place and time. You can remember where it was, what happened while you were there, and many other specific things about the experience.

We all crave a connection to nature in some way. When we take vacations, most of us want to spend time with the natural world. We go to the beach or the mountains, we spend time in our gardens or go for walks outside. The connection to our natural environment is a strong one. Spending time outside has a way of refreshing our spirits and gets deep into our souls if we let it.

I encourage you to go outside and paint. By painting a landscape on location, it immerses you in the natural world in a deep way. Creating a painting slows you down, allows you to use all your senses to really look, hear and feel the wonders that are around you, and brings the earth's energy into your soul. Find other people that also want to paint. The connections you create with others will enhance your life – and their lives as well. The light inside you will come out and it will create within us a calm and peacefulness we all can use more of – as a result, the world will become a better place.

Diane Hunt is a traditionally trained realistic oil painter who connects with nature through her brush. She inspires others by creating connections through the healing powers of art and nature.

Diane has used these healing powers to get her through traumas in her own life and empowers others to do the same by teaching aspiring artists to connect with the artist within. She helps them build confidence, self-esteem, and connection, which will bring a peacefulness to their heart and soul. As a result, beautiful works of art are brought into our world for all to enjoy.

Diane has a BFA, (Bachelor of Fine Art), from The Maryland Institute College of Art. She works from her studio on a small farm in Maryland's countryside. Diane has created paintings both in the studio and en plein air, (outside on location). She is a member of the Plein Air Painters of the Chesapeake Bay and a juried member of the Oil Painters of America and the American Artists Professional League. She has had paintings juried into numerous shows and private collections. Currently, she has a painting on exhibit at the Chesapeake Bay Maritime Museum, in the exhibition, "The Changing Chesapeake". The exhibition will be open for all of 2023, until it closes in February 2024.

14

LINDA DAMGAARD - Radical Self-Love/Care

When I was asked to write what radical self-love means to me, for this wonderful book, I most of all was grateful!! And happy and excited to share with all of you, my way into and definition of creative self-love.

My name is Linda Damgaard. I am a Danish artist, living my life here in southern Denmark, surrounded by my beautiful family who is; My husband, two children and children-in-laws and three amazing grandchildren. Beside my artist life I work fulltime as a daycare for 4-5 small children, in the age of 6 months - 3 years. To all the children who enrich my life, I LOVE to give them the possibility to see themselves as I see them. To make them believe in themselves, give them self-confidence and self-esteem and to make them bloom.

To describe to you what creative self love is to me, I have those three words coming through all of it. DARE, TRUST and BELIEVE. Self-love to me is to believe in me. To believe in that no matter what I would like to try out here in life and no matter what I am drawn to, I will find what is needed for me to do so. Self care to me is to dare follow my dreams. Dare to try out new things in life in the safe belief that everything will work out okay. e.g. Last year I started an education to become an educational assistant. This was a dream I have had for years. I didn't know for sure if I was able to, but I knew that I would do my very best and guess what...I WAS able to and in fact I did so very well!! I have had the most wonderful year filling myself with all this knowledge and wonderful relationships with people, who have enriched my life tremendously.

As I started to paint, about 15 years ago, I had no idea that one day I would be an art selling artist, shipping my paintings around the world. The only thing I knew was that I loved to paint. In our summer house, we had a neighbour, who was SO talented. He painted the most wonderful paintings, colourful and bright. I would have loved to buy one of his paintings but unfortunately, he had none for sale at the time. That was the reason why I started to paint myself. My journey as an artist has been filled with so much joy, laughter and happiness. Making space and time to be creative, also in everyday life, to me is so, so important. I have tried out new techniques and styles. Tried out different types of mixed media and while doing that, I enjoyed myself knowing that there was no right or wrong. Like trying on new clothes, see if it fits right? If it fits, it's a YES... I found a new technique to use in my next painting. If it doesn't fit, YES... Now I know this is not for me, let me try out something new!! In other words, to me there is no right or wrong. If I don't like it, in my mind I put some sparkle on it and let it go, I have learned from it and am ready to try something else. To me, it's as simple as that. Here in Denmark, we had this wonderful Danish theologian and philosopher Søren Aaby Kierkegaard who once said "Vi fødes som originaler og dør som kopier" and in English; "We are all born as originals and die as copies"...That's such an important reminder, I think. A reminder not to compare oneself with others. And a reminder that we don't have to be perfect, and we don't have to be like others. Always remember to go for _your_ dreams and make the space in your life to follow _your_ dreams and goals. Not for other people but for **YOU**.

These values I have always told and still do tell my own two children, my three wonderful grandchildren and all my daycare children. You are unique and special, exactly as you are. You are precious. You are so worthy of all the good things coming to you in life. Believe in yourself, I KNOW you can do whatever you want to do. Trust the process, the journey and enjoy!

To enjoy and to be happy, and to celebrate all the wonderful things that we accomplish and experience in life is so important. From my perspective, it's likewise as important to be able to rejoice with others when *they're* doing well in life. Do not let jealousy poison your life when other people succeed, but celebrate and be happy with them, and on behalf of their joy and success. Life isn't a competition, it's a journey where you have all the possibilities to feel joy and happiness. But it doesn't come by itself, it comes from within.

Xoxo Linda

Linda Damgaard is a Danish intuitive, abstract, and mixed media artist who creates art from her heart. As an educational assistant, she has focused on recognizing, acknowledging, and encouraging children and people in general to believe in themselves by creating art together. Her vision is to show people that spending time on being creative, playing music, knitting, or anything else that makes them happy – bloom and shine, is possible to combine with being parents, work, school, etc.

II

— Unapologetic Love Letter... To ME —

Transformative tales – designed to reignite your love for the person you truly are!

15

JOANNE ENDERS - Finding the Way to Me

When I was a kid I believed I could do and be anything. I also learned that there were few people I could trust and rely on over time. I struggled deeply to fit into groups, had few friends, and struggled with learning. I struggled with becoming acceptable.

Learning really well how to be a chameleon, to fit in the space that was available, in the way those around me needed me to fit. Yet never really belonging anywhere. I didn't share my true feelings on anything. If I shared ideas they were generally attributed to others for which I shrugged and accepted that at least the world moved further forward from my contributions in some small way. I learned skills like diplomacy, acceptance, patience, listening and learning. They were invaluable, they made me the grease in the cogs of the lives around me.

Throughout my life I've been a job hopper, never getting too close, never allowing people to know the real me. I'd become so frustrated with having to play that imaginary role of the person they hoped I'd be that it tore me up inside, literally forcing my body to respond with sickness inside and out.

My family couldn't understand me. They believed they understood what I wanted and who I wanted to be and then they didn't. Feeling like a wanderer in search of my place in this crazy world, the journey began, to start eliminating everything I did not want. Telling my husband repeatedly "At least I know what I hate!" and continuing to trudge ahead.

Suddenly, the pieces that had been stored away so carefully started to connect. Two years ago after finding an artist group on Facebook and a photography group on Twitter I slowly started sharing little pieces of my life and everything I'd learned.

Embarking on my artistic journey within the digital web3 communities, the concept of true community started to take shape in my life. It's been a whirlwind adventure filled with personal challenges, unexpected triumphs, and a newfound confidence that has transformed me into an internationally sold artist, a best-selling author, and a catalyst for innovation in this thrilling and sometimes daunting new world.

In my quest for self-love, I realized that I needed to take risks, particularly when it came to building connections and nurturing relationships. It meant peeling back the layers of my soul, exposing the hidden pieces of myself that I had kept sheltered from the world. It meant forging trust and learning to trust in return.

Each time that fear rose up I took a deep cleansing breath and just said "f***it" then kept going. All those skills learned to protect myself were starting to come in handy.

- Learn, learn and learn some more - you can never have enough understanding of new technology specifically. Even if it's not your thing, understanding how the tech works, how it will affect you, and your future life is invaluable.

- Communication and listening gave me a leg up in understanding how people tick. Most everyone just wants to be seen, be heard and be acknowledged.

- Uplifting others takes little effort if you're respectful, sharing in those same struggles, and showing you care.

- Time has a way of multiplying if you focus on your goals. Just keep taking those little steps forward, don't get stuck on the "ready, set" instead focus on the GO!

- Kindness goes a long way and then some.

- Be yourself, say what you mean and mean what you say. They may not agree but they will respect you for believing in yourself.

My grandmother used to tell me that if I shared my knowledge, experiences, and opinions with a gentle touch people would hear what I was trying to tell them. In the web3 space people wanted to hear what I had to say. Never feeling judged, little by little I let down my guard and started to share my life, my secrets.

Communication is a really nuanced dance, influenced by our diverse backgrounds, education, cultures, and personalities. Respecting others means allowing them to navigate their own paths and recognizing the immeasurable value of listening to their thoughts and perspectives. The more I shared of myself the more these new friends gave back.

Holding spaces open to the world, people began showing up for me. They felt heard and heard what I had to say with the care in my heart. Strangely, people started following me, not in the creepy way but in the way that they cared to see what I had to say and were curious about what I would create.

Next I began creating digital art using my physical art, photography, drawings on the iPad and utilizing AI and other technologies. All these years of holding all these little pieces were finally coming together in my art and writing.

That's when I, like the tight bud unable to hold in all the pain, finally began to bloom.

"And the day came when the risk to remain tight in a bud was more painful than the risk it took to blossom." ~ Anaïs Nin

We each travel our own remarkable journey of self-discovery, acceptance and eventually, empowerment. You have to be honest with yourself about what you don't want while opening your arms wide to everything you're too scared to admit is important to your heart.

I've learned that I was an iceberg, not cold, but well hidden in the depths of my soul. I am now working toward rising into a mountain reaching high into the sky touched by the sun, blooming with life. Never forget that the greatest masterpiece we can ever create is the masterpiece of our own selves—lovingly crafted, passionately lived, and unapologetically celebrated.

The end.

Lens–based Artist, Photographer, Author, Speaker, and Spacehost. It's always the little things that make the biggest differences. Joanne's journey, shaped by her mother's and grandmother's wisdom, exemplifies the transformative power of art.

As an internationally acclaimed multimedia artist, she embodies resilience, authenticity, and personal growth. Her emotionally charged work resonates with global audiences while her trailblazing multimedia creations captivate through digital art, AI, and photography.

Joanne's #1 international best–selling debut book, "The Creative Lifebook", showcases her narrative talent and promotes community building and collaboration among 64 artists. Her business savvy, combined with her artistic prowess, positions her as a driving force for change and inspiration. From her modest beginnings to her worldwide success, Joanne's life and creativity are testaments to growth, resilience, and authenticity.

16

JANE BELLANTE - Stop, Listen, and Breathe

In January 2021, I found out that my left coronary artery was 99% blocked. At the age of 49, I had to get a stent and go on blood thinners for a full year. At the same time, I had multiple fibroids causing me to bleed heavily. Add in the blood thinners and I had the perfect storm. I went from bleeding once a month to bleeding every day. It was like a murder scene. I lost so much blood in 2021, I had to have a transfusion in June, and was so low I almost needed another one before I could finally stop taking the blood thinners in February of 2022. What I learned over the course of that very long year was one thing: life is not guaranteed, and if I didn't immediately stop what I was doing and change directions, I may never get the chance to do it again.

I was a small shop owner selling painted furniture and mixed media art, along with home decor and some other fun items. Because I was so weak from all of the blood loss, I began to notice that I didn't really have the motivation to paint the big furniture pieces anymore. I also began to notice that I was just going through the motions of owning the store. Even though all of my pretty furniture was on the floor and my art was on the walls, it just seemed different. I really and truly thought that this was the dream. I had my own shop, and my own creative space, so why wasn't I happy?

Because I was losing so much blood all the time, I had no energy for anything, and I was still in shock, to be honest. Learning that my body actually grew new veins for the blood to flow through my heart to genuinely keep me alive was a lot to process – on top of 2 kids graduating from high school during COVID (2 consecutive years), running a business, and being a not-so-great wife. I was soooo burned out. Like, recycle me cause I'm done kind of burned out.

I started having really vivid dreams with imagery (I never remember my dreams, so this was kind of amazing). Brown bears, black panthers, kittens. I was very curious as to why I was all of a sudden remembering my dreams, and what this could possibly mean. So I Googled. Every single one of these images stood for rebirth and transformation. EVERY SINGLE ONE.

So you know that saying "God first gives you a pebble, then a rock, then a boulder"? This was my boulder. All of the things that I had been experiencing (yes- I'm saying the stent in my heart wasn't even the boulder), were clues that I needed to change – but I wasn't listening. I was lost in the doing because I wanted no part of the being. It was all way too much. So when I started having these images in my dreams and actually remembering them, I finally started to take notice. The universe was going to the extreme to get my attention. And it worked.

In mid-November of 2021, I took action to close my store. I didn't even care about upcoming holiday sales. I was so burned out and once I realized that, I was finished. It was the most liberating thing I had ever done for myself.

I have been a mixed-media artist for 30 years. I just wanted to make things and teach people how to make things. So I changed my business name from Morning Dew Creations to Jane Bellante Art and I started to let myself be seen. I had always kept my art journals a bit secret. They were mine, not to be seen by anyone else. But what I started to realize was that the art journal was the actual thing that would not only change my life, but the lives of so many others.

We tend to run on autopilot much of the time. When this autopilot is driving, we are nowhere near being present in the moment. And that is where so much negative self-talk emerges. We stop ourselves cold from creating anything. We compare ourselves to others, saying "Well, mine will never look like hers so why even bother", or we buy a whole bunch of cool new art supplies only to be too afraid to use them and never open them, much less take them off the shelf. We have some sort of idea of perfection that is never, ever defined, yet we tell ourselves we can't create unless we know it will come out perfect. Will we ever reach that undefined measure of "perfect"?

These stories that we are telling ourselves are just that– stories. And when we bring them to the light, it is very hard to push them back into the darkness. We need a stop sign – right in front of our faces – that shows through all of the veils we create for ourselves so we don't have to feel, be seen, or allow anything or anyone to penetrate.

We need to create space and time for ourselves to be completely quiet. To literally detach from everything. Because it is in all of this detaching that we can begin to listen. When we are running on autopilot all the time – our brains never stop. It's the reason we are never, ever present. It's the reason we can't sleep at night. It's why we are stuck in a holding pattern of negativity, lack, and distrust. Connection is non-existent because we do not even allow it.

So actually scheduling time to breathe, to be quiet, and to be detached allows you to listen. It allows you to receive the signs that the universe is screaming at you if you only give yourself a chance to receive them. You can't just keep giving and giving to everyone else all the time. I wasn't hearing these messages when I got my stent. I wasn't hearing them when I was living through COVID with my family – trying to help them navigate life, high school, and graduations, while I was trying to keep my retail business alive and suffering so much medically as a female human-person. I was just doing. I never detached. I never let myself feel, or cry, or lose my sanity because everything was unraveling all at once.

I went back to my art journal and decided to honor these messages for rebirth and change. My art journal is everything to me. All thought, all emotion. Pure flow state. It doesn't matter what I put down on the page. It's me and some color, some marks, some forms, and pure potentiality. Every message the universe wants to tell me is heard. There is no perfectionism, there is no competition, THERE IS NO FEAR. I put my phone on do not disturb for two hours EVERY DAY. Sometimes what I create is freaking amazing, and sometimes it's pure trash. But I am giving myself the space to stop, listen and breathe. And not just the super shallow breaths we allow ourselves to have in any given moment of our day, but real, full, life-giving breaths that allow reception and expansion.

I invite you to do the same. Whether it's an art journal, a journal for writing, a yoga mat, a bike, etc. Let go. Let yourself feel. Stop. Listen. Breathe. Then receive.

Jane Bellante is an expert at helping people let go of negative thought patterns so they can create the art and personal brand they have always wanted with joy, confidence and ease. She has been a mixed media artist for 30 years, is a

published artist and has a Masters Degree in Adult Education. She is founder of the 5 Day Letting Go Workshop, the Creating Confidently 5 week course, IGNITE your business cohort accelerator and is a married mother of 2 kids and 2 pets.

17

DR. ZERRI (DR. Z) GROSS - Pay Me First! With Love

In the first CLB book, I shared a snippet of a mindset shift about money. The full version of the ebook is totally available for purchase. I was listening to a coaching call with one of the six coaches I invested in the year of this writing, looking at my schedule, checking emails, looking at my sleeping teenager, completing my mid-year form for one of the masterminds I'm in, and taking a call from my cousin who has decided to write a book.

The title became effortlessly clear of what I wanted my section in this collaborative book to be as I have been noticing how much I give to the world via my intentional time giving and my gifts to the world. I wanted to share how spending time alone allowed me to have a chance at resetting what I'd like to call my functional feminine Goddess Vibe. And it hit me! Boom!

My time!

I gave love for everything and everyone else when I gave my attention and time. What others get is my knowledge, empathy, care, tools, and even money (money can totally be measured as different times of currency, such as emotional money). If I am giving, that means someone else is receiving because of my deposit into them and the withdrawal from me. My radical self-love looks like how much money am I giving myself, what boundaries do I create for who gets it, why, how, when, frequency, etc (just like a treatment for all the therapists and service providers).

My time is money! My energy is money! My gifts are money! My love is money!

How much money am I paying myself? This question brought me to snot tears, dry heaving, pain in my abdomen, and feeling physically ill and weak at the knees. I immediately understood how much I did not love myself as I looked at how much time, energy, and gifts I did not pay myself. Needless to say there is room for growth in giving myself radical love because my love to me bank account is depleted.

I immediately recalled actions, feeling, and processes that I have used haphazardly and in recent years and months of what allowed me to seriously feel like I paid myself and put my money tools to work for my own self-love bank to be fulfilled. Imagine everything having dollar amounts so you can totally externalize the feelings to actions that produce results of self-love that are tangible with the feelings being the cherry on top. Here's what it looked like:

1. **I am intentional with my time.** I spend time in places, with people, as I am available that allows me to be poured into and the reciprocity of me pouring into them. I go to places that feel good like islands, warm locations, good music, good food, and beautiful places. People that I can laugh with, dance with, eat with, make money with, and literally bring out the greatest versions of ourselves.

2. **I don't give away my services that cost money for free.** I have

historically given all the life answers to anyone who asked with no commitment or reciprocity for the knowledge and time. I volunteer when I am in a space of abundance, not lack.

3. **I don't accept all invitations.** I used to even for things that literally caused me pain. No is a complete sentence and I owe no one anything except myself.

4. I check in with my mind, body, and self for **"Hell Yes! Or Hell No!** (Definitely for major choices exploring my energetic chakra fields for blockages, overactivity, underactivity, and what's needed to get my answer).

5. **I spend time alone.** I take solo trips, sit in my home alone, schedule spa days, work out, allow silence, etc. to reset. It took decades to recognize how powerful being alone was towards being the greatest version of me with and for others.

6. **I schedule my life, career, self-maintenance, volunteer-ships, etc. for me**. I readjust monthly and quarterly as it does or doesn't work as best as I have knowledge of to benefit myself and everyone else.

7. **I put my money where my mouth is.** I hire help, coaching, support, food, and training and check how I feel when I spend it for the benefit of doing so.

I traveled more this year and embraced it to have more experiences with myself. It cost more but the alternative was a lack of peace, rejuvenation, refocus.

I didn't realize that I planned to unintentionally time to get away in a frequency that aligned with the stream of events in my life for business and family. I enjoy being at home but all of the events called forward the need for me to go spend time in other places, with new people, and familiar in different capacities.

I gained so much more of me and who I knew myself to be by allowing myself to be experienced through others, regroup and reintroduce the aspects I was willing to share.

I've definitely become more selfish with me as I've become more public for others. I do things that I don't invite others to. I enjoy my own gifts in silence, private, and fully when I am not providing an experience for others.

The more I give to me the more overflow I give to the world of greatness cultivated from self love, indulgence, and priority. This has completely gone against who I've programmed myself to be to be helpful to others. I've had to say no and notice I was the person most impacted by my no than the person, event, or things I said no to. No piece of cake ever had a feeling about a person not eating it.

If you take anything away from this become comfortable with being selfish of you, your time, and your gifts. This one act of love to yourself will allow you to become more selfless because you are full.

Dr. Zerri (Dr.Z) Gross is a Licensed Marriage & Family Therapist, International Best Selling Author, Trauma-informed Yoga instructor, and mindfulness facilitator that provides holistic psychotherapy in her group practice Greater Self Therapy. Dr. Z provides community support (therapists, healers, service providers, small business owners) via whole life coaching, cultural competency training and wellness retreats to intentionally shift, transform and manage how they spend their time making money as the embodiment of their Greater Self, LLC.

18

THERESA ALLEN - Radical Self-love When You are Functioning At 8%

Have you noticed that we live much of our lives focused on percentages? Phone battery life.

Chance of rain.

Report cards.

You get the point.

An 8% discount off the pair of shoes you have been eyeing probably wouldn't excite you. But what if you found out that a major, life-giving part of your body was only functioning at 8%? What if it was 92% dead? You would definitely tune in.

It happened to me. My kidneys were caput. My choices for combatting this were to start dialysis or find a new kidney.

Immediately.

I felt like I had an armed grenade rolling around my feet.

My kidney journey is a short story that started with an autoimmune disease rudely deciding to control my body. This disease, called Sarcoidosis, can attack any organ. In my case, it took hold of my kidneys and my eyes. I did not know I had it until routine renal labs showed roller coaster charts of blood markers going bonkers. A kidney biopsy proved that Sarcoid had set up shop and was making holes in my little beans like termites in a tree.

As for my eyes, Sarcoid's gift was soon to be permanent floaters that dart around like annoying bugs that do not land long enough to bat away.

I am a Type A personality, you know the ones; competitive, workaholics, who like to control everything. I mean if you want something done right... Yes, that's me. I love to solve problems. You can ask me a rhetorical question and I will go to work crafting the answer and its defense just in case you need citations. I am also a person who must show confidence, never vulnerability. For whatever reason, I see vulnerability as a weakness. It is one thing I truly wish I could change about myself, but I haven't had much luck doing that.

With the bombshell kidney news, my Type A brain locked into research overdrive. How do I avoid dialysis? How do I find a new kidney? How did this happen? And, most importantly, how can I fix it?

I was determined not to be tethered to a blood-filtering machine for four hours, three times a week. I turned to the next option; find a donor. There are two ways to do this. Secure your spot on the national kidney transplant list or find a kind soul willing to rip out their perfectly good organ and hand it to you.

Finding a donor or securing a spot on the transplant list are tasks that take months, or years, to complete. In fact, many kidney patients who start dialysis never get to quit their treatment. They are either not a candidate for transplant because of their comorbidities or simply run out of time waiting for their miracle to arrive. The reality was I was the latest addition to a grim family portrait of kidney warriors, and I was praying to be photoshopped out.

The very first thing you do, whether you plan to find a live donor or not, is to apply for the national kidney list. Members of this list hope to receive a kidney from a deceased donor. This lets the world know you are waiting on the gift of life which, unfortunately, comes at another's expense. You must endure weeks of diagnostic tests. They check everything from your colon, lungs, and breasts to your unique genetic material that can only find transplant success with the most carefully matched, almost-twin human you can find. Even a real twin human is no guarantee of a match.

My Type-A tendencies were squashed at every turn. It did little good for me to be well-informed with a computer full of research completed. Like everyone else, I had to work through the process. I had to wait on appointments and test results and gather mounds of information so the transplant center could "consider" my case. I had to sit waiting for emails not answered in the timely manner they deserved. I had to learn patience.

It is safe to say the control freak in me was nothing more than a big-shoed rodeo clown trying to distract the bull. That bull will take you down if it wants to, you silly clown.

Because of immunities built up from pregnancies and my hard-to-match blood type, my plethora of tests marked me at 92% unmatchable. (Here we are with percentages again.) I was placed on the kidney transplant list with ninety-thousand others who were waiting in front of me.

During this time, my beautiful wife Cooch, wanted to rescue me so she offered up a kidney. To be my donor, she had to prove herself a worthy subject. She endured the same testing and waiting and was turned down by the first transplant center we contacted. In the end, the next center approved her. We flew over that hurdle like Olympians on the way to the podium.

However, when the testing dust settled, she was not a match.

A little heartbroken, but nonetheless determined, she offered to enter the National Kidney Exchange Live Donor program. This exchange finds recipients for live, mismatched donors. Not all transplant centers work this program, and we had to find this option on our own. (Ok, finding that information was where my Type A won a small battle.)

In May of 2021, Cooch gave her kidney to a man in Tennessee. Two weeks later, I received a new kidney from a lady in Boston. We were part of a beautiful love chain with two complete strangers.

Because of Cooch's efforts, I only waited on the transplant list for three months. I was one of the lucky ones. Since I was removed from the list, we felt blessed that our use of the exchange program allowed someone else to get a kidney that might have otherwise gone to me. Cooch saved three people!

I learned many things about myself along this difficult path. If you are like me, perhaps you will appreciate one of these moments of clarity I experienced.

1. Letting go of control is sometimes your only choice. Lean into it.
2. Calm down. You cannot rush time or stop it, but you can live in it. So do that with your whole being.
3. Be vulnerable. It is the most human thing you can be so don't be afraid.
4. You are not measured by what you control, so just use that part of you when it is really needed.
5. Remind yourself that your value as a person is not solely dependent on your achievements or productivity. Embrace the idea that you are

worthy of love and care simply because you exist.

6. Accept gifts given in love. They are motivated by the purest center of the giver's soul, showing itself to only you. That's a real treasure on earth.

Cooch and I are two years out from the incredible journey we took together. We are both healthy and thankful for the generosity of others. We have also started living more fully. I hear that happens a lot when the grim reaper knocks on your door.

Not today, pal.

Theresa Allen is the CEO of Sanresa, Inc., a marketing consulting agency focused on elevating the success of small, passion-driven businesses. Theresa holds a BS in Advertising & Public Relations from Texas Christian University. She is also the owner of Heavenly Bound Rosaries, established in 1993. Her unique spiritual jewelry has been sold across the globe and featured in the renowned Kimbell Art Museum in Fort Worth, TX, as well as Buckfast Abbey in Buckfastleigh, UK. She is an American Business Awards nominee in Marketing and a guest MBA program lecturer at the SMU Cox School of Business in Dallas, TX.

With 30+ years of experience, Theresa is a highly sought after marketing maven and serial entrepreneur who levels up her clients' growth and revenue using a diversified set of tools and techniques.

19

COURTNEY BARNARD - Our Success Lies Within

Radical self-love. Three powerful words that can evoke drastically different responses from each person. For some, these words can bring joy, excitement, and pride, and for others can bring confusion, guilt, and fear. Not everyone knows, truly knows, how to love themselves. It sometimes seems that our ability to do so has been stripped away and sold back to us as a luxury. We're told that self-care is a treat when it really should be part of our daily or weekly routines. Self-love is more than just a massage or a bath once in a while, it is the innate ability to listen within and know what we need to feel connected in this world, connected to ourselves, to one another. Self-love is knowing on the deepest level, what serves our souls. While each of us is unique, we are all searching for the same things on the most basic level.

In 2019, I had an experience that opened my eyes to all of this. I had never known about mindset or self-love or any of the things I practice today. I was a young mom of 3, struggling with my own childhood wounds, and, after years of putting my needs last, my body started forcing me to change.

I grew up an only child. My parents had a volatile marriage. They were off and on a few times until finally calling it quits in my early teens. Even then, my parents remained codependent on one another and on me. Sharing my feelings wasn't something that was asked of me, nor did I feel like I could do so without repercussion, so I buried everything and never properly processed any of the things I had experienced. Like many, I continued living what seemed like two different personas: the one my parents expected of me and the one that felt like me.

As an adult, I tried to continue my façade as best I could while also starting a family of my own, but it became too much. The anxiety of balancing everyone's happiness was actually doing more harm than good and I reached a point that required me to put boundaries in place. Boundaries were a new concept to me. Never in my life did I have boundaries. Boundaries meant that others would be unhappy with me – and not just anyone, but my parents. The codependent relationship we shared made this seem impossible. But I needed to do it for myself and my family. Even now, after having 4 kids, I still feel like this was the hardest thing I have ever done in my life. But I have never regretted it. It was the catalyst that set me on the path of healing and learning to love myself.

Six months after I put these boundaries in place, I started having sleep issues which exacerbated my anxiety and led to depression. It started out as one night every few days and quickly increased over the course of the month. At its worst, I was averaging two to four hours of sleep a night. My mental state was so bad that I was truly terrified to live another day feeling the way that I was, but I also didn't want to die. I had three little people relying on me to be their mommy and I was scared for my life.

With the help of my doctors, I was able to start sleeping again. However, I knew that underneath it all was unresolved trauma. I wasn't dealing with my feelings from this incredibly traumatic event that I had just experienced, and on top of that was a whole life of unresolved, trauma. The weight of holding everything in for so many years was costing me my health. How was

I going to be the wife, mother, or person I wanted to be if I couldn't even allow myself to be human?

Once I had a solid week of sleep under my belt, I knew I needed to figure out ways to help myself mentally and emotionally, to prevent this or anything like it from happening again. If I was going to be successful with anything in my life, I had to make room for me. I had to love myself in the past, present, and future.

Not knowing anything about it, I began listening to small meditation segments online. I quickly took a liking to it and started to venture out on my own, just sitting outside on the porch or laying in the grass and connecting to what was around me. I was just being, without expectation, without judgment. I began to figure out who I was and what I really wanted.

Soon after, I began journaling. Again, it started small and in bursts, but it helped me release whatever I had on my mind and would almost always lead to some sort of epiphany, no matter how small. One of the things I struggled with the most was feeling like I had no time for myself to do the things I loved doing. Painting, for example, has always been my biggest passion. I had an art degree and big dreams but felt like there was never any time while having three kids in four years. So when I would write in my journal, I started with affirmations to change my perspective. I began writing things like "I am enough. I am worthy. There is always enough time. Things are always working out for me. I love me." I would write pages of affirmations, no two the same. It helped me be more optimistic and see the opportunities instead of the lack, but it also built me up with an energy I had never felt before. I had never really told myself that I loved myself, and for the last four years, I have signed every journal entry with "I love me". Not every entry is gold and I certainly don't feel like doing it some days, but I show up. Because that is what self-love is – showing up for ourselves even when it's hard. We must love and trust ourselves if we are ever going to love and trust others. It is that love and trust in ourselves that keeps us going when we start to have doubts. Our success lies within. Our joy lies within. Everything we want and need in life is within us, but we have to believe it and we have to practice listening to it, especially when it feels uncomfortable or scary. Those are the growth moments where we are making progress and stepping into the person we know we really are.

Since I started painting again, I've made it my mission to paint for those who feel unseen and unheard. I want to paint the emotions that people feel from life's traumas and let them know that they are not alone. We can feel and heal together if we just learn to lean in to that radical self-love and not be afraid to share our vulnerable sides. That love and trust is what builds community and connection - the connection we are all searching for.

So start small, but start loving yourself. Whether it's meditation, journaling, or spending time doing something you're passionate about, you deserve to love yourself, even if you don't believe it yet. It takes practice for many of us, but you will get there if you just show up for yourself!

Courtney Barnard is an intuitive abstract expressionist painter who acknowledges and validates people's experiences through her work. She helps create connections and community with her topics and encourages people everywhere to feel and heal.

She received her Bachelor of Fine Arts degree, with honors, from West Chester University and, after some time away to start a family, Courtney came back to painting with a whole new purpose. Having hit rock bottom emotionally and physically, painting became not just something she enjoyed, but a way to heal. Through meditation and journaling, combined with her art practice, Courtney unlocked a new way to express emotions and connect with those going through similar experiences. It has become her mission to help those struggling with trauma recovery to feel validated and part of a bigger healing community.

20

DANIEL COHEN - Loving Who You Are

The first time I danced on stage as "myself" was when I was eighteen. It's still vivid in my mind. The blinding lights and adrenaline, the reverberations of the music. For the first time, I genuinely could not stop myself from smiling. I remember the feeling of pure happiness and freedom. In that moment I realized that it was possible to want to exist, to be able to exist as someone who I thought I would never become. Or more accurately, as someone who I always was. This memory was the first time I was able to love myself. Everything on the outside was resonating with everything on the inside – it was the first time I felt like me. I thought my life would never be the same from that moment, and I also thought that I would only be happy from that moment on and all my problems in life would melt into the void, never to trouble me again.

This memory indeed marks a big shift in my life where some things changed. Simultaneously, many things looped back into familiar patterns of perfectionism, doubt, sadness, and ultimately trapping myself into feeling like I had to become someone I was not. In the years since, or more honestly in the last couple of months, I've begun to realize that radical self-love is an active process that continues to grow within you through time. It's a commitment to yourself. I was lucky that the planets aligned at that moment a mere couple of months after transitioning, when I was able to perform and the real me emerged. The feelings and voices in my head were my own and filled with nothing but love for myself and my existence in that moment.

For me, an initial step to committing to radical self-love, and one that continues to be an active practice, is questioning who is controlling my internal dialogue. Is it me and my intuition or is it someone or something that caused me harm in the past (whether intentionally or inadvertently)? Regardless, a lot of these phantoms exist in our subconscious mind, and usually, we don't even realize that their words are not our own. When a harmful thought or belief makes its way into your consciousness – perhaps it's one that focuses on perfectionism or traps you in a place where you cannot be yourself – start by asking whose belief this thought came from.

I know it's dangerous to speak in absolutes, but I guarantee that your actual voice and intuition are *only* capable of loving and supporting you. That first voice, or first consciousness, can easily become lost with traumatic experiences, toxic people, our oppressive society...the list goes on. But your voice is still there! And it is waiting for you to find it again. Once you've found it (and you'll know, it's a feeling that comes from your heart and gut, and maybe a bit of your mind), trust it. If you have an inkling that you need to do something, or something does not feel right, or you're craving a particular food, try listening to it instantly and see what happens.

Is it really that simple? Yes, and there is also more to it.

In our society, we are conditioned to ignore our bodies and natural super-powers of intuition and empathy. I've experienced this first-hand from training in both rhythmic gymnastics and ballet. We are taught to "break" our bodies through hard work and repetition, so that they may "become" the instruments to express our art. The irony is, wouldn't honing the practice of listening to our bodies help us express ourselves more? Wouldn't that allow us to achieve those unimaginable feats without destroying our bodies in the process? What if we used learning-centered emotional intelligence instead? What if we showed appreciation for our bodies by listening to what they need to create the art that we are so passionate about? Everything goes back to listening to our bodies and what they need. And, to respect and listen to your body, you *must* love it. Listening is just another form of love, which is yet another piece of loving yourself.

Of course, life is a multidimensional spectrum that requires a balance. There are also these wonderful and scary things called emotions that add more colors and layers to the ways in which we can love ourselves. Being present, which I believe is another form of loving yourself by appreciating yourself in the moment, might mean beginning to process and acknowledge emotions. Give yourself time. Keep coming back to yourself through it all. Life shifts and changes will happen, and you will shift and change too.

I experienced another big shift in a more recent performance. A big aspect was dancing outside of the toxic environment I was comfortable in, and collaborating with someone who has always loved and supported me. I've always had trouble watching myself on video, and yet, after that performance, I tried something different. I watched it from the perspective of a younger me, who had just been diagnosed with an autoimmune disease. A me that was unsure if I'd make it to tomorrow. I showed them my performance, and I loved watching it. I remember having an emotional moment, as I realized that for the first time, perhaps ever, I felt grateful that I was born. The biggest takeaway in this more recent performance, when looking back at the memory I shared at the beginning, was feeling love for myself the whole trip and the mix of emotions that came with it. It wasn't just a moment; it was an experience. During that trip, I felt an abundance of appreciation for how I'm alive, how I exist, and at the center of it was me loving myself both on and off the stage. Loving myself for simply existing and being grateful that for the first time, I was allowing myself to. Now, I find myself looking forward to every performance (or life) because I know it will be different and exciting, instead of hoping it will be the same, or that I'll be able to repeat something I deemed as "good." Instead, I choose myself. Things began to shift and align after that, the internal questioning began to come from a place of self-advocacy, especially within myself. You must advocate for yourself both outside and *inside yourself.*

And thus, we have reached the current part of my life with radical self-love. There is comfort in living while walking alongside the past or the future, letting the yesterdays and tomorrows of others trap us in a false web of our perceptions, emotions, and self-worth. And change can be daunting, exciting, and freeing all at once. Changing and growing into loving ourselves might be uncomfortable, and at the same time, perhaps it is something we've always known we are capable of. Let us choose to embrace ourselves. Let the past and future walk alongside us in the present.

When you love and support yourself, the whole world is led to support you. Because you are your whole world. You're inspiring people by just existing or learning to exist as yourself. There are people waiting to support you, waiting for you to love yourself the way they love you. Remember to ask for help. To admit if you're not okay. To celebrate that you are okay! Life is so much more than the binary of good and bad. We can experience multiple emotional truths simultaneously. The trick is to lean into it and guide life in the direction you want to go.

We can be angry at ourselves and still love ourselves. We can feel lost and still accept ourselves. We have the gift to choose ourselves. In that, we have the ultimate power, freedom, and opportunity. We are making the world a better place as a direct result of helping ourselves.

A last thing to remember, before we part ways. Sometimes it's easy to remove yourself from the equation. More than once I've found myself thinking, "I have to help others," or "I have to make the world a better place." Perhaps you have too. Remember that you are part of the people you wish to help. You are part of the world that you want to make a better place. Include yourself in your love.

Love who you were, who you are, and who you will be.

Daniel Rei Cohen is a healing artist who is learning to live life fully through radical self-love and acceptance. He strives to create movement, environments, and collaborations in which everyone is accepted as their authentic and wonderful selves.

Daniel is an elite athlete who won gold in multiple categories at the Junior Olympics for rhythmic gymnastics. He is currently training professionally as a ballet dancer at the University of Utah School of Dance and has performed featured roles such as Bluebird in Sleeping Beauty, and Basilio in Don Quixote as staged by the University of Utah's Utah Ballet. He also has experience in choreography, screendance, poetry, fencing, Wushu, psychology, and social justice advocacy.

As a Taiwanese and Jewish transmasc person living with an autoimmune disease, Daniel understands what it's like to struggle with identity, self-acceptance, and emotional and physical well-being. He also is beginning to understand the freedom and power that blooms from radical self-love and is determined to share it with the world. He wishes to foster healing in others through his compassionate art and believes everyone deserves to revel in all the iridescence that life has to offer. Everyone deserves to be loved for simply existing as who they are.

21

KATHY FREDERICK - Self Love Through Scripture

It happened around fifteen years ago. I walked into a church conference in New York, and a strange scene captured me. Right there during worship was a barefoot man with a ponytail playfully painting away. I blurted out to God, "What is this? Look at that guy doing art? But this is *church*!" I added, "It's so cool! Do you think I could do that?" Crickets! No answer!

Months later, I lay prostrate on the floor, a steady torrent of tears and snot persisting as I poured out my soul to God. I knew there were undeveloped talents trapped inside of me. My mind was the jailer: fear and unworthiness were my shackles. I lacked confidence and self-love. I knew I had to risk failure and trust the talent I'd been given, but I'd been stalling for years.

I wiped my face with my last tissue and checked my emails. A friend had sent me information about an upcoming art/worship workshop in Vermont. I'd never heard of such a thing. Intriguing! Money was a little tight, so I declined. Ann implored me to call the conference center; maybe they had scholarships.

To my astonishment, they offered me a 100% scholarship with lodging! I only needed to show up! I recognized this was God's response to my getting real with Him and making a shift. I acknowledged my call, accepted it, and the universe flung open its doors.

I drove up on a beautiful March morning, enjoying every stream with pillows of white on exposed rocks and snow-laden branches bending gently over the waters. Gratitude swelled. I was beginning a journey of radical self-love and discovery.

I knew I was where I was meant to be, and God was about to drop an astounding confirmation. Balancing art supplies, I carefully opened the studio door and the teacher turned to greet me. What? Are you kidding me? This man was that same barefooted guy with the ponytail that I'd seen a year earlier in New York! God was finally answering: "Yes, you *can* do that – and he'll be your teacher!" Imagine that!

During my prayer and meditation time, I wrote God a poem. I sensed His reply, and this is a snippet:

Stay humble, stay low,
And you will flow.
You are the paintbrush, and you are the paint.
When the brokenhearted and those who faint
Come to you, you be the paint.

When the tired masses need a lift,
I will give you the proper gift.
You give it out, you be the spout.
My Glory, My healing will gush out.

Space here doesn't allow for the many experiences I've had where my art or poetry has deeply touched the hearts of people, but the stories are astounding.

When growing up, there are endless things that can happen to a child to affect their self-worth. These things can take decades to recover from. I'd experienced some things that made me feel unworthy of love.

This is the thing, though: God is a healer, a restorer, a redeemer of time. He pursued me, using people to demonstrate His love, and I accepted his invitation to get to know Him. His love transformed me, and slowly caused me to accept my own worth and truly love myself. He showed me how my experiences were being sifted through a filter of unworthiness and I wasn't seeing things as they really were. Like a cornered cat, I'd swat my paw to reject others before they had a chance to hurt me. He gently began to show me a better way. I needed to watch my words and dismiss and replace thoughts that didn't serve me: these two simple things proved powerful.

I like to read, and I delved into the scriptures. I found some real nuggets that fostered my self-love.

Psalms 139:16 (NIV) says, "Your eyes saw my unformed body: all the days ordained for me were written in your book before one of them came to be." Wow! There's a book about me? My life was carefully planned? Mine? So, I am valuable!

I saw in Mark 12:31, there's a command to love our neighbors as ourselves. We can only love our neighbor to the same degree that we love ourselves. Because I've accepted my call and perceive the open doors that serendipitously appear, self-love is nurtured, and love for my neighbor grows.

Have you tried to get others to love you so that you can feel loved and valued? I have. Stop! That's a sign of self-hatred. When we do this, we allow them to tell us how to live and who to be. When someone asks you to do something, can you say no without giving a reason? If you can't, you are prey to their manipulation. When they inevitably disappoint you, you recoil and don't feel loved. This cycle repeats until you stop it.

I stopped by learning my identity and becoming secure in God's love. I no longer depend on others' opinions of me. It doesn't upset me if other people don't love me because I am grounded in purpose and love. I am free!

God spoke to Jeremiah in Jeremiah 1:5 (NIV) saying, "Before I formed you in the womb I knew you, before you were born I set you apart; I appointed you as a prophet to the nations."

Wow! God has specific assignments for us. We are His heart's desire and can sense His pleasure as we navigate our destinies.

Grounded in increasing self-love and knowing our identity, we find courage to step out to do those things that are in our hearts. We don't stress over mistakes: He's no more upset with us for a misstep than a mom is when her baby stumbles when learning to walk.

Years ago, I had a vision. I was seated high in the Heavenly realms. I was laughing and overflowing in joy as I leaned toward the Kathy who was down here on earth, and I was tossing down paintings and dollar bills to myself! (I had not even begun my painting journey yet.) I was in two places at one time. Quantum, right? God reminded me of a scripture found in Ephesians. Part of it says, "...And (God) has raised us up together and made us sit together in heavenly places...for we are his workmanship, created in Christ Jesus to do good works, which God prepared in advance for us to do." When doubt or fear try to rear their heads, I remember I'm a masterpiece!

If you are struggling with doubt and self-love, begin to declare the things that you want to see manifest. Do that each night right before you sleep. Write them out as well. Close your eyes and see yourself having or doing those things. Feel the emotions. In the mornings, thank God. Do that until you see change.

One declaration you might add is this: I am God's masterpiece, fearfully and wonderfully made. He will never leave me or forsake me, and I love myself as He loves me.

Invite Him to help you. As healing begins and hope rises, you will soar and never look back.

Kathy's mixed-media and intuitive abstract art lives with collectors on four continents. In addition to her studio work, Kathy creates live art at churches and venues during worship; God has profoundly impacted people through her gift. She speaks at events and churches, teaches workshops on Art & Worship, and encourages youth to step out in their creative giftings.

Kathy is on a mission to touch the hearts and spirits of people through her Spirit-inspired, Christ-centered poetry, prose, and colorful artwork. Many experience hope, joy, peace, encouragement, and confirmation. A common thread that runs through her poetry and art is how God makes use of every mistake and every heartache: nothing is wasted and every person is valuable. Many recount how her art has transformed the energy in their spaces.

Kathy is also a Christian minister with a theology degree and credentials through Christian International Ministries.

22

ANGIE NORDSTRUM - Quitting My Job as an Act of Self Care

The most loving thing I've ever done for myself is quit my job.

I was 46 years old. Single mom. Working full time and running myself ragged shuttling my son to before-school care as the sun was coming up, commuting to work, toiling all day in a job where my creativity was not appreciated, rushing back to after-school care to pick up my son, sprinting to ball practice, throwing tacos together every night because there was no way I could even make a plan to meal prep, trying to remember to change the laundry before it starts to smell and collapsing in bed. Repeat. My life felt like I was running in never-ending circles on a merry-go-round.

This was not the life I wanted for myself or my son. I was running ragged and exhausted. This lifestyle was a disservice to both of us. We both deserved better.

I got really quiet and walked and meditated on how to make this enormous change in my life.

I created my exit strategy and I quietly submitted my resignation. I firmly believed if I could give all of my creativity to someone else's business and success, surely I could apply it to a business of my own.

This is how I took my life back. I combined an unwavering belief in myself, movement, community, and creativity to craft the life I wanted. It wasn't easy, but so worth all of my hard work.

- Start with a firm belief in yourself. I've known since I was a child that creativity is my superpower. I took all the skills I had acquired over decades in the workplace and created my own art and design business. I have always had an entrepreneur's spirit and always wanted to work for myself. Want it, believe it, build it.

- Find clarity through movement. Walking away from a reliable paycheck is very stressful, especially as a single parent. Income may become a wild card and that is scary. You need to get those endorphins going and move stressful energy out of your body. Do whatever speaks to you. I rode my mountain bike every day. I ran around the lake over and over. I went to yoga.

- Find your people. Every time life has dealt me a difficult hand, I have learned to find my people. These are the people who have already experienced whatever challenge or crisis you are currently going through. Find the people who are at least one step ahead of you. Go out and find them. I reached out to professional connections and friends. I set up a bazillion coffee dates. How did they get their new business off the ground? Where did they find their clients? They will understand where you are and how to best support you.

- Create and make every day. Creating and making things with your hands releases endorphins. Get those happy chemicals flowing! I'm always working on multiple creative projects at once. Painting fuels the digital work and crafting inspires the design for the next mural project. Creativity is like a wildfire, it picks up momentum the more you feed it. Keep creating and igniting that creative fire. Let the creativity flow!

Building my own business allowed me to create on my own terms and be the Mom I wanted to be. I was present for ball games, holidays, school events, appointments, and meals. I showed my son perseverance, resilience, and how to take inspired action to create the life you desire.

Today I work full-time as an artist. I paint and make and create every day. I teach workshops and I mentor. I put my soul into my work and create art that others enjoy. This is the most gratifying work I have ever done.

You can do it too.

Angie Nordstrum is a dynamic and passionate artist and creator who breathes life into her art on various mediums such as canvas, walls, windows, and even clothes. Her vibrant and colorful paintings have the power to inspire and ignite the flames within your soul.

Angie's artistic journey has taken her to fascinating places, including the design and creation of eclectic decor for eight renowned restaurants across the country. Fueling her love for public art, she has adorned numerous walls in Colorado with captivating murals. Sharing her expertise locally and internationally, Angie imparts her knowledge through engaging workshops.

Currently, Angie is immersed in an ambitious large-scale project in Mexico, showcasing her artistic prowess on an expansive canvas. As an active member of her community, she generously gives back through various family art experiences throughout the year, while also mentoring high school students in the art of mural painting.

Driven by her wanderlust and thirst for adventure, Angie has pursued her passion for travel, living in London, immersing herself in the culture of Paris, experiencing the thrill of landing on a beach in a plane, and swimming in enchanting jungle waterfalls.

Additionally, Angie, a single Mom, has demonstrated tremendous strength and resilience in the face of adversity. Confronting the challenges of cancer, divorce, and trauma head-on, she emerges as a symbol of bravery and perseverance. Her unwavering spirit and unwavering support from loved ones have provided her with the strength to overcome these obstacles and continue to create art that touches the hearts of many.

Angie's remarkable artistic journey has garnered recognition and accolades, with her work featured in esteemed publications such as The Turquoise Iris Journal, Better Homes & Gardens Do It Yourself, and Creative Kids magazines, as well as The Denver Post. Though her adventures take her across the globe, Angie's home base remains nestled in the scenic foothills of Colorado.

23

ARIELLA COHEN - You are Enough

The best way I know how to communicate is through stories. They have most often inspired my creativity. They have shown me what is possible. I want to show you radical self-love through a story of my own. Take a break with me for a while. – Ari

Today, all I could do was hold on.

I remember when I could barely muster the energy to reach out. I was a lot sadder at that time, yet hopeful. It's funny, those things I hoped for are the reality I walk through now. I need to remember that every once in a while.

As rays of starlight flecked into my room, I quietly opened the window and hopped out. I crouched in the makeshift maintenance cradle that hung from the side of the ship. The cradle bobbed gently looking like a decrepit, if well-loved cat toy. I huddled in its cage, my injuries from yesterday's battle ebbing a familiar melody. I tried to tune my senses to the breeze that hummed contentedly past. But the dull, uneven beat of the old song cleaved numbly and dully into it. My fingers gently stroked the soft bandages that Xiaogou had wrapped around my arms. I clung to that feeling, trying to ground myself where I was. The old melody didn't have that softness. After a while, I was able to uncurl my head and watch the stars and clouds as they drifted past. In this part of the immortal realm, there were no sky isles or constellations or rails. There were only the spider webs of rivers, suspended like threads in the endless sky. My hand reached out. Unconsciously, my fingers found the bead in my pocket. Tracing its cool, smooth surface – time and again finding the crack etched into it like a scar – I started to breathe again. The wind carried the cool, sweet scent of the stars and warm, blooming incense of life from far away. I pulled the bead out of my pocket and cupped it in my hands. The scent of melting snow drifted from its lightly sparkling surface. I could have seen it as progress. The fallen star had used to smell like decaying autumn leaves, and vast smoky darkness swirled within its body. It had taken immense effort to get it this far, pouring my scarce magic into it bit by bit. But all I could think about was the full-blown anchor it should have sprouted into by now. Its surface felt as cold and dead as when Xiaogou had given it to me. *Enough.* I took a deep breath. *It's okay.* A sense of urgency, of fear, spiked through my chest and back like lightning. The emotion still caught me off guard and overwhelmed me.

I had spent so long believing I was never meant to feel. I knew now that emotion was possible for someone like me and that it was a lot better than feeling numb, even if it shook my entire body and made me feel like I was going to explode. I tried to calm myself, but my thoughts surged stubbornly. *I need my anchor to grow, soon.* Anchors kept gods and spirits alive. Here, they most commonly took the shape of floating isles - a manifestation of an object, place, or idea in the mortal world. They were an immortal's domain, their funnel for power. Without one, a being here would eventually fade. Being neither a spirit nor a god, no one was sure what could happen to me without one. Most likely, I would eventually be rejected back into the Frame, the reflection that sat between the mortal and godly realms. My old, lonely home. I wanted to be able to stay *here* in this realm. I wanted to be able to help people like Xiaogou. But as I held the broken gift, I couldn't bring myself to summon any energy. The fallen star remained cold and dead in my palms. I might have fallen back into the old song then, but something happened. A sound called to my mind, breaking the calm before dawn. A rustling, a shifting, a sparking, like the lullaby of a campfire. I climbed on top of the cradle and leaped straight up, landing on the edge of the ship. I clung there for a moment like some humanoid beetle, then scrambled up, over the side. The soft moss embraced the soles of my feet with each step. The ship was made up of the bodies of various vessels, earth, and architecture. Wings, doors, and sails, formed of metal, stone, and wood sprouted from across its surface in a manner that defied logic. Nestled in the vessel's core, its roots running across every surface, lay an enormous tree. The roots pulsed gently, the veins and arteries to the ship's body. A canopy of branches and leaves sprung from the top of the ship, an exposed rib cage protecting its cabin. This was Xiaogou's anchor. Accompanying a symphony of crackles and sparks on one of the great tree's branches, something was moving. Slowly, almost imperceptibly, a tiny bud was beginning to grow.

I had sundered a part of myself to look after her. We had both gotten pretty battered up yesterday when we collected that spirit's soul. Even as a god, she could still get hurt. It was a fact that gave me overwhelming feelings that I wasn't ready to think about yet. To my surprise, the part I had separated from myself, reported that Xiaogou had left her room. I tuned into its senses immediately. I saw the hallway of the ship and – a big fluffy ghost? It...was Xiaogou. From my part's vantage point as it floated near the ceiling, I could just see her head peering out from deep within a mass of blankets. She slowly inched forward down the hallway, a giant sentient burrito making its solemn pilgrimage. I let my part continue to follow her. Xiaogou made it to the kitchen. She reluctantly unwrapped the blanket and hung it on a chair. She put on a pastel pink apron with a kitten on it. She started...to cook. I watched quietly as she plucked a sun fruit and cracked it into a pan. The oil sizzled, shimmering like the stars around me. She grabbed batter that had been stored in a bottle and spooned some in. The pale substance, fluffed up like a cloud. Xiaogou flipped it over to reveal the little cake had become golden brown. As she worked, my gaze was drawn to her. A lattice of pale scars reached across her brown muscular back, while her new injuries were enveloped with blue bandages that I had wrapped last night. Her arms flexed and relaxed with her movements. They were so, buff. *Focus, Dae.* She knew that I was watching her. Xiaogou had seen my part many times: a tiny round ethereal blob with the vague features of a cat. For once she wasn't trying to hide her emotions. She looked as exhausted and sad and depressed as I felt. There were moments when she stopped, and I could feel that she was grounding herself. Like I had to, when the old song began to play in my head. But, she kept going. She was still caring for herself.

We had both changed a lot since we had taken each other's hands. Since we had caused a rift in the Frame, and I had been displaced in the realm of the gods. Since the odd pair of us, an emotionless undead and a broken reaper, had started on our journey, laying to rest and collecting the souls of gods, mortals, and spirits fallen to the Bloom. I didn't have the courage to come inside yet. I let the little blob cat me sit in front of Xiaogou, to remind her she wasn't alone. And all the while I watched as the tiny bud grew from her tree. I had thought it was supposed to be a solitary process. A growth rent with pain and work. Could it really be as simple as being?

All of a sudden, Xiaogou was bringing the food to the table. She had done it. A feeling rose in my chest. Before I knew what was happening, I found myself at the side door of the ship. The feeling split down my veins. I opened the door. I met Xiaogou. She was sitting at the table. Her eyes met mine. Relief and warmth and nervousness thrummed in her gaze. I walked unsteadily over to her, and I let that emotion fully take hold. I hugged her. Hesitantly and gently, yet firmly, she hugged me back.

As we talked and ate and laughed, the unspoken words fell between us. *It's going to be okay. You are enough.* A delicate crackle kindled from the star in my pocket: like the sparkling dew of a fresh dawn.

Ariella (Ari) Cohen is a queer, mixed, Taiwanese American animator and comic artist who strives to create stories that change people's hearts.

As someone given a second chance at life, Ari is determined to pursue what they love. It is often not easy to live, and healing is a continual journey. They are learning to accept themself as a work in progress. They strive to make art that helps people feel seen and comforted. To reach out a hand. To help others like them feel less alone.

From the ages of 9–15, Ari trained in elite sports including rhythmic gymnastics and competitive dance, winning numerous awards. They have since retired and enjoy more relaxing hobbies like martial arts (they find punching things pleasant and therapeutic). This physical background gives them a unique perspective and skill set when animating. Since childhood, Ari has helped their mother foster kittens. The ability to have helped save lives is something they cherish. They were as much saved in turn by the thirteen fluffy companions they live with. In 2022, their first gallery piece Yet to Meet You was accepted to Queer Spectra.

As they cultivate their art and self, Ari is completing an animation degree at the University of Utah.

They are currently working on their first webcomic: the odyssey of a god and demon through a dying world. It features parallel realms, world-building rooted in Asian mythology, very gay characters, long cats, and a magic system tied to emotions.

24

CATE RAPHAEL - The Joyful Soul Journey – How I Found Radical Self-Love

I was born with my third eye open. With this special gift, I was able to live in a sacred world filled with high vibrational beings, angels, ascended masters, and ghosts. I received messages that can't be obtained by our everyday channels of perception and reasoning. Within my many years of self-discovery, I realized I could not only envision and listen to this world but share the gift of its interpretation with you. I call this the *Joyful Soul Journey* because working in the Akashic Records taught me how to live a more joyous life.

The angels, whom I have known since childhood, came to me in their most powerful form when I needed them the most. I learned to recognize and appreciate them deeply, connecting with my own spiritual world. Eventually, this relationship as well as with the other "members" of my ethereal team enabled me to find a greater clarity in my life.

Growing up with both parents having addiction issues, I followed that familiar path later in life and married a narcissist who was sick with alcoholism. I thought then – like many who marry into addiction –I could help my husband, but he was not ready to change his life, and as I discovered, it was not my job in the long run. It took me eighteen years to find the courage and strength to leave the relationship.

Throughout my marriage, my passion as a painter took a back seat to survival, and to motherhood. Determined to find a creative outlet, I used cooking and crafts for my artistic expression. After my divorce, I realized I had been living in a state of lack: Lack of clarity, money, trust, belief, forgiveness, self-worth, self-compassion, and self-love. I was always giving and never receiving. I was empty on every level.

It was then the Angels re-entered my life in a powerful way. They were sending me messages through repetitive numbers that appeared daily. These number codes led me to a numerologist who became my teacher. She then introduced me to the next six teachers with whom I would study. My life transformed with a greater understanding of how to live a more joyous life.

These teachers guided me toward a clearer recognition of my gifts and healing abilities but it was when I learned how to read the Akashic Records (everything AND anything one has ever experienced in any lifetime, stored in a place of energy called the Akasha), I discovered I could use ALL of my gifts here. Not only was I able to find healing for myself but also was able to help clients find the root of their issue. Together we can heal, clear, and release whatever isn't serving them so they can live a more joyful life.

I am sharing with you the five essential steps that I have learned working in the Akashic Records with my clients over the past 12 years. It is my desire that you too, find *Radical Self Love* by working with these steps. As you will see, it doesn't begin with Self Love; that comes later.

Step One

Self-Care - This is a priority. Make time for your basic needs for a healthier life. Eating healthy foods, exercise that you enjoy, taking time to connect to the divine, looking money in the eye, and a time out when you need one. For your spirit, try meditation, yoga, sound healing, and breath work. Get more rest if you are tired. This is about taking care of **you**: mind, body, and spirit. Focus on those things that bring you joy! Do you know what brings you joy? I suggest making a list to identify and practice what brings you happiness and self-fulfillment.

Step Two

Gratitude - I believe gratitude is the most powerful form of prayer there is. I believe there are 2 ways to use your gratitude practice. First, saying *thank you* for what you already have notifies the Divine you are ready and open for more goodness. The second is saying *thank you* in advance for that which you desire to bring to yourself. This allows the Divine to manifest for your highest good. Gratitude changes your mindset and view of life to focus on a more positive, open-hearted one. In this way, you will find yourself searching for and attracting more *goodness* to your life. Try daily gratitude for 30 days and see what happens!

Step Three

Connection to the Divine— I believe we are not alone in this world but are supported by a Divine Source (God/Universe/Higher Power) along with angels, guides, and guardians. Their purpose is to assist you. To connect with them, simply *ASK* for their assistance. Tell them you wish to connect and need their help. Take the time to speak to them and trust they are here to support you. Trust, believe, take action steps, and turn it over. This is when you learn to let it go. I believe you will find if your request or prayer is in your highest good, it will happen. And quickly too! Don't forget to say thank you. My favorite saying is: *set it and forget it!*

Step Four

Self-compassion- This is about acceptance. Self-compassion is not a way to judge ourselves. It is a way to embrace who and what we are, with kindness. It's being patient with ourselves and our shortcomings. It's about embracing who we are! Instead of dwelling on your shortcomings, focus on what you are doing well. Acknowledge what you have done well that day. Here's something you can practice on your own. Look at yourself in the mirror and congratulate yourself on one thing that made you feel good that day. This will shift your focus to something positive about yourself. You are a human being worthy of love. When we learn to be compassionate with ourselves, it is only then we can be compassionate with others.

Step Five

Self-forgiveness - Why is forgiving ourselves so hard? We are *ALL* imperfect. Remind yourself that you are not the only person on earth to have made a mistake. It's how we learn as human beings. The shared human experience is imperfection! Shut that critical mind down and call in your "team" for help. Try separating from the situation by having a conversation with yourself. To do this, simply discuss it as though the issue belongs to your best friend. When you separate forgiving yourself from judging yourself, you will be better able to learn from the past and fully love and accept yourself. Remember, we are all spirits having a human experience.

When you can embrace and master these five steps of self-care, gratitude, connection, self-compassion, and self-forgiveness, you will experience the ultimate goal: *Self-worth*. Your creativity will flow with love and confidence.

Cate Raphael was born with her third eye open. She is a natural medium, healer and Spiritual Consultant. She works directly with the Ascended Masters and

Archangels. It is her soul purpose to get to the root of the issue that is holding you back from living a more joyous life. With the assistance of both her team and your team, it is healed, cleared and transmuted for all times. Past, present and future.

Cate Raphael is known Internationally as a Level 3 Certified Master Akashic Records consultant. She is Certified and Authorized as a Heal Your Money Story coach, Angel consultant and reiki 2. Cate spent 2 years studying the Chakra System at School For Modern Mystics. She is contributing author for the bestselling book "Courage Under Siege– Book series, Bewilderment to Enlightenment."

Cate Raphael is also a professional artist whose mission as an artist is to preserve the uniqueness, serenity and beauty of the landscapes she walks. She infuses each painting with peace, serenity and joy. Collectors have shared with her that this is how they feel when standing before them.. She seeks inspiration from peaceful, open spaces, then transfers that onto the canvas. Her style is uniquely her own, and could be considered nontraditional realism. She has been a professional artist showing in galleries since 2010.

Cate believes that it is everyone's innate ability to create. Creation is a gift given to us through Divine Source to find peace, and keep us grounded and present. She believes that creating is a spiritual act in itself, healing one's own spirit. She looks forward to bringing this belief to the classroom to assist you in healing your inner desire to create, by integrating meditation, healing ceremony's, mindset and intuitive creating, all in one setting.

25

ESTHER JOY MARUANI - Embracing Self-Care, Setting Fantasy-Type Goals, and Finding Purpose Through Backyard Chickens and Unleashed Creativity

Life has a way of throwing unexpected challenges our way, and it is during these times that we often discover the true depths of our resilience and the power of creativity. In this chapter, I explore my personal journey of navigating depression, financial loss, life's curveballs, and the isolation experienced during the COVID-19 pandemic. Through the exploration of self-care rituals, the setting of some very large, unrealistic goals, and the creative pursuit of sustainable living, I uncovered a transformative path towards self-love and a fulfilling life.

As the world went into COVID lockdown, I found myself trapped in a cloud of depression. Isolation and uncertainty weighed heavily on me, as it did on the rest of the world, leaving me adrift in a sea of despair. As the mist of chaos grew and the days started to blur together, my inner voice grew faint, as I struggled to navigate my life and manage the lives of my children. Recognizing the need for change and the support of an amazing husband, I embarked on a journey of self-care and self-discovery. On July 1, 2021, I announced to myself and on social media that I would no longer view the proverbial cup as half empty, that I would stop feeling sorry for myself and find a purpose in something. This mindset shift led me to meet a wonderful person named Ingjerd Jensen, who has since become a dear friend. Ingjerd is a coach through the *Proctor Gallagher Institute* and guided me through the *Thinking Into Results* program. She believed in me, taught me to dream big, to stop being so hard on myself, and to embrace small steps of self-care and accomplishments. One of the significant goals I wrote down was to become an author, specifically a best-selling author. I learned the importance of writing down all your ambitious goals, and the need to not give up on yourself.

I dedicate time to nurturing my mind, body, and soul each morning. Starting with a 5-to-10-minute meditation, I allowed myself to find stillness and try to embrace the present moment. It has been and still is challenging, but it has also been incredibly beneficial for my personal well-being. This practice has provided a much-needed emotional anchor and a space for inner reflection. Following meditation, I engaged in 20 minutes of yoga, deeply connecting with my body and grounding myself in the physical realm. The gentle movements and conscious breaths served as a reminder that I was capable of resilience and strength. I began to cherish this dedicated time for self-nurturing, realizing that to give to others, I must first fill my own cup.

In addition to meditation and yoga, I have adopted a simple yet powerful self-affirmation ritual. Each morning, I stand before the mirror, look into my own eyes, and with a genuine smile, I give myself a high-five. This small act of self-celebration is accompanied by words of encouragement: "Good job, you got this! You are amazing!" These daily affirmations have helped me to cultivate self-love and foster the positive mindset necessary to face all the challenges ahead.

During these times of introspection, memories from my childhood resurfaced. In particular, I recalled a children's book I had written when I was

10 years old, called "On The Farm". This nostalgic recollection ignited a spark of creativity within me, reminding me of the joy and wonder that accompanies storytelling. Driven both by a desire for personal purpose and a connection to nature, I embarked on a mission to create a small chicken operation in my backyard, for myself and my children to enjoy. Despite my upbringing on a small farm, I recognized the need to refresh my knowledge and immersed myself in two years of extensive research. I explored all the intricacies of raising backyard chickens, emphasizing their safety, health, and well-being.

The birth of Backyard Chicken Academy was inspired by the fulfillment that my backyard chickens brought me. I felt compelled to share this journey with others who are thinking about getting backyard chickens or may be feeling the attraction of sustainable living. Combining my newfound expertise with my passion for teaching and helping others, I founded the Backyard Chicken Academy. With four comprehensive modules, the academy guides individuals from "Chicken Thought" to "Chicken Parent", offering valuable insights and practical advice for embracing sustainable living.

As my passion for backyard chickens grew, so did my creative endeavors. This inspiration found its outlet in the form of writing children's books centered around these captivating creatures. As I poured my imagination onto the pages, my children expressed a desire to contribute, both in writing and illustrating. Together, we embarked on a creative journey, weaving tales of adventure and joy, bringing laughter and learning to young readers.

Additionally, the pursuit of sustainable living sparked innovative ideas within my family. Motivated by our chicken set-up, my son proposed a collaborative project aimed at improving the functionality and comfort of the chicken coop during the egg-laying process. My children and I brainstormed ideas and sketched designs, working together to invent a device that would alleviate stress for our beloved hens.

My journey from darkness to self-discovery and creativity has been transformative. Embracing self-care rituals, such as meditation, yoga, and daily affirmations has allowed me to cultivate a deep sense of self-love and resilience. These practices have become the foundation upon which I build my creative endeavors and pursue a fulfilling life. By reconnecting with my childhood passion for storytelling through the creation of children's books about chickens, I have not only ignited my own imagination but also inspired my children to explore their artistic talents. Together, we eagerly embark on these creative journeys, anticipating the day when our stories will come to life and inspire other young readers.

The development of the Backyard Chicken Academy has also given me a platform to share my knowledge and passion with others. Through the online course I developed, families who aspire to embrace sustainable living can navigate the intricacies of raising backyard chickens with joy and confidence. The satisfaction of seeing other families embark on their sustainable living journeys has been immeasurable, as it reinforces the idea that our experiences and knowledge can positively impact others. Innovation and collaboration have also become central themes in our lives. As my children and I work on inventing a device to improve our chicken set-up, we find ourselves bonding over shared ideas and aspirations. The process of problem-solving and bringing our inventions to life has not only strengthened our relationship but also allowed us to contribute to the well-being of our feathered friends.

In conclusion, I hope this chapter reflects the transformative potential power of embracing self-care rituals, rediscovering childhood passions, and pursuing sustainable living. Through self-love and creativity, I have not only emerged from the depths of depression and financial loss but have also found a profound sense of purpose and fulfillment. As I continue to nurture my growth and creativity, I am excited to see how my journey will inspire others to embrace their own unique pathways towards a creative and fulfilling life.

Esther Joy specializes in helping families who dream of raising their own backyard chickens but feel overwhelmed, or unsure of what it takes or where to begin. She understands the challenges and concerns that come with starting a backyard chicken journey, and provides you with the knowledge, support, and resources needed to make your chicken-keeping dreams a reality.

Esther Joy was born and raised in a large family on a small farm in Wisconsin and spent many years working with chickens. After college, she made the decision to stay in the city, but despite her love for the bustling city life, she always missed the tranquility and simplicity of rural living. As a mother of four, Esther Joy recognized the importance of instilling in her children the values of sustainable living and understanding the origins of their food. Balancing the roles of a dedicated mother and wife, she got her Masters in Learning Technology so she could also pursue a successful career as a full-time instructional designer. However, it was the passion for backyard chickens and sustainable living that truly ignited her.

Esther Joy is an author of a children's book On The Farm that she wrote when she was 10-years old. Currently, she is diligently working on expanding the acclaimed "On The Farm" series, while simultaneously collaborating with her children to create captivating literature centered around backyard chickens.

Esther Joy has founded Backyard Chickens Academy, an online class and community where she can help families all over the world with their backyard chickens journey.

26

PRISSY ELROD - How Embracing Loss Created a Mosaic of Art and Eternal Happiness

"Hardships often prepare ordinary people for an extraordinary destiny." C. S. *Lewis*

Readers often refer to me as **The Butterfly Girl** since I metaphorically portray my personal journey of transformation with semblance to the epic **caterpillar to butterfly** metamorphosis.

When a brain tumor stole my husband, it also stole my identity. I was faced with an unfamiliar, colorless landscape. But I chose to believe when one person dies, two people should not. With this belief, I began an excavation of self to find my new purpose in life.

My journey began when I challenged myself to step out of my comfort zone and author a book I could never find – what happens behind the closed doors of a life-changing event. In doing so I would help the next person sabotaged by the unexpected in life.

The first page of my first book **Far Outside the Ordinary** became my **Second Chapter in Life**. It propelled me from the shadows to the spotlight. It also created a new career and my new identity.

The caterpillar dies so the butterfly could be born. And, yet, the caterpillar lives in the butterfly, and they are but one.

It was just another ordinary day – until it wasn't. My healthy, vibrant husband went in for his routine, annual physical. He was told he had a year to live. The terminal diagnosis stamped on him that day was catastrophic. I sought anything I could find to tell me what I should say, do, or be, to somebody with no hope. I found books on death, grief, and loss—a plethora of psychology, religion, and self-help books. But I needed to know how to travel the path of **losing**, not **loss**. The difference is profound. Surely someone wrote a step-by-step, minute-by-minute, day-by-day guide on how *they* navigated the arena of shock, despair, and hopelessness. What does one say to a terminal husband, wife, children, and friends who don't know what to say to the dying? I found no books anywhere. A yearning to write it seeded in the depth of my soul but never sprouted.

There is nothing in a caterpillar that tells you it's going to be a butterfly.

I cycled through grief on the overused road called survival. I retreated within my own being to search for answers – mainly, how to find joy again. I pulled out my combat boots and went to work rediscovering my original self, the girl who was forgotten. Piece by piece, day by day, came strength and resurrection.

I gifted all my beautiful jewelry to my daughters and began to replace it with funky treasures made by local artisans. Soon I donated all the clothes and shoes that stifled me and replaced them with the boho-chic style I loved. I joined a Tae Bo class and kicked ass three times a week. And, after almost three decades spent with one man, I entered the dating world.

"For a caterpillar to become a butterfly it must change."

Without realizing what happened I allowed myself to appear naturally from a trapped cocoon. I became the left-handed version of my right-handed self. I barely knew who I was. I lived as two people. Or maybe, I was layers deep, peeling them off in sheets.

I'd never taken a painting class before. But I loved art and art history and thought I'd give it a try. The class was called *Introduction to Oil,* but it appeared from looking at everybody I might be the *only* one getting introduced to painting. Everyone appeared to know what they were doing. I was a nobody looking for somebody to teach me something.

I couldn't know I would uncover untapped talent trapped inside me. Or that one day soon, I would paint children, landscapes, barns, and pets that would hang on the walls of family, friends, and perfect strangers.

The writing came next. I wasn't mentally prepared to revisit the pain and wanted to forget that period in my life and enjoy my present life. But I couldn't. Sometimes, there are things we shouldn't forget, but rather, try to understand, so we can better accept them.

Start by doing what's necessary; then do what's possible; and suddenly you are doing the impossible. ~Francis of Assisi

With no writing experience, and no idea how to begin I knew I needed to study the craft. It was my birthday, a significant one. I bought five presents for myself: *On Writing* by Stephen King; *Bird by Bird: Instructions on Writing and Life* by Anne Lamont; *The Year of Magical Thinking* by Joan Didion: *You've Got a Book in You* by Elizabeth Simms; and *90-Day Novel* by Alan Watt. I'm still laughing about the last one. That day I began my self-taught learning and read the books over and over, with yellow highlights and dog-eared pages, marked, bent, and worn. Five books became a library of 48+ books on how to.

I read *how, why, and when* to do *this, that, and everything* until it seemed impossible to succeed. Each person had different opinions, styles, verse, and commands. They poisoned my confidence, voice, and self-worth – through no fault of their own. It was my *not* believing in myself.

Sick of learning how to write, I decided to just write...what I had lived and the lessons I learned. I could be a flashlight for those with no beacon of light. I would share how I watched a kind man stolen from us in the prime of his life – but also, how I navigated through it with my imperfect footprints. Finding meaning in a situation that is meaningless, random, and unfair is hard.

In the words of Dr. Seuss, *"Be who you are and say what you feel because those who mind don't matter and those who matter don't mind."* I held that truth next to my heart the day I began my authoring journey. I still do!

As I pushed through writing *Far Outside the Ordinary,* I knew I might not make the world better, or different, but it would make a world of difference to me. My readers would know tragedy– but also comedy. So, I included the humor buried inside our pain, the laughter through our tears, incorporating all my imperfections, mistakes, and regrets. I believed doing something for others would give purpose to Boone's stolen life, his death, our pain, and all that suffering. I kept my manuscript hidden and allowed no one to read it in those first three years. Why? I can answer in two words: *no confidence.*

It would take four years and 14 drafts before *Far Outside the Ordinary* was complete. After which, nothing was ever the same again. Sometimes unanswered prayers are answered only in a different way.

"Just when the caterpillar thought the world ended it became a butterfly."

You miss 100% of the chances you don't take. So, I took a leap of faith when

I chose happiness. From there I discovered me, the girl left behind, the one with buried talent, undiscovered. It is simple to write but it was complicated to live.

When asked "What's the biggest mistake we make in life?" Buddha replied, *"You think you have time. Time is free but priceless. You can't own it, but you can use it. You can't keep it, but you can spend it. And once it's lost, you can never get it back."*

In the end, my narrative inside **Far Outside the Ordinary** and **Chasing Ordinary** became mosaics and butterfly art. My **Mosaic of Art** was created from the pieces of our broken life to show beauty can come from brokenness and transformation from courage.

I read once if you have a talent and don't use it, your life can collapse in on itself like a black hole. You must find inspiration in your struggles and live the life you have. What began as a story to help me has now helped thousands more. When you step out of your comfort zone is when you grow, blossom, and change. The formula is simple; we make it hard.

Everyone has untapped potential, something they long to do, be, or create. Yet, they sacrifice this discovery by sabotaging themselves with self-doubt. *I'm too old, have no time, no talent.* Believe me, none of that is relevant when it comes to dreams and potential. The death of joy is comparing oneself to others. Please, don't!

Inspired by my personal experience, I encourage you to embrace *your* landscape of choice, chance, and change and then reimagine, recreate, and resurrect the talent waiting to ooze out of you. We are all braver than we know.

"What lies behind us and what lies in front of us pales in comparison to what lies inside us." ~Ralph Waldo Emerson

Prissy Elrod is an artist, inspirational speaker, and the published author of two books: Far Outside the Ordinary and Chasing Ordinary as well as three Meditative Coloring Books: Far Outside the Ordinary Butterflies; Flowers; and Circles.

Her memoirs are populated by book clubs around the country and have been profiled in multiple Florida and Georgia newspapers. Bloggers from California to New York have reviewed and shared her books with their readers. She is a contributing columnist to Flamingo, an award-winning Florida's Lifestyle Magazine, and pens her column - PANHANDLING - from her home in Tallahassee, located in the panhandle of Florida.

From large auditoriums to living rooms, Prissy shares her inspirational message of hope in the aftermath of loss. Her audiences have included Florida State University; Flagler College; SunTrust Bank; Merrill Lynch; Contemporary Women Authors of the South; Philanthropic Education Organization; Rotary Clubs and Writers in the Round, to name just a few.

With her first book, Prissy partnered with two non-profit organizations to help raise money for bereaved widows: Fresh New Start: an organization whose primary purpose is to support and advocate for young widows who lost their spouses to cancer. Also, Construction Angels: The first responders to the construction families in need of assistance when a disaster happens.

She has been featured on the cover of Tallahassee Woman Magazine, highlighted in Writer's Digest Magazine. The cover of her first book — Far Outside the Ordinary

— was spotlighted in *Print* magazine, after winning one of the top 350 Best Designs in the U.S. for the butterfly design.

Elrod has been seen on CBS, NBC, and ABC and featured in Thrive Global (Humor); Medium (Second Chapters: How I Reinvented Myself), as well as NPR, Blog Talk Radio, and multiple podcasts.

Referred to as 'The Butterfly Girl', she metaphorically portrays her incredible journey of transformation with semblance to the epic caterpillar to butterfly metamorphosis.

"Just when the caterpillar thought the world ended it became a butterfly."

She hopes to inspire others to believe in themselves and achieve the extraordinary.

27

KRISTEN HOARD - Sculpting Self-Love: Embracing Creativity to Shape a Life of Passion

Despite growing up in a household that celebrated creativity, I denied possessing any artistic skills. I found myself drawn to art, frequenting art shows and gravitating toward creative individuals. I often envied a colleague who enrolled in a metalworking class, and yet believed that such a pursuit was not possible for me.

One day, a close friend and psychic told me that she saw metal sculptures in my aura. I invited her to my house to see some sculptures I had purchased, but she shook her head. She had envisioned MY very own sculptures and insisted that I take a class to explore this untapped potential. At age 40, I embarked on a transformative journey to become an artist.

It was then that I realized the wellspring of creativity had been residing within me all along. The decision to embark on this artistic odyssey was terrifying, but also empowered me to embrace my true artistic self. Listening to the guidance of my psychic friend and taking that courageous leap of faith represented an extraordinary act of self-love.

Indulging in creative pursuits is an act of self-love. It allows you to express your talents, passions, and interests, celebrating the remarkable abilities and creativity that reside within you. By giving free rein to your creativity, you celebrate your unique abilities, which fosters a sense of self-worth and appreciation... What is radical self-love but celebrating your innate uniqueness? You will feel a sense of accomplishment just by creating, even if it's just for you. Express your unique viewpoint to the world because no one else is going to think up or create the things the way YOU do... it is wholly yours to own. So own that sh*t!

I was blessed to grow up with a mother who oozed creativity in everything she did. Whether it was adorning our home for every single holiday or stocking a room with craft supplies. My three sisters and I were surrounded by a philosophy of creativity permeating our lives. We are all over 60 years old now, you can see the lovely imprint it left on our lives. We are all creatives, author, painter, sculptor and decorator, even the nieces and nephews are creatives!

But what if you didn't grow up with a magical creativity fairy? My mom was also a preschool teacher and she taught me how to share...So fear not, with some help from my mom, even though she's no longer with us, we are going to sprinkle some cosmic tips to help you on your journey. So, let's get radical, shall we?

Take a Leap

Embracing creativity for self-love requires courage and a willingness to risk failure, ridicule, and rejection. But remember, with risk comes freedom. You are free to explore your wildest ideas, bring them to life, and experience the profound love that comes with birthing something unique and beautiful into the world.

So, when you find yourself on the precipice of that desire, don't just look, leap! There is no courage without fear – taking the leap is the perfect vehicle to find and utilize your bravery – which in turn fosters that feeling of self-love. This was the step I took in going to that metal art class in my 40s. Self-love means having faith in yourself. So take a leap of faith.

Just Make Sh*t!

Start by immersing yourself in the creative pursuit of your choosing. Get some materials, make mistakes, embrace imperfections, learn from them, and keep growing. Create a multitude of prototypes, even if you end up discarding most of them.

When I got a commission for a 4 x 9-foot heart, I was intimidated and scared. I made 4 prototypes before I got it right... so lots of mistakes and frustration. I walked away and came back several times... I had to fight the fear and imposter syndrome every step of the way. In the end, I was extremely pleased with the sculpture and felt it was my best work ever. Talk about accomplishment.

Sometimes you will gain confidence and at other times, you will be frustrated. Working through the frustration is a messy but necessary part of the process. That's when the "aha" moment of your creative masterpiece emerges (or unfolds)! Each breakthrough builds a stronger foundation that informs and encourages your next step into the unknown. Self-love means giving yourself permission to make mistakes, knowing they lead to the growth you need.

Break the Rules

Don't be confined by instructions and norms. As my mom used to say, "Ask, What if?" Challenge conventions, experiment, and push the boundaries of what is possible. The possibilities are endless. "What if" I take apart this clock and use the gears in a piece of art? "What if" I try to weld these 2 pieces of metal together even though you aren't supposed to? Well sometimes they stick and sometimes they don't!

Mix and match ideas, squint your eyes, turn things upside down. I once kicked over a twig sculpture in frustration because it was not meeting my vision... but with that kick it turned into a jellyfish, which became one of my signature sculptures... all from my mistake! Combine concepts and explore unexpected connections.

Are you still afraid? Afraid to take that leap and stumble upon obstacles along the way? Here's some ideas to help you gather the courage to jump:

- **Play** – doodle, build with blocks, go back to crayons, fingerpaint, scribble, make a mess!

- **Make a List** - Take a moment to think about what things you do with flair, glitz, flamboyance, and a pinch of panache? Do you whip up delicious dishes, dive into coding adventures, sew fabulous creations, tend to blossoming gardens, color magic on hair, explore hidden treasures in thrift shops, fix things in unconventional ways, or decorate with your own personal touch?

- **Look to nature** - For shapes, texture, and lines. I sat under a tree on my deck and all of a sudden, I saw art in the lines of the branches spreading out from each other and I went and cut the design out of metal.

- **Visit an art store** - get your supplies at a flea market, garage sale, antique store, fabric store, furniture store, craigslist...There are many inexpensive ways to find materials.

- **Be a little bit crazy** – go nuts with the things you like...don't hold back to appease others. Be crazy, unleash your eccentricities, and create for the sheer joy of it.

- **Take the damn class!** - you don't need a psychic to give you permission, I'm giving you permission. Go! Get to that class you have always wanted to take and explode your mind.

- **Embrace being a beginner—** the willingness to be a novice is a scary step that will help you discover your courage and allow you to learn something new – use a different part of your brain, give yourself permission to let go of perfection, ask questions and forgive yourself as you learn.

- **Keep asking "What if?"** at every step of your creative journey. Curiosity fuels creativity, propelling you to explore new possibilities and breakthroughs.

Expressing your uniqueness is a fundamental part of the human experience—it's what makes you, well, YOU. Creativity is the oxygen that breathes life into your soul—it's a profound practice of radical self-love. So, protect your creative time fiercely, make the time to indulge yourself. Allow your talents to grow, glow, and flourish. It's a beautiful gift you bestow upon yourself—one that will unlock your true potential. Creativity is yours—Step into it and surprise yourself! Above all, love your creativity, because it's part of you!

Kristen Hoard is a metal sculpture artist who helps people beautify their homes and workspaces and immerse themselves with color, creativity, and joy. Her artistic journey was ignited when a psychic recommended that she explore metal sculpture classes.

With an inherent passion for the art form, Kristen eagerly enrolled in her first welding class and has been captivated ever since. Her artistic mission revolves around playing her part in preserving the planet by transforming recycled metal into captivating and thought-provoking metal art.

Her artistic style carries an organic essence, reminiscent of nature and the primordial origins of our planet. Adding a finishing touch to each piece, she employs vivid colors infused with various dyes and inks, resulting in bold and brilliant artwork.

Drawing inspiration from her numerous visits to Burning Man, Kristen delves into the realm of sculptures that incorporate flames and LED lighting. This passion led her to create a stunning 5-foot metal lotus flower firepit for Siegfried and Roy's residence in Las Vegas. Her recent sculpture, a 5 x 9-foot flaming heart sculpture recently shipped to a collector's home in San Miguel Allende, Mexico. Additionally, she has completed several notable projects, including corporate sculptures and public artworks showcased throughout the Bay Area and Sacramento.

Her dedication and relentless pursuit of artistic excellence have garnered recognition, leading to appearances on several morning shows on KCRA, Fox News 40, KXTV, and the Art Infused Life Podcast, where she has shared her creative journey and showcased her extraordinary talent.

28

KYLE HOLLINGSWORTH - COURAGE: The Key to Radical Self-Love & Creative Expression

I was afraid ALL THE TIME. I lived my life white-knuckled, anxious, and braced for the next blow.

Trauma for me began in early childhood with my mother's mental health issues, her suicide when I was eight years old, being tossed back and forth between family, sexual and verbal abuse, my father's alcoholism and drug use, his imprisonment, and eventual death, and being bullied and outcast in my hometown. By the time I hit adulthood, I had no sense of self, and I allowed my fear to keep me in a chokehold. I also blamed myself for all of it.

From the outside, most people saw me as high-functioning, lively, creative, and together. Inside, I was terrified – I constantly shapeshifted myself to accommodate what I thought the world wanted me to be. I lived in fear of losing everything, believing that I was somehow broken, lost, and unlovable. I did not trust or love myself. For decades, I shouldered the responsibility for everything and everyone around me, overachieving and running myself ragged to be liked, loved, wanted, accepted, and safe. I worked 60–70-hour weeks and I barely slept. I said yes to each and every thing that came my way, afraid to say no for fear of not being wanted, liked, or financially stable.

I hit rock bottom 14 months ago when I broke down sobbing and said to my husband "I can't do this anymore." I meant it. I had finally reached my breaking point after years of depression and anxiety, anger, resentment, and feeling trapped inside my own life. I knew at that moment that if I kept up this constant state of stress, of self-judgment, of trying to live up to my outrageous expectations of myself, I would not be long for this world.

I chose at that moment to love myself, to put my own needs first, and to save my own life.

It took some real soul searching, radical honesty, and a lot of courage to sell our home we'd only just bought 3 years prior, let go of many of our belongings, say goodbye to family and friends, and leave our stressful yet familiar surroundings and launch out into the unknown.

We spent the next 6 months living nomadically, with no plan. During that time, I committed to doing deep work with cognitive behavioral therapy, EMDR, and tapping. I worked with healers, shamans, and most importantly, my inner child. I did medicine journeys, prayed, and used every modality available to me. It was intense to do the inner work of reconnecting with my younger self, and giving her what she never had: radical, unconditional love. To tell her she is safe and that I am here.

I dove into mindset work, finally realizing how much my thoughts and beliefs had been keeping me small, in a state of fear, and how much agency I truly have in changing them. As each thought, belief, and way of being were challenged, I felt layers of pain and the heavy weight of shame dropping away. I was finally able to let go of the tight grip I'd had on life and to open my arms and heart to allowing, to trusting the universe to hold me, and above all, trusting myself.

I spent our nomadic months drawing, journaling, crying, and loving myself. I created with no plan or attachment to, "Will this make me money or make someone else happy?" and instead, I finally gave myself permission to create for ME, to write whatever wanted to come out, and to release any judgment I had about whether it was good enough.

The more I opened to possibility, to trust, and to love myself, the more life kept guiding me and unfolding with a flow I'd never experienced before. My husband and I ultimately were drawn to New Mexico, where we now live among the big skies and wild horses, and our life is unrecognizable from what it was. I now make *myself* my priority each day. I have practices in place that create balance and flow, and I can say for the first time in my life that I truly adore myself. I love Kyle and all her messy, imperfect, wildly creative, deep, wise, and beautiful ways.

I now am clear that no matter what life brings me, I am here for myself, I love myself, and I have my own back. That is radical self-love to me.

Are you ready to start?
Here's a potent list of tools that have had a profound impact on my own healing:

1 – Give your inner child love. Find a quiet place to sit with paper and pen. Take a few moments to imagine yourself as a young child, in as much detail as possible. Open your eyes and write out a description of that child. Be loving, kind, bold, and lavish in your words. Then read it out loud, as if you were speaking to that very young child in a tone that feels safe, loving, and warm.

    Example: "Kyle, sweetheart, you are bright, creative, funny, and kind. Nothing that happened to you was your fault, and you are safe now. I am here for you. I love you so much." Feel into every word. Now, do that same thing in the mirror. Remember to smile.

2 - Step into courage. Do one thing each day that pushes you out of your comfort zone. Take a step towards something you want, learn a new skill, ask for the job, the raise, the connection you want with someone. In my experience, if it scares me, there is freedom on the other side of it.

3 - Take 100% responsibility for your life. What does this mean? It's not about placing any blame on yourself. You've done plenty of that. It's about taking your power back, about realizing that *you get to choose* how you feel, what you believe, and how you live your one, wild, precious life.

4 - Tell yourself - and those you love - the truth. Be willing to be uncomfortable, because asking for what you truly want is an act of self-love and can feel strange if you've spent your life denying it. Say it out loud. Write it down. CLAIM IT. Then do the work to believe it's already here: imagine in your mind that the life you want is already yours. Feel the joy, the peace, and the contentment of having your desires fulfilled.

5 - Forgive yourself. Remember that you did the best you could at the time with what you had. It's OK to not have all the answers. If you find yourself thinking or speaking unkindly towards yourself, remember that little child and speak to them with love, patience, and kindness.

It takes courage and commitment to love ourselves fully. And it's the key to freedom, full self-expression, and joy. As we love ourselves, we let the love of the world in, and radiate love out to everyone and everything we touch.

You are worthy of your love. Love yourself wildly and completely. It starts with you. You've got this.

Love y'all.

Kyle Hollingsworth is a vibrant and dynamic force of creativity, inspiring others to embrace their true potential.

A survivor of countless challenges, she ignites a fire within to empower others on their courageous journey of healing and self-discovery through the transformative power of creativity.

As the owner of Kyle Creative, she fearlessly explores art, design, illustration, and animation. Her Emmy-nominated designs, award-winning illustrations, and captivating fine art have earned her global recognition.

Kyle's talents extend beyond the canvas; she's a sound healer, writer, medium, and captivating public speaker. Through her private community, Courageous AF, she shares her stories of triumphs and holds a safe space for authentic expression, creating a vibrant tapestry of courage, creativity, and community.

Kyle's mission is to inspire others to find the courage to heal while leveraging the transformative power of creative expression for personal growth.

SUSAN PEPLER - Create A Life That ROCKS!

Introduction:

As an artist, I'm sitting here, theoretically, with a pen in one hand and a paintbrush in the other to write my chapter on love.

And it dawns on me that this concept of radical self-love just might be one of the magic keys to life!

Today, I can turn a blank canvas into a work of art that transforms my clients' lives and living spaces. Getting there has taken some time and practice, but it's happening. And as I embrace the new (to me) concept of radical self-love, I can see that it is enhancing my vision, sharpening my awareness, encouraging me to seek guidance, and fueling my painting and teaching practices. Radical self-love breathes life into me and my art and sets me free to create a life that rocks!

Having a Vision:

My life and art vision are increasingly fine-tuned, with radical self-love as my guiding light. I'm encouraged to dream audaciously and take precious time to play, rest and explore.

After losing my parents in recent years, when my super cute mini poodle died this year, I indulged in three holidays ... *in a row!* First, I took comfort in the company of beloved relatives in Ottawa, followed by a deluxe vacation in Cuba, and, on my return, I accepted a friend's invitation to join her in South Florida for ten days. I let go of my misbeliefs about taking holidays when there was so much still to do in my life and business at home ... *it was so worth it!*

That indulgent (for me) holiday experience opened my eyes to see more clearly where I want to go and how I want to live, and that is with purpose and meaning that nourishes my creativity and propels me forward to live life well.

Noticing Details & Awareness:

Learning to radically love and accept myself, with all of my quirks, ADHD and dyslexia challenges and all things positive or "negative," is allowing me to relax more and experience being uber present. I've always noticed the beauty of the world around me, but even life's seemingly mundane and ordinary things appear beautiful. I drink up the enticing and intricate details I see, and they breathe life into my art *and* my daily experiences. And in my art practice, I'm immersed in the moment with each brush stroke, intuitively applying paint with ever-increasing sensitivity to the nuances of colour, texture and form. This heightened awareness extends beyond the easel and is permeating my life. I savour the richness of connection with family and friends and find joy in the simplest pleasures. My senses are alert, allowing me to soak up the magical details that make life extraordinary.

Developing Skills and Seeking Guidance:

Radical self-love has allowed me to dive into so many cool things ... For example, I've already got a degree in Fine Arts, a diploma in Illustration and Design, 12 years of drawing and colouring for Advertising companies and more than twenty years of full-time painting behind me ... You could say I've done my 10,000 hours. Yet, I took a fabulous painting course this year; it was a deep dive into all the exciting principles of making art. I learned so much, including a more sophisticated way to mix colours which I'm already incorporating into my work ... *and people are noticing!*

There's always so much more to learn. That will never end. Fine-tuning skills and seeking guidance or help in our life's journey are vital to our well-being and contribution to the world. I'm embracing personal and professional growth as a lifelong pursuit. I'm always keen to develop new skills, broaden my perspectives, and deepen my understanding of myself and the world.

Practice:

Radical self-love reminds me to approach my painting practice and life with patience, kindness and compassion in all things and with everyone. I see life's challenges as stepping stones to growth rather than barriers to success. I'm encouraged to nurture my physical, emotional, and mental well-being to show up as my best self in every area of life. With radical self-love, I'm more forgiving and compassionate all around. And I love celebrating every little victory.

Conclusion:

Embracing radical self-love has been a game-changer for me. My vision is clearer: I want to continue painting big canvases. That really lights me up and keeps me sane. It's the ultimate "getaway" for me. And ... this is new; I'm creating more space in my life to guide others into a painting practice because it's so good for you and so much fun! Learning to love and honour myself, which is radical self-love, encourages me to slow down and notice the exquisite details of this wild and wonderful world. And I'm more committed than ever to living big and expansively and won't hesitate to seek guidance from great thought leaders, mentors, therapists or life coaches.

So, my creative friends, let's embark on this incredible adventure together—indulging in radical self-love to unlock our creative spirits and create an extraordinary life that ROCKS!

Susan Pepler is a renowned and award-winning realist painter, captivated and inspired by the astounding beauty of this world. Her lush, large-scale paintings grace elegant homes across the globe, touching the hearts of her clients and transforming their lives in the process.

As the visionary CEO of Studio Susan Pepler, she not only wields the brush but also revels in sharing her expertise as a painting instructor, igniting the flames of creativity in others.

After dropping out of business school, Susan's indomitable spirit led her to triumph in the realm of art, earning a Bachelor of Fine Arts Degree from Concordia University and a Diploma in Illustration and Design from Dawson College, where she later taught drawing and painting. Before becoming a full-time fine arts painter, she further honed her artistic skills as a television storyboard artist in the advertising industry for 12 years.

Susan's artistic journey has been featured on esteemed media platforms such as CBC, CTV, CJAD, The Montreal Gazette, and Le Tour. Her illustrious life as a painter has led to unforgettable encounters with fellow creatives Jim Dine, Bobby Burgers, Joseph Plaskett, Martha Wainwright, and more.

30

TAMARA MULKEY - Embrace the Moment and Move

I can remember the incident vividly. I was with my parents and husband and we were looking for my daughter who had run off to play at a nearby school ground. I was in a deep depression and plagued with anxiety. It was relentless despite medication and counseling.

Upon finding her and heading back to my parent's home, I decided I was done with it all. I noticed a car coming up the road. I began crossing the road at a snail's pace in hopes that the car would hit me...that it would kill me. Suddenly, I heard my father's voice telling me to hurry up. I snapped out of the trance and caught up to them. My tears flowed as I realized what I had just done. It's 2023, as I write this, and I'm still here.

"Embrace the Suck", is a military saying I discovered and have adopted. It means, to consciously accept the current situation, no matter how bad, and keep moving forward. In retrospect, my suicide attempt would have never worked. The car would have never gotten to me – it was so far down the road. I want to say it was laughable, but at the time, it shook my world.

My depression and anxiety have been with me for about 30 years now and

I am on disability because of them. I've taken meds and seen my share of counseling. My sweet husband has weathered my storms and tears for almost as long. He could have given up on me but hasn't yet. My beautiful girl has struggled through her own episode. We think it may be genetic.

One of the ways I use to move forward is by creating art. Like any skill, it must be practiced to be retained and improved upon. Early in my marriage, I tried to draw a portrait of my mother-in-law's mother. It looked nothing like her. Everyone loved it and saw the resemblance. Still, I didn't see it at all. "I have an art degree!", I thought. I couldn't accept what I saw. In my eyes, it was a failure and I wouldn't draw again. I felt like my talent and muse had abandoned me. In later years, my mother begged me to draw anything. I tried a few times in a small sketchbook, but I just saw scribbles.

Fast forward to 2017, after losing our beloved dog and my daughter moving out, I faced what I saw as a long, dark winter. My husband worked nights and I would be alone with myself. While online, I discovered a year-long art course, called Lifebook, by Tamara Laporte. The host was a delight to watch in this video. And, we had the same first name. It was kismet! I knew it was time for me to create art again and I signed up. This would be my Christmas gift to me.

It's been an amazing, creative adventure! I can now call myself a professional artist. I love creating paintings for others. I've been doing commission work since 2018 and in May became a member of an online art gallery that specializes in monthly auctions. I"m painting more than I ever have. I have created 12 paintings in the last 3 months for their shows, sold 5, and have a commission currently in the works for a collector.

Martin Luther King said, "If you can't fly then run, if you can't run then walk, if you can't walk then crawl, but whatever you do you have to keep moving forward." Every day, I get up and do what I can. Do I think it's enough? Never. In addition to my mental illness, I have developed some physical ones as well. I have had to learn to accept the days that I have limits and the days where I can do more.

When I find myself stuck, like a soldier in the mental mud and muck, there are a few things I do to free myself. The first thing I turn to is sleep. Most of the time sleep will reset my brain and break the cycle of overthinking an issue, real or imagined. It's like rebooting a computer. When I wake up, I find that my thinking is more flexible and positive, and I can move forward through my daily journey.

Chronic illness is a thief. At 50, I was diagnosed with both Fibromyalgia and ME/CFS. If you know anything about this duo, you will know exhaustion is one of the numerous symptoms listed. It has become my constant nemesis. It keeps me home and indoors. I find myself becoming a shut-in. Today, anything can be delivered. As an artist, I need to be alone to create, yet I have never been so lonely. Social media helps, but it's nothing like connecting with real people. I watch others having adventures and long to as well.

Anyway, another way to jump off the negative hamster wheel you may be running, is to change your environment. Get out of your current space. Go for a walk, a drive, or window shop. The different sights and sounds will help alter your way of thinking. Do something – it will move you forward.

The final idea is to exercise gratitude. It's that simple. I've heard it many times. Just think of three things you are grateful for. It doesn't have to be anything epic. Keep it simple. You could express it in prayer, meditate on it, write it out, etc. I'm challenging myself right now, and you're my witness – I am going to put my three "gratitudes" as the first layer of each piece of art I do. Only then can I create the painting or drawing I intended. I invite you to try it too. You can do it, I know you can!

So let's do a review... Think like a warrior and "embrace the suck" that you may find yourself in. Accept it and move forward. This isn't a race – pace yourself. Remember the three ideas that I've given you: sleep/rest, change your environment, and find your gratitude.

You want to know a secret? I've written this as a reminder to myself as well. This is easy stuff. We are both capable and strong enough to do this. You and I are worth it!

Tamara Mulkey is an award winning, mixed media artist based in Utah, U.S.A. She has always had a fondness for art and studied Graphic Design. After earning her degree, she found herself in the glamorous world of retail, followed by marriage and motherhood. She experienced a long struggle with the darkness of depression, and once she healed enough to look to the future, she invested in herself and fell in love with mixed media and the freedom of expression they offer.

Currently, she is an artist specializing in commissioned portraits of both people and animals for her collectors. She is also a full time artist with Facebook group Artistic Souls Gallery.

31

TINA MARIE ROMERO - Cultivating Self-awareness as a Path To Radical Self-love

"You have no need to travel anywhere. Journey within yourself, enter a mine of rubies and bathe in the splendor of your own light." – Rumi.

When someone you love commits suicide because you're not ready to marry him, "love" morphs into a confusing word. What's worse, his family blames you for it and proclaims they can never forgive you. In an instant, the "Tina" I knew vanished and I became a villain unable to defend myself in my own life story. How I rediscovered myself is a gift I am compelled to share so it can help someone who feels lost, find and love thyself again.

My traumatic experience started months before when my ex warned me of a morbid outcome if I did not change my mind about marrying him. He made me question myself and my dreams. I felt trapped. Am I being selfish? Am I wrong for listening to my heart? Am I not entitled to make my own decision? Do I not matter? As I continued to stay true to myself, the threats elevated.

I lived in fear for some time, not knowing if and when he would fulfill his threat or put me in harm's way. Until one hectic Tuesday morning at work when I got the dreaded phone call that changed my life forever. The aftermath was far worse than the months leading to it. The incriminating voices around me got louder as my own voice and identity faded into oblivion. I believed and accepted I was to blame for everything. More so, I felt I deserved to suffer to redeem myself.

Retreating from everyone, I took refuge and found solace in my pen and paper. Reflective writing is an analytical practice that forced me to describe my traumatic experience and delve into what it meant to me personally. It required me to think deeply about what happened, how it happened and what I could have done to change the outcome.

It was overwhelmingly painful to relive the trauma, but the authenticity of reflective writing served as a nonjudgmental path to see myself and cultivate self-awareness. It also demanded a significant amount of creative thinking.

As I became more self-aware, I discovered psychological research suggesting that illeism can bring cognitive benefits. Illeism is the practice of talking about oneself in the third person, rather than the first person. The linguistic switch is intended to make the statement feel more like historical fact recorded by an impartial observer.

By switching to the third person, my description of a situation sounded as if I was talking about someone else rather than myself. This detachment helped me assess my situation more objectively and see the bigger picture instead of getting caught up in my own emotions.

The use of illeism enabled me to get to know "Tina" through a distinct set of fog-free lenses. I learned to see her clearly, understand her values, know her strengths and weaknesses, acknowledge her dreams, catch her sad tears, hear her heartbeat, feel her beautiful soul and finally learned to love her. It infuriated me that she got blamed for something that was not her fault. For the first time, I found myself defending "Tina" and realized my foremost responsibility to advocate for her as I would for my best friend.

This simple shift in treating myself like my best friend ignited a radical self-love absent in my life before. And ta-da! I discovered I was enough. Like pulling wool over my eyes, I finally felt freed from the need to overcompensate, overachieve, and seek validation from others.

Self-love is not being selfish. On the contrary, lack or absence of it will deplete your limited energy and dim your own light. It is necessary to fill your cup first, then to give to others from the overflow. This is what gives you the capacity to heal and to move forward into your next chapter of life.

In my current world as owner of a homecare agency, self-love is a big challenge for family caregivers who care for their loved ones with cognitive, mental, chronic, and terminal illnesses. A wife taking care of her husband with dementia gives herself selflessly every day to her husband who un-knowingly demeans her and forgets she is his wife. She gives all she has willingly until there is nothing left to give and burns out, but that is what love does. Sadly however, studies reveal silent heroes like her often end up dying before their loved one due to severe stress.

So, it is essential to be aware and recognize that our cup needs to be filled so we can continue being the light to those who rely on us. According to research on self-awareness, 95% of people identify themselves to be "self-aware." However, research shows that just 10-15% of people actually are. Self-awareness is a sign of emotional maturity and intelligence. It allows us to see and understand who we are and how others perceive us.

So how do we know if we are self-aware? Here are five ways:

- You unapologetically know your worth, who you are and who you are not.

- You don't let others' perception of you define and affect you.
- You don't let society and others dictate how you should live your life.
- You don't blame yourself and carry guilt for someone else's misery.
- You don't let the dreams and expectations of others override yours.

Self-awareness led to my metamorphosis from a villain to a heroine in my own life story. And so can you. It is our birthright to be a doyenne, but first we need to truly know ourselves and our gifts. If you are feeling lost or do not resonate with any of the five essential statements above, I invite you to follow these three simple steps to find and love yourself again:

Step 1. Reflective writing.

Step 2. Use Illeism. Talk about yourself in the third person.

Step 3. Treat yourself like your best friend.

Tina Romero is a creative entrepreneur and intuitive aging expert passionate about helping others see life as an evolving creative process, age gracefully, grow bolder and reinvent themselves so they can live their life's purpose.

As CEO of Synergy Homecare of N Central NJ, she provides creative solutions so our loved ones can age and die at home with dignity and independence. Her agency grew from zero to seven figures in less than three years and has consistently received Best of HomeCare Provider of Choice and Caring Star Service Excellence Awards.

Uprooting herself from the Philippines in 1995, Tina created the life of her dreams starting from scratch as a fearful undocumented worker into a self-made millionaire employing 100+ immigrants, a board member collaborating with business leaders and a lobbyist advocating for seniors and immigration reforms. She was also a cancer survivor whose recovery propelled her to be a triathlete, marathoner, Spartan trifecta finisher, yogi, and dancer.

An international bestselling author, Tina has been featured on NJ News 12, The Lisa Show, The FilAm, Authority Magazine, Thrive Global, Medium, Life Expressions and various podcasts.

32

JOANN RENNER - Turning Adversity into Positive Life Changes

Radical self-love can have so many different meanings. Deeply embracing it has helped me to heal, and to continue healing. I have discovered that life is not linear but is more of a spiral. And that's okay. Physical injuries/chronic pain, and the trauma of verbal, emotional and financial abuse throughout my life gripped my soul with extreme self-doubt, anxiety, depression, mom guilt, social anxiety, bitterness, and imposter syndrome. I put others as my top priority while sacrificing my own basic physical and mental health needs.

That said, I am not the type of person to abandon someone I love. My art career and personal life were sacrificed because my brothers left me with the responsibility to care for our mom for 13 years after she was disabled in a car accident. My now grown kids have also struggled with mental health issues. It was their bravery and determination to heal that convinced me to rethink all of society's crap I was programmed with all my life. It hurt A LOT! It made me angry that my daughter's life was nearly destroyed because of the very same expectations that ate away at me.

Creativity can help open you up to that self-healing and self-love regardless of your circumstances. You don't need to be rich, or live in the "right" neighborhood, or be famous, to find whatever feeds your soul. I am a very stubborn person and when I saw what my kids were going through, I turned that anger into determination. It empowered me to make tough life decisions. My painting kept me from giving up hope because I could express my feelings in them freely, even the crappy ones.

So I made the conscious decision to "take the bull by the horns," look him in the eye and say "No more".

No more wishing for something better. No more backing down. No more bitterness. No more negative anger (it can be used for good if there is self-control). No more letting the jerks get in my head. No more poverty. No more dependence on a man for identity or income. No more blaming others or circumstances for my situation. No more expecting to be rescued. It's about making the decision to be empowered.

Everybody's experiences are different. I am an artist, not a life coach or therapist and I won't pretend that I am. But there are some things that I learned over the years that maybe can help someone who just needs some encouragement to overcome whatever they are facing.

Doing these things changed my life and my art drastically for the better!

- "Wise Mind"- a positive mindset that a therapist for my daughter explained as a way of handling stressful situations that deescalates negative reactions you might have. It helps you resist feelings of anger or frustration that rob precious energy. An example might be a server at a restaurant makes a minor mistake. They apologize but seem distracted or upset. Instead of getting angry, making the server even more upset, try thinking that maybe they are worried about a sick child at home, or if they can even pay their rent this month. That would make me screw up at work! It helps with manifesting positive results in a practical way.

It works great for staying sane while driving!

- Financial independence-so many volumes have been written about this. Get your own email and get a bank account and credit card in your name only. There are so many online now that it makes it much easier. It will be key to your financial freedom. Build your own credit history, not one based on a husband's credit.

- Do the little day-to-day things that give you joy. Not everything costs money. Enjoy the feel of the sun's warmth, the sounds of the birds, and breathe in the clean fresh air after it rains. Mindfulness exercises and art journaling have enabled me to process my thoughts in a safe, creative way. Change something in your environment like curtains or pictures. Stay in the moment and tell that annoying voice in your head saying you have to do the dishes to shut up for once!

- Name that annoying voice in your head anything that reminds you that it is not you and realize it is not in alignment with your authentic self. Mine is a swear word! It gives you more control over those thoughts.

- Say "Please" and "Thank You". You will be SO surprised by how much better service you will get at the store or anywhere else. Our culture is so impressed by bravado and loud nastiness, that it takes an incredibly strong person now to be kind and polite. It is NOT a weakness. Of course that doesn't mean be a victim just to be polite. Politeness is a social skill that pays huge dividends when you treat others with basic dignity. This works in business relationships too. And yeah, there will be idiots who make fun of it or act stupid because they never learned anything other than rudeness. Just let it "roll off your back" as my mom would say, "It's their loss!". I even had someone say they never heard of saying "Excuse me" to go past someone. Really?!

- Acting as a mature adult instead of a spoiled brat builds self-confidence, self-awareness, self-respect and self-love. Be proactive, not reactive.

I found healing through some amazing creative connections online during the pandemic. The last few years have given me hope for the first time in my life. We women no longer have to dress like men, degrade other women, or treat others like garbage just to feel worthy of recognition. Now we can be our authentic selves, do what we love, still be awesome moms if that is our path, and be there for our loved ones.

Born in the early 1960's, I witnessed the beginnings of the women's liberation movement in the US. I and so many others bore the brunt of the backlash, struggling for the fundamental right to be seen and heard, to be respected as free-thinking human beings, and still do. I lost sight of that after marriage.

Society's expectations and priorities dampen creativity, oppressing it especially for women and for children's learning, like teaching girls that their value is only in their appearance. "Marrying well" should not be a career option! It hurts boys and men too by denying their humanity. It seeks to suppress compassion, creativity, healing, intuition, and empathy which are at the core of our human existence and are so necessary for good physical and mental health.

It is time to break the stigma surrounding mental health issues, acknowledge its existence, treating it with seriousness and compassion. By doing so, we make ourselves and our families stronger, more resilient, more loving. It has the ripple effect of making communities better. Take time to heal, to love yourself and others even if from as far a distance as possible. This path is not easy and is lifelong. It's messy and complicated but worth it. Please remember that it's okay to make mistakes. Maybe try some drawing again. Who knows?

Joann is a formally trained fine artist who has overcome family trauma and medical issues by "grabbing the bull by the horns" and refusing to give up on herself and her passions.

She earned her BA in Studio Art/Art History at the University of Pittsburgh in 1986 and is a member of the Pittsburgh Pastel Artists League.

She seeks to inspire others to go fearlessly forward regardless of their circum-stances and to break the stigma of mental illness by exhibiting her paintings so that people are encouraged to thrive on their own unique paths. Joann is deeply passionate about helping others manage their day-to-day mental health issues, and about exploring spirituality, climate change, and community preservation with her public speaking engagements, content creation, and educational workshops.

33

LAURIE KORALEWSKI - My Favorite Things

Art. Music. Flowers. Dogs. Loving Family and Friends.

My passions, my happy place. My pieces to the puzzle for radical self-love.

Loving and accepting yourself is key to caring for and loving others. Most important to me is loving God and others as yourself.

Art allows me to get to the core of what God uniquely designed me to do. Creating art helps me relax and to see the world and its constantly changing challenges in a positive light.

Growing up in a family overflowing with mental illness, rage and brokenness, I found myself searching for an outlet of peace and security. There were two places I could go and feel nurtured and light-hearted. My grandmother and great-grandmother's house was one, and my childhood best friend's house was the other. We were free to play, laugh and explore new hobbies. Also, our schools had excellent art classes, with teachers who inspired us to appreciate and love art. My love of art has grown immeasurably ever since.

My love of music lifts my spirits and creates a joyful and energized environment for painting. Of the 1000's of songs in my playlist, most are fun and upbeat, reminding me of good times and favorite moments. While painting, you can hear me loudly singing all the lyrics, if slightly off-key. Okay, maybe a lot off-key!

Daily workouts are a priority for me. Walking is my favorite way to be in God's presence and to be surrounded by His beautiful creations. He is the master artist. I am always in awe of His meticulously formed and detailed flowers, trees, clouds and more. The colors always amaze me. Flowers and flower fields are typically the primary source of inspiration for my paintings and creations. Vivid colors, patterns and textures make my heart sing.

Dogs. I adore dogs and would own dozens of them if I could. Each has a one-of-a-kind personality, keeping me entertained and laughing like nothing else. Dogs are loyal, non-judgemental and calming to the soul. They somehow make my world feel more balanced.

Self-love means finding your own small support group of family and friends who truly love you for who you are, paint splatters and all. Those who genuinely pray for you and want the best for you (even if that means moving further away from them) are priceless! My group constantly encourages me, laughs and cries with me and are my biggest cheerleaders. They are irreplaceable and I am so blessed by them and beyond grateful for their love.

As you go through this crazy life of tragedy, heartache, bullying, unrequited love, illness, economic crises, relationship turmoil and so much more, it is more crucial than ever to take the time to greatly care for yourself and others. Remember, we get to choose who to surround ourselves with and what we take in. It really is okay (and healthy) to have boundaries with others and their behaviors. I urge you to make sure you have a tribe who will be there with you through thick and thin, forever. Also, take the time to find what your true life-altering, heart-fluttering, passions are. Take classes, go exploring and let your fears fade. Learn to be content, give freely without strings attached, and to forgive others (yourself too). You never know what wonderful things God may have in store for you!

Creating art has always been Laurie's life passion. God gave her a heart for spreading joy to others through vivid colors, fun patterns and light-hearted themes.

After receiving her very first box of 64 crayons, she was over the moon in love. In second grade, she won her first blue ribbons at the County Fair.

Laurie studied art and interior design at Texas Tech. She enjoys working with acrylic paint and ink/markers. Laurie's style is happy, whimsical and care-free. Her artwork has sold at galleries and art websites, and is currently available at Karen Stephenson Photography, where she partners with her adorable sister.

Laurie lives in Springfield, Missouri with her amazing husband, Rick, who makes her laugh like no other.

34

KAREN STEPHENSON - Creativity Can Ease Your Grief

Grief is part of life. We don't ask for it, but must go through it if we live long enough. There are tons of reading and counseling resources from churches, community centers, and social networks about grief.

I am no expert on grief. I am an artist, photographer, wife, lover, mother, grandmother and friend. My specialty is offering love, a sympathetic ear and a caring shoulder to cry on. I also create works of art that I hope convey the beauty of nature in God's magnificent world. What I'm sharing about grief is simply based on my experiences throughout the last few years and how I have used creativity to help myself on that path. I hope my ideas might motivate you to create a path to a happier and fulfilling life. We may never feel "normal" again, but by adding creativity to our lives, we can at least begin to feel better.

You've probably already read traditional information on the stages of grief we must go through. I'm going to try to focus on providing you with creative aids and small projects to get you through some tough days and help shine some of Hope's rays into your life.

If your Grief is from the Death of a Loved-One or Close Friend: Concentrate on the Positives. These may be turning to Biblical examples, rereading old love letters, taking up offers of support from close friends. Keep the love for your special person at the front of your heart. Continue to love yourself throughout this hard time. Never hesitate to ask for a doctor's or counselor's help if your grief starts to harm your health!

Read great literature, soul-touching poetry, or some light reading through-out the different phases of grieving. Read what helps you feel better to move toward healthy outcomes. The poet John Roedel has a gift for writing about grief. His modern poem "Grief is a Coral Reef" is on his Facebook page. Look it up for a sweet emotional swing-ride. You will cry, then smile through your tears with new hope. Write a story about your someone or list beautiful memories you shared. Sketch a portrait of your love from a photograph. Make a scrapbook of special shared trips through the years.

If your Grief is from the Death of a Pet: Things can seem unfair when our furry family members die. We go through all the usual stages plus we're saddened that we couldn't communicate with them before their death. We may feel anger towards friends, family, vets or ourselves for not knowing what could've been done better. Others may try to invalidate our feelings saying "it's silly to grieve over an animal." In our hearts, we know that the love-bond between a pet and its owner is just as strong as it can be with some people. To help heal after losing your little furry friend, continue to walk the same trails for a while. Have a simple, funeral service, tailored to your family and giving everyone a chance to speak heartfelt words. Create a drawing or a poem in memory of your sweet pet. Pick or buy flowers to set by the grave. During family nights share funny pet stories. Miniatures that resemble your pet, family-made or store-bought, make great keepsakes for birthdays and holidays.

If your Grief is from Divorce, a Breakup with a Long-time Love, or a Loved-One with Mental Illness: Although technically not a death, losing the devoted love of a spouse or a long-time love can be just as devastating and inflict just as much pain and grief. Heartbreak-related grief is unique because although it feels like a death to you, outsiders don't see it that way. They expect you to just hurry up and find someone new.

We still go through the phases: Shock, numbness. Intense pain. "I have nothing to live for."

Guilt: "What did I do wrong?" Anger, "But this is what they did wrong!"

Bargaining: "Please, God, I'll be perfect if you'll bring them back."

Reconstruction, Calm: "Life seems to be a little better."

Acceptance: "He/she was doing the best they could at the time. They needed love too. I forgive him/her."

Hope: Seeing a future again, "I want to study art again", "I forgive myself." "Maybe my heart is open to falling in love again."

And experiencing the devastation of mental illness is one of the saddest and most anger-inducing forms of all grief. But, I believe forgiveness is the highest form of love and can truly lift us up from anger and despair. Forgiveness is a gift of healing for ourselves and anyone we've ever held anger for.

Some want to seek revenge after a breakup. You may have heard that living well is the best revenge. I say forget revenge. Just live well and start forgiving. Except in cases of abuse, if we've ever lived through a breakup, it's because we've been fortunate enough to have loved! Whether we've been hurt by breakup or mental illness, for those we've ever truly loved, a piece of our heart will always stay with them. The best way we can live in peace is for us to truly wish them happiness and peace as well.

Here are more creative must-dos to keep you moving toward peace and healing:

Force yourself to smile! Lots of research has shown that forcing yourself to smile can interrupt the cycle of sadness. Just before that deluge of tears wells up again today, break out into a smile for a while instead. As odd as it seemed to me at first, it really works!

Along with smiling, read a humorous novel, search for jokes online, listen to an upbeat song, get up and dance! My favorite must-do: watch the official music video of "I Smile" by Kirk Franklin. That will have you singing, dancing and feeling joy in no time.

Not ready to be around people yet? Get outdoors, to walk or just to sit. Absorb the beauty of nature with a camera, a sketchbook, or tape recorder.

Visit a gallery or museum (most are free once a week). Take in one artwork up close, or a whole room.

Pick up lots of books at the library. Let friends who want to help in some way return your books on their due date.

If you're an artist, and you've been missing your art, take baby steps into getting back into what you love. You know the healing power of art! Start taking a class once a month. Gradually work up to weekly classes or even teach if that brings you joy.

I hope you have found some of my ideas helpful. You're in my thoughts and prayers as you make your way down this often confusing path. Don't forget to be kind to yourself!!

Keep believing. Keep loving. Keep grieving (healthily). Keep forgiving. Keep smiling. Keep creating!

Karen loves to capture the emotion in scenes or subjects she photographs. When a colorful flower or magnificently lit landscape attracts her eye and trips an emotional response, she tries to convert that feeling into an image others can hold and treasure forever.

Other favored subjects, besides grand landscapes, are intimate vignettes, architectural elements, nature, and wildlife. Karen's art runs the gamut from lightly-enhanced realistic photos to those sporting wildly textured or painterly effects, creative composites, double exposures, and inspirational scenes doubled with inspirational quotations.

Karen's constant desire for creativity led her to photographic arts. The joy photography brought to her life, together with the steadfast love of her husband of 51 years, Dale, has been her saving grace through the darkest times.

35

SHANNON HEAP - Power of Positivity and Perspective

After the gym, I went home and before heading out for my walk in the cold rain, I put on a jacket I haven't worn in a while and found $40 in my pocket! I decided to drive to my favorite community coffee shop to grab a warm drink to soothe myself as I walked. However, it did not stop there. I decided instead of a walk I'd take a trip to my favorite place – the Centre Street stairs (a grueling climb up a never-ending staircase).

During my short excursion on a small winding path through the park toward the stairs, I happened upon an elderly homeless gentleman perched on a bench underneath a low-hanging tree. I should have felt unsettled as he and I were the only ones inhabiting the park on such a day, but strangely I did not. He sat with his legs crossed right over left with fingers intertwined and clasped over his knee. His smile was warm and inviting. "Good afternoon! Beautiful day today!" As he gestured to the solemn sky and surrounding area. I gave a small chuckle and said "Yes I suppose it is." He then engaged me in conversation for a while and motioned, inviting me to have a seat beside him. I declined and chose to remain standing but thinking back now I feel regret, hoping he did not find me rude. As we chatted about 'his park' I could not help but notice the pungent smell which wafted past me. He unfortunately had not had the privilege to bathe in some time. As we chatted, the rain would pool in his ball cap and stream down, landing in his long hair that now had formed into ringlets. Then drip, one drop at a time from the curls down into the breast pocket of his jacket. My eyes flitted back and forth from his mismatched socks to his toothless grin and the significant dirt beneath his fingernails, and the sparkle from his deep blue eyes contrasted with the weathered, leathery texture of his face and the unkempt grey-white mustache and beard with yellow stains around the opening of his mouth – I guessed probably from years of smoking.

What began as a light conversation gradually deepened, and I found myself opening up to a total stranger. He told me how he enjoys when the city gets quiet and the melody of sounds he can then hear, like when the rain hits the puddles or tin garbage cans. I waited for a break in the conversation and then asked him if he was cold, as I was starting to feel the effects of the weather.

He said "You get used to it. It's really all in how you view it. It could be snowing!", and then gave me a large gaping smile.

I told him how I was fortunate to find money in my pocket today and I wanted to offer it to him so he could get a hearty meal and a hot drink to help him through the long night ahead. As I pulled out the money, he was reluctant, shook his head "No" and waved it off.

He then eloquently stated "The company of a beautiful lady on a day such as this, has warmed me enough...I've enjoyed our conversation and am thankful you've entertained this old man's ramblings. Then he said "Oh" with wide-eyed exuberance, "I forgot to tell you this, "Don't ever strive for extraordinary, instead, find the wonder and marvel in an ordinary life and make the ordinary come alive!" With that, he stood up and shook the rain from his clothing, and started to walk away.

As I stood there watching him, in awe of what I had just experienced, he turned back toward me, paused and pointed his finger at me, and said, "There is always something in us that we feel we are lacking. We are constantly searching for something elusive, something we just can't put our finger on, but that's a lie someone has sold us or we created and now believe it to be true because of the culmination of circumstances from our past." With his yellow-tinged forefinger still pointed at me, he cocked his head to the side, gave a little nod, and winked at me. "I know you feel lost, alone, like no one can find you, but really you are only hiding from yourself. I see you. I see your pain", he said, putting his hand to his heart. "Stop it! It serves you no purpose now. There is a tiny spark deep within you, it's not gone out. It's wanting to become a raging fire-you have to find that spark and pour gasoline on it! We only have a finite number of days on this earth, if we're lucky we will see 85 summers. I have seen my share and my numbers are few now, but you, you have many. What are you going to do with them?"...and with that, he stomped his foot splashing water up onto the hem of his pants, while clapping his hands, then flashed that beautiful gaping smile again and continued walking down the path away from me.

That hit hard. I needed to sit down so I positioned myself on the bench that was still warm and just stared off into the ether letting his words reverberate inside my head, while the rain ran down my back and soaked my yoga pants. How poignant and profound chance encounters can be. From this unassuming and faceless man to many of us – who would pass him by without a thought – I was fortunate to experience an amazing soul, who taught me a plethora of life lessons in mere minutes. He was right. You have a choice in how you view your world...we as humans lean toward seeing the negatives in people and life. Why is that? Why not choose to find the positives instead? We're really not here for very long. Why not make it the best experience we can?

As I sat there floating in contemplation, it became clear to me. There are many iterations of me out there. Versions I created to help me survive.

However, there is one in particular that longs for healing – that little, bare-footed four-year-old, golden-haired, wild child. The search to find her will be challenging as she protects herself by hiding away, curled up in the deepest, darkest corner in the back-bedroom closet (the one where no one ventured and old things were stored, the dust so thick you could write your name in it), Or perhaps I will find her in a tree or a rooftop - up high and out of reach, is the only place where she feels safe and free. She is where it all began - the epicentre. She is the foundational brick in the wall that has built me and without her, I am in danger of crumbling to the ground. I must rescue her and show her unconditional love. When she is healed, I am healed.

That old man's words resonated in me for many years...

I had received a gift that day, packaged in a wake-up call. I realized there were parts of me I had been hiding from or running away from, and those are pernicious things. If your demons aren't dealt with properly they will find a way to resurface and manifest in very negative ways.

I am a work in progress and I'm okay with that. I am learning to embrace my authentic self, unapologetically, and to live intentionally and on my own terms-by doing this my hope is to embolden others to do the same.

To live intentionally and unapologetically you need to choose to disconnect from the barrage of messaging that tells you you are not good enough. It's self-preservation and this act of defiance can completely transform your life. Change your thoughts, your routines, your habits. Find sanctuary in nature. Put yourself first, be true to yourself, and speak kindly to yourself. Practice grace and live in a state of gratitude. No longer be available for things that disrupt your peace. Follow your intuition, don't put off your passions and stand up for yourself. If you implement even some of these things your life can be so beautiful.

Manifest a life of wonder and excitement. Find simple pleasures, no matter how small to be appreciative of - open the windows wide to the fresh air and the songs of birds. Savor the smell of the coffee brewing or the taste of freshly cut lemons or peas from the garden and the solace of the touch of a hand or a long hug from a loved one and certainly appreciate that you opened your eyes this morning – not everyone was granted that miracle.

It takes some work but I'm not running anymore, I walk, and sometimes I stumble, but I'm okay with that. I won't give up on myself nor will I invite negativity to stay long anymore because I found myself, and I believe I am worthy, and that I have value, and I am enough exactly the way that I am and simply because I am breathing and alive on this earth, I am deserving of love and respect, and so are you! To truly believe this, you must find your way to self-compassion, and the confidence to embrace your experiences, and all your lovely idiosyncrasies and imperfections. There are no experiences wasted. No matter how dark, broken, or scared you are, you can always find yourself again. Live in awe and wonder and authentically show up. Love your human nature in all its entirety. Fully choose yourself and like me, live out loud!

Shannon Heap is an artist and best-selling author residing in British Columbia,

Canada. She is a multi-faceted creator who is always searching and finding wonder and beauty in what would seem to be 'ordinary' things. She is inspired by nature, her environment, and art making experiences where all the senses are used. She shares joy through her work and helps people fill their homes with beautiful creations.

36

WENDY DREWS - Put Your Oxygen Mask on First

I feel that we are all originals. That every single one of us has something to offer to the world. Self-love is important and I have always heard in an airplane emergency put your oxygen mask on first! To have a radical love for oneself you must understand basic self care. Some hard decisions in life based on self-love can really leave one isolated. I was grateful to be a part of The Creative Life Book living from a fully expressed artist life. In my chapter I offer some tips and guidance for oneself. It takes a lot of bravery and strength to love yourself enough to cut toxic ties and trauma bonds. That's the first act of radical self-love. Stepping back and releasing all and everything if needed. I feel to fully heal you must reveal and nobody heals in silence. It takes a silent toll on the heart and the one's that don't have self-love don't last. Humans are wired for connection so it's important to heal to make new relationships. Future re-entry into the world requires you to reprogram the mind. You have to have self-love to survive otherwise you will not be able to function properly.

Self-love is taking the healing and the levels it brings. Healing is not linear; it may take several years to get to where you need to be. It's not easy and by having the self-love you can make it and get there one day. Working hard is the same way, it takes years of sacrifice and working to make it. Don't give up as your life can change overnight for the best. Reflecting on this moon we have had the past few nights, it's interesting. Right now it looks like a dot not like the slice or silver of a crescent like last night. It's barely visible. It's May 23 and it's the anniversary of when I quit smoking in my youth. I should have never smoked. I will say if you smoke quit now before you can't breathe. That's the best form of self-love right there. It's not easy but I would help anybody achieve that dream. It's all about following a simple timeline. You have to have self realization and self-love. Sometimes you can barely see the moon but it's always there and it's always whole. You have to have that same faith in yourself and in God. You have to trust yourself to take the leap and go for your dreams. Things may not always work out but I think the most important rule, if you have any in life, is to love yourself. What got me through my first semester in college was the motto F.L.Y. first love yourself. I wrote a poem which I featured in The Creative Life Book One: "Pilots Belong In The Sky." That's opened new opportunities for my hard work with the promotion of this book. I was offered a spot into a program that's going to change the rest of my life. Taking the risk working hard without getting paid and sharing the knowledge - that's powerful. We just have a small moment of time here to make the best of your life. I feel community care is so important to make sure all citizens are honored, especially children. Far too often people fall through the cracks and the effects can be devastating. I loved myself enough to go back to college and academics was fun until the last college class. It wasn't easy and it didn't provide the stability that I desperately need to get on my feet. That's how we all are, we want to thrive and others will see that light and you should be cherished and protected. The best advice I can give is to establish healthy boundaries with others and yourself. This is especially vital if you're a single Mom. Sometimes your light will attract it all and it's about personality and self protection. I recently learned from a public figure about how interpersonal relationship skills are so important to know. That EQ, Emotional Intelligence isn't enough to have to protect yourself. So, that's where I am in my personal journey to continue growing with self-love.

One of the biggest steps that I took was to jump at making my website official recently. I have worked on my blog to share my college and artist history. I always wanted to help people achieve their dreams. I know I have inspired countless people with my perseverance. Colleges didn't provide the path yet it gave me greater self confidence. I gained academic titles but I need to make a portfolio or professional plan. Community care is so important but self-love is just as important. It's so important to know who you are to achieve that level of love for yourself. There is power in truth if you are honest you have nothing to ever remember. With my website I originally chose a creative life happy life but I changed it to a creative life happy future. Having many new connections here is truly life changing. It will lift me higher than imagined. For me being a part of this was self love investing in my co-authorship was self love. Putting myself out there was fun for the first time. I wasn't scared. I was happy and making sure your life is fulfilling is a good plan to have. Become the warrior you always had within yourself. You can create that generational wealth and help others all over the world. My own personal statement is Fly Dream Remember Sky. Just don't lose hope as many do give up and still struggle daily having self-love is survival. It's time we all drink from a full cup. When yours is overflowing make sure you fill your people's cup. If you don't have people donate your abundance we must uplift others so that they can learn self-love and pass it on. Many mentors will say be kind always but I say love yourself first. It's time to put on your oxygen mask and take care of yourself.

While I mentioned the moon above I want to leave you with this poem, "Be Like The Sun." My mentor Jess Hughes doesn't know this but she inspired me to write this poem last summer. She's all about the good things in life and helping me leave this legacy as a creative visual artist and literary artist.

Be like the sun which comes up everyday. Fireworks are temporary; they last seconds to minutes; they are for many holidays, celebrations, and traditions. But, the sun it's here everyday no matter the occasion. The power is so immense that the sun provides life on Earth. Fireworks fade and go away as soon as they are seen. Be like the sun to stay everyday not just for when times are good for celebrating. We can harvest the power of solar from the sun but can we really harvest anything from a firework display? Other than temporary light and time to light up the sky? The sun can be depended even on a cloudy day. The sun rays are always here even if we can't feel or see them. The sun is a living legacy. Be like the sun.

Wendy Drews is a International #1 best seller and #1 Amazon best seller. A visual artist and writer, working at the intersection of math, science, photography, and art. She came up with the acronym SKY– Somebody Knows You. She created this to inspire people not to give up hope.

III

— Steps to Spark Self-Love —

Empowering techniques for embracing your worth, showering yourself with kindness, and celebrating the most important relationship you'll ever have – the one with yourself!

37

COLLEEN BROWN - Awakening the Financially Empowered Creative Woman

For many creative women — artists, sculptors, writers, dancers, and other visionaries — the concept of money often feels at odds with pursuing their passions. The prevailing notion of the "starving artist" can perpetuate harmful stereotypes and instill a mindset that creativity and financial prosperity are mutually exclusive. This mindset can form a significant barrier to recognizing their worth and pursuing a stable income from their craft.

However, creativity and wealth need not be at odds. By shifting your mindset around money, you can reconcile your passion with prosperity, enabling you to pursue your creative endeavors while securing your financial future.

It's not surprising that many of us, myself included, struggle to implement healthier beliefs around money, wealth creation, and the overall value of our products and ourselves. Many women have been discouraged or prevented from acquiring the financial knowledge crucial for navigating the modern world. But financial literacy is about more than just knowing how to balance a checkbook or save for retirement. It's about understanding money's power and how to harness it to support our aspirations and dreams. In my family, money, or lack of money, was often a source of contention. My parents were great people but lacked the education and resources to even know how to make a change. However, they instilled in me a hunger to do better and a belief that I could "be anything I wanted to be" if I worked hard. And so, I did.

At almost 30 and after my divorce, I enrolled at university. I was one of the first members of my family to pursue further education. At times, I had to take my two small children to classes with me, all while working a part-time job and supplementing my income with government assistance. I didn't say changing your life was easy, but I can say it's definitely worth it. After years of grinding at a full-time job and two "side hustles," I could retire earlier than I had originally thought and now participate in my art studio business more fully.

My new e-book and online course, "Empowering Creative Women: Financial Literacy for the Dreamers" is designed to provide creative women with an introductory guide to mastering money management. We understand that the language of numbers may not always resonate with individuals who have dedicated their lives to the language of art. We will explore topics like financial independence, reducing financial stress, budgeting, saving, investing, managing debt, and educational investment in clear, straightforward language that resonates with your creative spirit.

I realized I had to shift my mindset first to make a true shift in my life. Here, I share a few practical exercises that helped me change my beliefs and, ultimately, my financial wellness. It's a starting point, and we all have to start somewhere. I was tired of being broke and having more bills than dollars. Available cash flow limited my opportunities to participate in creative pursuits and projects. So, I set about creating a change, and while it hasn't always been a flawless transition, I know I can help you on your journey to better wealth creation and management. Let's go!

Unraveling Old Beliefs

The first step in shifting your money mindset is understanding and unraveling your long-held beliefs around money and wealth. Ask yourself what views you hold about money. Perhaps you think, "Money corrupts creativity," "Real artists starve," or "I am not good with money." Consider where these beliefs came from and if they are truly serving you.

Activity: Keep a "money beliefs" journal. For a week, write down any thoughts or beliefs you have about money as they arise. At the end of the week, review them. Are they helpful or hindering? Are they based on facts or societal myths?

Developing a New Narrative

Next, it's time to craft a new narrative. Instead of viewing money as a necessary evil, consider it a form of energy, an exchange of value that allows you to continue creating and sharing your work with the world.

Activity: Write a new money narrative. In your journal, rewrite your harmful beliefs with empowering ones. For instance, "real artists starve" could become "my creativity is valuable and deserving of fair compensation."

Visualizing Abundance

Visualization can be a powerful tool in shifting your mindset. When you visualize something, your brain can begin to believe it's possible. Visualizing abundance can help you embrace the idea that you can be successful and financially secure with your craft.

Activity: Spend a few minutes each day visualizing your life as a prosperous creative. Imagine having a steady income stream, being able to afford the materials you need, and earning recognition for your work. See yourself in your ideal creative space. How does that look, smell, and feel? I set about implementing some of the small things I imagined my studio would look like – a few new cushions, candles, paint, and lighting helped me believe this was truly attainable.

Investing in Your Worth

Understanding the value of your time, talent, and effort is crucial. Many creatives underprice their work, undermining their worth. Recognize that your creative output has value and deserves to be adequately compensated.

Activity: Review your pricing. If you're undervaluing your work, gradually increase your rates. Conduct market research to understand how others in your field price their work.

Embracing Financial Literacy

A common hurdle creative individuals face is a need for more understanding or interest in personal finance. However, mastering the basics of budgeting, investing, and wealth generation can be transformative.

Activity: Dedicate time to learn about personal finance. Read books, listen to podcasts, or take online courses. My new course and e-book: "Empowering Creative Women: Financial Literacy for the Dreamers," may be a great starting point.

Building Multiple Income Streams

Having multiple income streams can create financial stability. Not putting your "eggs in one basket" can offset potential losses in one area by having other income streams. Consider selling prints of your artwork, creating online courses, writing e-books, licensing your work, or offering workshops.

Activity: Brainstorm ways to diversify your income. List your skills and interests and consider how to monetize them.

Practicing Gratitude

Lastly, practice gratitude for the money you do have and for your ability to create. Cultivating gratitude can positively influence your mindset and open you up to receiving more. We, the creative dreamers, bring things into reality that never existed before! We can do that with money as well!

Activity: Keep a gratitude journal. Every day, write down three things you're grateful for related to your creativity and finances.

Shifting your mindset around money takes time, patience, and consistent effort. But with each step, you're moving closer to a reality where your creativity thrives alongside prosperity. Remember, your creative abilities are unique and invaluable. You deserve to be rewarded not with applause, "exposure," and accolades but also with the financial stability that allows you to continue creating and inspiring the world. You can do this!

Learn more over at https://empoweringcreativewomen.com

Colleen Brown shares her knowledge of financial literacy with women & girls so they can live the life they want without limitations. Colleen has risen from being a struggling single parent, often attending university classes with her children in tow, to becoming financially independent and retiring early to pursue the artist's life.

As an entrepreneurial business woman with an MBA, she has both the experience and education to support others in their journey toward financial independence. In the Fall of 2023, she will launch a new website and online course: "Empowering Creative Women: Financial Literacy for the Dreamers."

38

CAREY KIRKELLA - The L.E.N.S. Method™ & Connecting with Your Higher Self

I woke up feeling out of place in my sterilized bed and glanced at my sleeping roommate in the maternal mental health ward. Had I said out loud that I had been convinced she was my sister even though my sister had passed away a few years before? In my exhausted meds-induced haze after 26 hours of labor and subsequent c-section – not to mention the vague understanding that I was there for postpartum psychosis – I wasn't completely sure. As I collected myself and walked down the hall looking for the hospital-grade breast milk pump, I felt a sense of determination wash over me. There were two things I was sure of: Even though I didn't yet know how – I was going to be the best damn mother I could be. And somehow, I was going to use my mental health journey and my creativity to help others with their mental and emotional well-being. I decided I was going through all of this for a bigger purpose.

Each of the three times I was hospitalized for bipolar disorder-related manic episodes, months of crippling anxiety followed. Looking back, I can see that every time it happened, a new brick was laid for the foundation of The L.E.N.S. Method™. After the first episode, I instinctively knew I needed to reconnect with nature. I already knew that I was a highly sensitive empath and a dedicated photographer, and I could use these gifts to help my well-being. I began creating a series of photos that symbolized concepts I wanted to feel more aligned with - grounded, peaceful, beautifully designed, and belonging among the stars in the sky.

Through my journey, I have learned that the *lens* through which we see ourselves affects how we show up in the world and how we experience our life, on a profound level. If I want to change the world and my experience of it, I *must* start by being self-compassionate and loving myself.

As a pre-teen, I knew I wanted to be either a photographer or a psychologist. The word psyche is not just about the mind, it is also about the spirit, the human soul. I learned that embracing radical self-love requires the unshakable belief that we are all inherently worthy of love – from ourselves, from others, and from Source Energy, no matter what we have been through. I am committed to being conscious of my energetic state and knowing that I am so much more than my thoughts, feelings, and past experiences.

We are all spiritual beings going through a human experience and our souls are composed of the energy of unconditional love. Radical self-love involves prioritizing how you feel about yourself and directing your thoughts and actions *based on the life you envision*, rather than being dictated by your current circumstances.

How do we become a conduit for experiencing more wonder, connection, and joy in this life? How do we become capable of receiving clear guidance from our higher selves? Every moment offers a choice – to live from a place of love and empowerment or from a place of fear and disempowerment. Staying attuned to the present moment and giving myself opportunities to get into a *creative flow state* deepens my connection with my intuition and reinforces my love for myself and this miracle of life.

The key to manifesting more miracles in your life lies in expanding your capacity to choose self-love consistently. You do this by aligning yourself with the frequency of your higher self, which is always in resonance with the energy of love.

The L.E.N.S. Method™ came through me by healing my mental and emotional well-being, and from my lifelong love of creative photography. I invite you to use this process to align with a life fully expressed through the lens of radical self-love. The framework is about taking inspired action to practice the five pillars of emotional resilience through creative photography. Doing this sends a powerful message to yourself and the Universe.

Images are powerful. Creativity plays a vital role in soothing the nervous system and is essential for emotional well-being and cultivating self-love. A practice that gets you into a creative flow state helps you live more intentionally and be more present so more of what you want can flow toward you.

L.E.N.S. stands for Light, Empathy, Now, and Storytelling.

Light represents our inner luminosity, reminding us that we are beings of pure light and love.

Empathy refers to having a compassionate lens through which you perceive yourself and the world.

Now emphasizes embracing the *present moment* and reconnecting with your senses and breath.

Storytelling helps us acknowledge that it is not events themselves that shape us, *but our beliefs about those events.* The creation of storytelling photos is a powerful part of this process.

The L.E.N.S. Method™ & The 5 Pillars of Emotional Resilience

Your emotional resilience grows stronger through self-love. Building emotional resilience through practicing these five pillars helps prepare you for the challenging circumstances that life throws at you; you will be more capable of truly *feeling your emotions with grace, integrity, and compassion.*

You can use any camera, including the one on your smartphone. I encourage you to use your phone because it makes this process easier and even more accessible to do regularly.

Your mission is to create a visual journaling practice that intentionally incorporates these five pillars of emotional resilience:

Mindfulness, Self-Awareness, Self-Care, Positive Relationships, Purpose

Photo Story Prompt Examples:

· **Mindfulness**

Spend time in nature, connect with your senses, put your bare feet on the ground, or hug a tree (try it! feels like coming home to me), and then begin making photos that symbolize words like 'grounded', 'growth', and 'flow'.

· **Self Awareness**

Are my thoughts and beliefs reflecting the energy I want more of? What are 3 things I'm grateful for that I can create photos about? Look for the 3 L's: Light, Love, and Laughter for inspiration.

Create a folder of your photos on your phone or computer as your own personal L.E.N.S. Method™ visual journal. Turbo-charge this process by pairing your images with inspiring quotes and affirmations and making them into a book. This is a powerful process even if you are the only person who sees what you created. L.E.N.S. can be an ongoing process done just for you, or it can be for helping you resonate more authentically with those you serve, through the content you share about your work in the world.

When you commit to a practice that helps you shift your perspective and your energetic state, those feelings of joy and peace become an integral part of your existence. Commit to this practice of radical self-love, and you will become a beacon of light for others, spreading love and creating a ripple effect in the world.

Time to dial up your inner light and let it shine! You, yes *you*, are a loved and powerfully creative being and you truly deserve to receive the infinite love that is here for you now.

Visit the link in my bio below to download a free gift and connect with me.

Carey Kirkella is an award-winning photographer, the Founder of The L.E.N.S. Method™, and the CEO of Carey Kirkella Creative. As a heart-centered creative entrepreneur and mental health advocate, Carey is an expert in harnessing the power of photography as a way to elevate socially conscious brands, and as a tool to help others regulate their nervous systems through creativity.

A graduate of Pratt Institute in NYC, her fine art photography has been exhibited internationally, and published in top industry publications worldwide. She has collaborated with household name brands, creating emotionally compelling story-telling advertising campaigns that connect authentically with their audiences.

Carey's passion for mental and emotional well-being grew out of overcoming serious mental health illnesses, and she openly shares her journey as a regular guest through multiple media platforms, helping to inspire others and break down stigmas. Her mission through her proprietary framework, The L.E.N.S. Method™ (LENS = Light · Empathy · Now · Storytelling), is to empower both adults and teens to use the process of creative photography as a way to connect more deeply with their inner selves, and to elevate human consciousness.

39

REBECCA ROSAS - Radical Self Love Is Listening To Your Heart

And learning to love yourself, over and over. This has been my journey.

I was five years old when we moved to Walla, Walla, Washington. I remember being this cute little Hispanic girl with short, dark hair and dimples that was a bit shy and quiet, but also happy. We had an orchard with lots of fruit trees next to our house. I would climb the trees, play with the neighbor kids and eat fresh fruit and homemade pies. Life was good. It was here that I developed my free and creative spirit, but it didn't last long.

We moved to Nebraska two years later. That move forever changed me. It was such a different environment and I attended a stricter Catholic school. I found myself retreating more and more into my shell. I became more introverted, continuing to stay quiet and just do what I was told. I didn't express myself much except through art. I loved art projects! I was always so excited to come home and show my mom all the pictures and mementos of things I created that day. Creativity was the place I felt most at home. It was where I was free to express myself. It's taken me decades and an intense spiritual awakening to help me reflect and see all the times in my life when I didn't love myself, held myself back, didn't speak my truth, or let myself be the truest expression of me.

I've been learning to love myself since I was a teen. Over the past seven years, I prioritized my self-healing journey. I was tired of playing small, feeling not seen or heard, not speaking my truth, and hiding behind the excuses of being an introvert. I was truly tired of not seeing or loving the real me. This journey has brought me to the depths of self-love. Radical self-love.

And, if I had to share just ONE thing that would help you learn self-love, it would be this....

Listen to your intuition, your inner voice, and the musings of your heart. Learn to strengthen your intuition and connect to your heart.

When you learn to connect to your heart, you make good choices that are in alignment with who you are on a soul level. When you strengthen your intuition you create a closer connection with spirit and with yourself which enables you to trust more, believe in yourself more, and overcome limiting beliefs more.

So, how do you strengthen your intuition and connect to your heart? Reflection, introspection, and creativity! These are some of my favorite tools you can use to strengthen your connection with yourself.

Here are some tips to help you connect to your intuition and your heart, as well as doing the creative exercise below:

Start by asking yourself these questions for any decisions you need to make, or anything that's coming up for you in your life, such as goals, dreams, and wishes.

- What does my heart want?
- What is my inner voice saying to me?

- What would make me feel good?
- How would it feel if I made this choice vs. an alternate choice?
- How do I feel in my body when I think about this situation? Am I excited or do I feel stressed?
- What's the first thing that comes to me when I think about an answer?

Reflect on your answers and continue to journal to help you gain more clarity on your feelings, emotions, and what your heart is saying to you.

Once your journaling is complete, let's go a bit further and strengthen your intuition through creativity! Below is a simple, but effective creative project that will help you get to know yourself better, strengthen your intuitive muscle and learn to trust yourself while being creative and giving yourself permission to express yourself!

Let's get started:

Grab a mixed-media art journal and a few of your favorite art supplies. *See below for a full list of supplies.

We want to start the groundwork by first helping you find your own style.

1. Open up your journal and start playing with lines. You want to determine what sort of brushstroke you like. Start adding all sorts of lines and shapes on your paper with black paint. Do you like straight lines, curvy lines, dashes, dots, circles, swirls, or spirals? What speaks to you? If you need some inspiration, start looking at some of your favorite pieces of art. Search on Pinterest. Ask yourself, what do you like about them? Notice what type of shapes or lines they use. For example, search Pablo Picasso. He was well-known for his Cubism work. He used lots of geometric lines and shapes. Do you like lines like that or are you drawn to softer abstract work? Once you've filled your paper with your favorite lines and shapes, move to step 2.

2. Now we want to play with color! Take out some of your favorite colors to make color swatches. Tune into your heart to decide which colors feel good and make you feel excited. Start adding a box or circle on the next page of your journal. Try adding different colors side-by-side or slightly overlapping. Play with different color combinations to see which combinations are your favorite. Don't overthink it. You can try adding white to your color to lighten it or adding a little black to it to darken it. You can take a color and add the complementary color to mute it down a little. The complementary color is the opposite of that color on the color wheel. For instance, the complementary color of yellow is purple. You can look at a color wheel or search online if you are not sure. Note, if you have any transparent colors (see-through) see how they show up differently - especially when you overlap them with other colors.

Now that you have a better idea of your own style of colors and lines, you can start creating!

3. Go to the next page of your journal. you are going to start painting hearts. Grab one color and draw three or four hearts in one row about one or two inches from the top and left of your page. Make the hearts proportionate to your page, (one and a half up to three inches in height). Grab a new color and create a second row of hearts. Do the same and create another row with another color. You should end up with three or four rows of hearts, depending on the size of your paper.

4. Here's where you can start having fun styling your hearts! Look at the lines and color pages that you created. Use these for reference. Start adding a second color to your hearts with some of your favorite lines. Then, maybe you start adding some dots around one of your hearts. Maybe you use a second color and paint a thicker line on the inside edge of your heart. Use this time to play and start adding more color combinations and a variety of brush strokes to make each heart unique. Follow your intuition of your favorite lines and color combinations for all your hearts until the page feels

complete!

Whether it's creating art, making a decision about a relationship, a career, or an opportunity, connecting to your heart and tuning into your intuition will help support you in making the right choice for you. You can't go wrong making choices from the heart. And making choices from your heart is radical self-love!

If you'd like to watch a quick demo of this creative project, go to my website, or if you'd like to dive deeper into self-love, check out my new self-love workbook launching soon. Visit the link below for details.

Rebecca Rosas is a Divine Feminine Empowerment & Creativity Coach, Abstract Artist, Creative Visionary/Entrepreneur, Energy Healer and Author that inspires and uplifts others to do the inner healing work to shine their light.

Motivated by her own transformational spiritual journey, she empowers women to use the healing power of creativity to express their emotions, heal their heart, connect to their feminine energy, deepen their self love and raise their vibration. Her approach helps women see their unlimited potential, align to their true soul essence and illuminate their soul. Through Becky's creative endeavors, she awakens the creative light of others and touches the souls of those around her and through her work.

She is a certified as an Usui/Holy Fire® World Peace Karuna Reiki® Master & Creatively Fit™ Art Coach and trained as a Soul Coach. As a creative entrepreneur she has a background in marketing & advertising.

40

REE FREEMAN, GRIGSBY FREEMAN & WALKER FREEMAN - Reclaim your Time, Energy, Money & Support (and Beat Burnout!)

We didn't think Self Love pertained to us until we hit a wall going 100mph.
The wall was burnout. We crashed hard. Everything burned up in a fiery blaze. It forced us to take a hard look at how we live and work.

Our business tanked because the workload and stress were overwhelming.
We were on a speed train to Success Station but forced to call it quits. People kept trying to buy. We shrank into a shell of shame to hide. We couldn't take payments when we couldn't deliver services. We didn't have the bandwidth to train or manage anyone. We had poured so much into our business. Then watched it crumble into ashes, unable to stop the volcano raging through it.

Our personal life turned into a dizzying array of problems.
Our relationships had seen better years. Those in our inner circle were battling their own crises and demons which added to the weight of it all. Our daughter was bombarded with health issues that our team of doctors hadn't been able to solve. She struggled with school and self-esteem because of a

bully. We worked 7 days a week to help her Health & Mindset.

Then our dog died, best friend died and my dad died. My mom almost died several times. It was a lot to deal with in a short timeframe.

We felt broken, again.
The other times were when we spent tons of money, years and tears fighting Infertility and a debilitating life-long injury with chronic pain. We were exhausted.

It got clear fast who our real friends were.
We were no longer the "good vibes" people everyone wanted us to be. That's the bad thing about burnout and a boatload of bad stuff, it's hard to be positive and happy. We still showed up for parenting, school and soccer games. Beyond that, we reduced interaction with everyone. We disappointed everyone but had nothing left to give.

NOTE: You really never know what someone is truly dealing with, so please, give people grace and be kind.
We are really private so looking in from the outside it probably looked like life was great. Unfortunately, it wasn't and it took a toll on our attitudes and vibe.

We were stuck in survival mode and it sucked.
Sitting in a 50-foot steamy pile of poo, we didn't know how we got there. More importantly, we didn't know how to get un-broken or unstuck. We didn't know where to start.

For years we grappled with burnout.
As soon as we thought we were ok, it would come back tenfold. We hadn't escaped. It was like being a yo-yo and getting snapped backward.

Desperate to break free, we consumed hundreds and hundreds of books,

articles, podcasts and scientific studies.

Being a shell of our former selves wasn't easy so we were on a mission to do everything we could. We were determined to stop the burnout cycle & misery.

Luckily, years of research paid off. Turns out, Self Love is the secret ingredient we were missing. Before burnout, we had no understanding of Self Love. Now, it's clear. Self Love boils down to taking care of yourself.

Thankfully anyone can tap into Self Love, no matter their age. Even you!

Your most precious resources are Your Time, Your Energy, Your Support & Your Money.

If you don't take care of them, you'll end up in a bad place. We learned the hard way. It's a difficult road back so you're better off taking action RIGHT NOW. The sooner you prioritize them, the better you and those around you will be.

Working as a Team is a tremendous boost to success.

If you have a team you can work with, please do. Every step of the way we helped and relied upon each other. Our family has come a long way from the early days of surviving. **Now we show up consistently as Leaders, instead of Victims.**

We Transformed the way we Live & Work by reclaiming our Time, Money, Energy and Support.

We have so much more control now. Instead of feeling helpless and fried all the time, we are empowered, happy and energized. We got Unstuck, Beat overwhelmed, Reduced Anxiety and Stress.

We cracked the code to lay a new path for the next generation while young, so decades aren't wasted.

Since age 6, Grigsby has been able to make choices that positively impact her future on an exponential level. Other kids can too.

Accountability is powerful when you have the right mentors and cheer-leaders.

Luckily we did. Burnout is no joke. Don't tackle it alone.

As a family, we created Frameworks, Guidebooks, Worksheets and Templates to keep us accountable and progress as individuals and as a Team-that anyone can use.

We tested and tweaked them many times. We continually educate ourselves and update our tools so they are more effective. We are excited and honored to help others reclaim their Time, Energy, Money and Support. Kicking burnout is cool too.

Kids make great feedback loops because they don't hold back.

They will tell you exactly what they think. They will also cheer you on and believe in you so much that it makes you believe in yourself. Grigsby was quick to point out when we weren't doing what we said we would. She would happily tell us what we should do differently and why. She taught us a lot about the power of Accountability and cheering for even the tiniest of victories.

The same habits that made us successful Students and Employees were what created burnout.

Changing habits isn't easy. We have to unlearn to progress. Fortunately, with our tools, it can be done faster and easier.

This is a problem for our Businesses, Schools and Communities.

We can no longer view this as a personal issue. There should be required education & support in every school & business on Energy & Time Management, Support & Money.

Building foundational habits to Manage Time, Energy, Money and Support

is something everyone should prioritize.

This is crucial for Leaders, Managers, Executives, Parents, Entrepreneurs, Coaches, Teachers and Students.

12 acts of Self Love to Beat Burnout and Reclaim your Time, Energy, Money & Support:

1. Analyze your Time, Energy, Money & Support.
2. Get Clear on Your Goals & Milestones.
3. Track Your Habits.
4. Ditch Habits that Drain You.
5. Add Habits that Power You.
6. Setup Your Support Routines.
7. Setup Your Support Systems.
8. Build Your Support Circle.
9. Review (Weekly, Monthly, Quarterly, Yearly).
10. Set & Enforce Boundaries.
11. Use Internal Motivation Triggers.
12. Get Accountability (multiple layers).

If you are reading this, it's exactly what you needed to see today.

Hopefully, our victories inspire you to keep going and not give up. The time and money we devoted to this battle was a privilege most don't have access to, and for that, we are very grateful.

Grab free printables & check out our videos, courses & VIP options at POWERMODE.co.

Please pay it *forward*.

Send a copy of this book to 5-10 people. Be a great friend, and send 20+ books! Friends, family, colleagues, book clubs and churches would all be excellent candidates.

You never know who needs this right now. Especially after the last few years. We can tackle this together and we're waiting to help you.

We believe in you!!
Hugs & High 5s!

Ree, Grigsby & Walker Freeman
(& Team POWERMODE)

Grigsby Freeman is an 11 yr old Author, Artist & Creative Entrepreneur whose work empowers people to be strong, confident & happy. At 5 she created her first products & business and at 8 years old she founded her second business & wrote a book on Gratitude. Her books, cards & Gratitude decks can be found at LoveG.co.

Ree Freeman is an Author, Speaker, CEO & High-Performance Consultant featured on top-rated International Podcasts & Media outlets.

Walker Freeman is an Author, Speaker & CTO; His 25-year Tech Leadership, Innovation & Strategy includes VP Software Engineering, Cloud System Architecture, Information Security Management & Software Development.

*A powerhouse team, Grigsby, Ree & Walker Freeman Co-Founded **POWERMODE**, a High-Performance Coaching & Consultancy firm, to help you Take Back your*

Time & Energy, Shift your Mindset & Habits and Hit your Goals Faster. It's time to step into YOUR POWERMODE.

They coach and consult on Productivity, Time & Energy Management, Burnout, Organization & Decluttering, Mindset, Systems, Support, Habits, Routines, Goals, Teams, Leadership & Creativity.

41

KELLY CLARK - Unveiling the Menu of Intention

"Transformative" - that's how I'd label the strategy that turned my life around. My mom, with her unique knack for imparting wisdom, offered me an unexpected lesson about life. She taught me that people are often quick to share what they don't want in life, but rarely can they express what they truly want.

At first, I struggled to grasp her words, so she gave me an easy-to-understand example. Imagine walking into McDonald's, she said, and telling the cashier that you don't want a burger, a milkshake, or chips. The cashier would surely give you a confused look before asking, "So, what do you want then?" Once I'd clarified, "I want chicken nuggets," the cashier would register my order. And within minutes, I'd get exactly what I ordered - my desired chicken nuggets!

This insightful story was too complex for my ten-year-old self. But as I got older, the underlying lesson of the story started to grow on me.

As a 21-year-old grappling with an assortment of failed relationships, both business and personal, I started comprehending the depth of mom's words.

What I truly desired from life, I realized, was not in the avoidance of what I didn't want, but in the clear articulation of what I did. I had to place my order, and in doing so, I had to get specific.

This began my journey into the realm of list-making, my creative way of establishing self-awareness and empowering radical self-love. The first list was my vision of an ideal partner. It was like penning down a character in a novel - every detail mattered. His age, his hair color, his build, his aspirations and goals, his finances, his relationships with friends and family, his wanderlust - everything. I poured my heart and mind onto the page and then carefully tucked it away. Although the paper was out of sight, the dream was etched vividly in my mind, especially when I considered entering a relationship.

For a while, nothing significant happened. The world, it seemed, was taking its own sweet time to align. Then, almost magically, a long-lost friend reappeared in my life. A casual conversation about future children jolted me. My mental list, buried yet alive, unfolded. One by one, I checked the boxes. And then, just like that, I was living my dream. Fast forward five years, I'm abundantly happy being married to my best friend.

The first list had worked wonders, and so, I kept making more. I made one for traveling, one for my business, another for friends. I used this strategy for every aspect of my life, transforming dreams into realities. No, the results didn't come instantly. But the lists inspired introspection. They made me question who I needed to become to open my heart and life to my dreams.

For someone with OCD, creativity doesn't always look like painting or songwriting. My creativity finds expression in structure and organization. Lists are my canvas, my song sheet. I channel my creativity into detailed, comprehensive visions for my life. It's a strategy, a mechanism, that fuels my sense of self-worth and helps me shape my future exactly the way I want.

By articulating my dreams and desires in lists, I've learned to embrace radical self-love. This approach has led to an indescribable sense of self-fulfillment. This isn't just about writing lists; it's about acknowledging what I truly desire and believing I'm deserving of these dreams. It's about consciously crafting my life's direction instead of leaving it to fate. It's about acknowledging that I am the author of my story, and every choice I make, every list I pen, carries the potential to create a new chapter.

Mom, thank you for weaving tales that unknowingly guided me towards shaping my entire future. Your storytelling has truly been a gift.

I encourage you to embrace this creative strategy.

- Begin by writing your lists: include your dreams and desires.
- Make a conscious decision to live life intentionally, not by default.
- Embrace the concept of radical self-love, accepting and valuing yourself wholly.
- Decide exactly what you want in your life, akin to ordering from a menu.
- When you've identified precisely what you desire, the next step is to determine the kind of person you need to evolve into to turn your dreams into reality.
- Be patient and persistent, and you'll soon see your desires becoming reality.

This is my story, and perhaps it can be yours too.

Kelly Clark, a dynamic CEO and Director, has a distinguished track record of spearheading 2 multi-million dollar location-based businesses to success through systems. Leveraging her expertise in devising systems, she bravely pivoted to the digital realm, dedicating her talents to nurturing online businesses. Her goal is to use her passion and elite skill to help online businesses reach the desired 8-figure mark and beyond. Kelly's know-how applies to all types of industries, showing off her ability to adapt and her dedication to helping businesses grow.

42

MAGGIE O'HARA - Artful Affirmations

Nurturing Self-Love through Affirmations & Creativity

In a world that often tells us we're not enough, cultivating self-love becomes an essential act of rebellion and healing. Self-love means fully embracing ourselves and our flaws and recognising our inherent worthiness. It's about reclaiming our power and celebrating the uniqueness that makes us who we are.

I'm Maggie and I'm an intuitive digital artist who creates artworks using colour psychology and one-word affirmations to raise the frequency so anyone in their presence feels uplifted and inspired. This is the story of why I create, how I use affirmation card decks, and why affirmations are good for finding self-love.

I invite you to explore the transformative power of self-love by integrating art and affirmation cards into your life.

"For me, self-love is an unapologetic embrace of myself. It starts with acknowledging that I am enough just as I am."

Society often bombards us with unrealistic standards of beauty, success and worthiness. However, self-love challenges these notions and encourages us to redefine our own values. By embracing our imperfections, strengths and vulnerabilities, we can develop a deep sense of self-acceptance and self-compassion.

My journey of self-discovery and empowerment through art and affirmations started several years ago after becoming a single mum with the sole goal of ensuring my daughters understood the value of being independent and strong and not requiring validation from others, they would learn the importance of self-love.

Art has long been recognised as a powerful tool for self-expression and self-discovery. Through various art forms, such as painting, drawing and writing, we can tap into our emotions and inner truths. When engaging in artistic practices we create a safe space to explore our thoughts, feelings and desires. Art allows us to communicate our experiences beyond words enabling a deeper connection with ourselves and others.

As a creative, I struggled with self-doubt, confidence, and the need to be perfect or to be accepted by my peers. The more I let go of the recurring thoughts of *not being good enough* or *perfect,* the more creative ideas came to me. During COVID, I created a set of 30 digital artworks using colour psychology and a concealed one-word affirmation on the base layer. I transformed them into affirmation cards and found that they resonated more deeply with others.

Affirmation cards are an effective tool for cultivating self-love and building a positive self-image. They contain empowering statements that reinforce our worth and capabilities. By repeating affirmations regularly, we reprogram our subconscious mind, replacing negative self-talk with empowering beliefs. I use affirmation cards daily to remind me of my values and strengths.

What can you do to embrace art and affirmations?

The synergy between art and affirmation cards creates a powerful combination of self-discovery and self-love. An inspiring way to integrate art and affirmation cards into your self-love journey is to create your own artistic affirmation cards.

Design your own affirmation cards using your preferred artistic medium and experiment with a different style each day for 30 days. Challenge yourself to use colours you're not normally drawn to and see if you can discover why.

Write down empowering affirmations and incorporate them into your artwork. Each time you look at your creation, you will be reminded of the love and strength that resides within you. By the end of the month, you will have 30 cards you can be proud of.

I have witnessed the incredible impact that integrating art and affirmations can have on transforming our relationship with ourselves.

By creating your cards and using various art forms, you infuse them with your unique creative energy, making them even more meaningful.

· **Watercolours**: Embrace the fluidity of watercolours to create vibrant backgrounds for your affirmation cards. Allow the colours to blend on the paper, symbolising the dynamic nature of self-love. Add affirmations in elegant calligraphy or playful lettering to infuse each card with empowering words.

· **Collage:** Dive into the realm of mixed media by creating collage affirmation cards. Collect images, quotes, and materials that resonate with you and reflect self-love. As you piece them together, witness how elements harmonise, just like the many facets of your beautiful self.

· **Zen Doodles:** Engage in the meditative practice of Zen doodling to create intricate and mesmerising patterns on your affirmation cards. Each stroke becomes an affirmation in itself, guiding you toward self-love and inner peace. Let your creativity flow without judgment, knowing each line represents a step on your self-love journey.

To truly harness the transformative power of self-love, it is important to integrate art and affirmations into your daily ritual.

1. **Morning Affirmation Ritual:** Start your day by selecting an affirmation card that resonates with your intentions. Take a few deep breaths, hold the card close to your heart, and recite the affirmation aloud or silently. Allow its empowering message to infuse your being and set the tone for a day filled with self-love and self-compassion.

2. **Evening Reflections:** Before winding down for the night, reflect on the day's experiences and lessons. Choose an affirmation card that aligns with any challenges you faced or victories you celebrated. Spend a few moments journaling or creating a small artwork inspired by the card, expressing gratitude and appreciation for your growth and resilience.

After working with an app developer to create **Australia's first fully interactive deck** using a FREE app to make each artwork come alive and fill the room with butterflies, I knew this was the future. It offers a holistic and embodied experience, as it engages your senses and connects with your physical and emotional being. This experience deepens your connection to self, fostering self-compassion and self-acceptance on a profound level.

Interactive affirmation cards and art can play a crucial role in assisting with self-love by creating active engagement and personalised experiences. Interacting with affirmation cards and art requires active participation, inviting you to engage with your thoughts, emotions, and creative expression. By actively choosing and engaging with the cards, you take ownership of your self-love journey. This level of engagement fosters a sense of empowerment, reminding you that you can shape your own narrative.

As a creator of affirmation cards, I specialise in crafting healing artworks that elevate the soul. The artworks are intentionally created, channeling healing energy, colour psychology and positive affirmations into each piece. Incorporating these artworks into affirmation cards creates a deeper connection with your inner self.

Embracing self-love is a transformative process that ripples into every aspect of our lives. As we learn to love ourselves unconditionally, we become more resilient, compassionate, and authentic

Remember, self-love is an ongoing journey, and affirmation cards and art serve as invaluable companions along the way by creating a positive feedback loop and rewiring your thoughts and beliefs. As you actively affirm your self-love, you reinforce positive neural pathways, gradually replacing self-doubt and self-criticism with self-compassion and self-empowerment.

I encourage you to follow these steps and embark on your own transformative journey. I'd love to see photos of what you have created.

Maggie O'Hara is an award-winning intuitive digital artist, author, and creator of healing artworks and affirmation cards. With her use of color psychology and affirmations, her work raises the frequency of the viewer. Maggie is the visionary behind Australia's first fully-interactive deck of affirmation cards, amplifying their impact through a free app. After years of low self-esteem and low confidence, Maggie uses creativity to heal her soul and her mission is to empower others by unleashing their inner child, boosting self-confidence, and restoring self-worth. Featured in digital art magazines across Australia, New Zealand, and the USA, Maggie's work has garnered praise and success. Her debut solo exhibition 'Transcendence' in 2022 achieved a remarkable 60% sales on opening night.

43

ELIZABETH KING - The Dance of Self-love and Fertility

As a best-selling author, it would have been unfathomable for me, a few years ago, to foresee the road I was about to tread – the complex journey of natural conception at the ripe age of forty. Yet, there I found myself, standing on the brink of a new chapter, newly married for the second time, my heart excited with a new longing for a family of my own, a cherished unit that would be a reflection of our collective love. For years, I had been entangled in a relentless struggle with self-love, a complex tangle spun from a multitude of interwoven threads, including my ongoing battle with weight and the distorted perception that I harbored about my body. Never once did my reflection in the mirror suffice to instill within me a sincere sense of self-worth, much less self-love. Moreover, my failed first marriage had planted deep within my psyche a gnawing sense of self-loathing, an incessant belief that I hadn't tried hard enough. Then I experienced a different level of pain from the silent agony of miscarriages, further cementing my chronic lack of self-love. It was through these tribulations, the daunting task of confronting the demons that fueled my self-hatred, that I managed to painstakingly chisel away at my old self, ushering in an era of profound self-love—an unparalleled metamorphosis.

Navigating the path towards procreation often plunges us into a labyrinth of societal narratives, biologically dictated timelines, and personal expectations. It isn't surprising, then, that we may find ourselves being swept away by these swirling currents, losing sight of an essential element of the process—ourselves.

The voyage to fertility, akin to any other life-altering journey, necessitates the cultivation of a robust, loving relationship with oneself. You may not be on a fertility journey per se but we are always looking to "birth" something in our lives. It may be a business, a relationship, a family or birthing radical self-love. As a best-selling author and a professional coach, I have dedicated my life's work to assisting individuals like you in discovering and rejoicing in that critical relationship. The cornerstone of this journey lies in embracing radical self-love—a kind of self-love that permits us to harmoniously dance with our fertility, without friction or conflict and finally feel like you can surrender to a magical flow in your life with yourself.

Radical self-love, particularly in the context of fertility, extends beyond mere self-kindness. It encompasses the wholehearted nurturing of your holistic being—your mind, body, and spirit. The pressing question, however, remains: how do we foster this radical self-love in a world that often seems devoid of room for it?

Section 2: The Dance of Self-Love, Forgiveness, and Care

The rhythmic dance of self-love is a harmonious union of the physical, emotional, and spiritual facets of our being. I propose three unique dance steps to choreograph your dance of self-love:

Step #1: Self-Love: Let each day begin with the recognition of your inherent worth. Practice the art of gentleness towards yourself, particularly in the face of adversity. Cherish and respect your body, irrespective of where you stand on your fertility journey. We go through times that it is difficult to get to that place but find one thing, as tiny as it may be to love and that will soon begin to blossom into more. Push yourself when it doesn't seem possible, that is when you need it most.

Step #2: Self-Forgiveness: Clinging to guilt, blame, or regret can cause emotional barriers that affect our overall well being and fertility. Embark on the journey of self-forgiveness, unshackle your spirit, and make room for love to flow freely. Look closely at the people in your life to see where there is still some self-forgiveness that needs to happen in order for you to move forward. Often the people who are closest to us can help us reflect back to us what we may still need to work on.

Step #3: Self-Care: This isn't about indulgence, but self-preservation. Regular exercise, a balanced diet, adequate rest, and engaging in activities that nurture your soul can significantly bolster your wellbeing and fertility.

Section 3: Choreographing the Dance Steps for Fertility

While the prospect of embracing these dance steps may seem daunting, it need not be. I offer some simple, actionable ways to weave self-love, forgiveness, and care into the fabric of your daily life:

- Usher in each day with an affirmation of self-worth. Be sure that it resonates with you on a cellular level.
    - Compile a 'Joy List' of activities that sprinkle happiness into your day, and pledge to indulge in at least one every day.
    - Carve out a tranquil moment each day for self-forgiveness. Discard guilt or blame and replace them with love and acceptance.
    - Allocate 'Self-Care Hours' each week. This time is solely for you—non-negotiable and essential for your wellbeing.
    - Start and end each day with positive visualization, envisioning the life you are in the process of creating.
    - Write out the details of what you want your life to look like with your

radical self love in place and set an alarm to read it outloud to yourself each day.

Conclusion: Your Dance Awaits

This chapter offers a sneak peek into the beautiful dance of radical self-love and fertility—a dance that acknowledges your inherent worth and power. As you prepare to step into this dance, remember you are an exquisite creator, capable of harboring immense love and fostering magnificent life.

Whether you choose to continue your journey through the pages of my upcoming book or via personalized one-on-one coaching, rest assured that you're not alone. I stand by your side, eager to guide you through each step of your dance.

You are seen. You are heard. And you are ready to embark on this empowering fertility journey, rooted in radical self-love. The stage is set, dear reader. It's time to let your dance begin no matter what you are wanting to birth in your life.

Elizabeth King is the CEO and Founder of Elizabeth King Coaching and the Fertility Coach Academy, where she trains other women on how to build successful, heart-centered businesses.

When multiple women approached her with the desire to grow a business from home that would create a positive impact and allow for a consistent income, Elizabeth founded the Nationally Accredited Fertility Coach Academy (FCA).

After having 3 children of her own naturally after the age of 40, Elizabeth believes taking a more holistic approach is the key to success when attempting to conceive. As a Master Certified ICF Life Coach, Birth & Bereavement Doula, and New Parent Educator she has helped thousands of women achieve their dreams of conception and parenthood in 20+ countries around the world. She supports clients through natural fertility, infertility, IVF, miscarriage loss, early pregnancy PTSD, and new parent support. Elizabeth works from a spiritual aspect and focuses on clearing potential subconscious blocks that could be preventing pregnancy or full-term birth.

With over 25k followers on Instagram, Elizabeth is the host of the Creation Innovation podcast and is a contributor to two Best-selling books, Naturally Conceived and The Creative Lifebook. For her expertise, she has been featured in Forbes, BBC, New York Magazine, Entrepreneur, The New York Post, Newsweek, Romper, Parade Magazine, and on Good Morning Washington, Sacramento's Your California Life, and The Tamron Hall Show, and on podcasts like, The Transition Channel and The Bachelor to the Burbs.

44

KIM BRUNSON - Chasing to B Seen

Growing up I was fortunate to be surrounded by so much love. My parents were raising three children, ages newborn to age 5. As their second born was diagnosed with cystic fibrosis, they suffered the loss of their fourth child. He was just weeks old when he passed from complications of suspected cystic fibrosis. At the time, my parents were informed that my sister's life expectancy was age 12. The specialized care my sister needed required our family to travel several hours from our hometown for her medical appointments. My role, be unseen.

As a young child, my beliefs and personality were being formed. I watched... I learned... my young mind perceived my role as the youngest sibling & "the baby" of the family to remain unseen. Innately, I was a helper and wanted to do what I could for my family. As long as others' needs were being met, then I equated that to my needs also being met.

My survival blueprint was locked in. I followed it as a daughter, as a sister, and into my adult life. Twisting and turning to people please, while silently chasing to be seen. That feeling of being invisible was numbing. It placed a heaviness on my chest, like I was wearing a weighted vest that was filled with overwhelm, trapping me and keeping me silent.

My "chasing" had me attaching my value and self-worth based solely upon the approval & recognition from others. You see, as an empath, this superpower gave me the ability to pick up on the energy and emotions of those around me. I used this to gain attention wherever possible, even if it meant keeping my true self hidden. I would pretend and disguise myself to be who I thought others expected me to be.

At the same time, the comparison game was also being played full out in my mind. From where I was standing, it looked like everyone else had what I needed. I had thoughts of, "Once I have this job....or after I get this new......then everything will fall into place, then I will be seen." This chasing of things and status was grueling. It was impossible for me to just be because my mind was constantly filled with thoughts of worry, judgment, fear and overwhelm. I don't recall the single event that woke me up to the realization of this existence conflict that I was living in. I just remember being desperate and exhausted from listening to the voice in my head repeatedly asking, "Who are you?", "What do you need?".

This immense pain is what pushed me to have the courage to ask for what I needed. I realized that I did not need to hide anymore and that it was ok to ask for help. Actually, it was necessary in order for me to be seen. My first step was reaching out to a dear friend who was a life coach. I was not sure what I was going to gain by meeting with her and I was certain she would think I was being ridiculous or worse, unsavable. Why would meeting with her be any different or make any real change? Multiple times the fear and shame nearly had me cancel my appointment with her. I had all of the excuses at hand and was ready to back out....Honestly, I am not sure what kept me from canceling my appointment, but I am forever thankful that I didn't.

Through our work together I began to recognize that I was carrying a tremendous amount of shame around the need to be accepted. These shadows of my past needed to be brought out into the light. What I learned was that I didn't have to eliminate this part of me. Instead, I needed to recognize the beautiful mess that I was, not judging it as bad or wrong, but instead extending compassion and the deepest love to this part of myself.

Throughout my journey I continued to connect with more teachers and coaches. They taught me to question what it was that I needed to heal. They encouraged me to ask my inner child what she needed, while teaching me practices to strengthen my love of self. In order to do this, I needed to listen and to trust my inner most desires. These practices allowed me to show up and to be seen unapologetically!

Now I ask you. Are you ready to get curious? To claim your brilliance? To love yourself unconditionally? Then when you find yourself in that "chasing" mindset, I invite you to put pen to paper. Grab that favorite journal, find a quiet place and listen to your deepest intuition. You will witness your words transition as your thoughts pour out from your heart. Best of all, you will begin to recognize and honor your divine right to be seen.

I created the following framework, **B. S.E.E.N.** This is a process that has changed my life. It is my deepest desire that it will transform you by increasing the love you have of yourself. My prayer is that it will help you to acknowledge your true self-worth and finally eliminate the need for external validation.

B. S.E.E.N.

1. Bravely

It requires bravery to ask yourself what you need to heal. I know that this question can make you feel vulnerable & exposed. Take your time and allow yourself the space to answer. Remember that you are safe and supported.

2. Surrender

Fully surrender. Turn down the chatter in your head. Sit quietly and place your hand on your heart, feeling the chair or floor beneath you. Slowly inhale through your nose to the count of 5; hold for the count of 7 and then slowly exhale through your mouth to the count of 8, making an audible sigh. Repeat this pattern three times. This practice will move you out of your head and will connect you with your heart, to where your deepest intuition lies.

3. Expose

Expose the limiting beliefs & mistruths that you have been living by. WARNING: It is important to avoid blaming yourself for these old beliefs. Instead, be curious and ask, "How did these beliefs serve me? What are they trying to teach me now?" Acknowledge all of these lessons and thank them for the learnings they have provided you.

4. Explore

You are the **only** one responsible for creating your place of belonging! Explore and be curious about the activities, opportunities and people that light you up! These connections and experiences are not a coincidence!! As your love for self deepens, so will your sense of belonging. Remember, don't get hung up trying to control your outcomes. Have complete faith knowing that your God & the Universe are always supporting you.

5. Now

Now is your time! You are uniquely you. You are the only you in the entire universe! Perfectly designed. Placed where you are supposed to be at exactly the right time.

Your first step is a click away. Connect with me at the link below and get ready to B Seen!!!

*Kim Brunson is a Transformational Life Coach who shares her expertise on avoidance with others, helping them move from **Stuck** to **Starter**! Kim guides individuals as they uncover what is blocking them from claiming their authentic & soul-purposeful life through forgiveness work. Kim's education includes a Masters degree in Special Education alongside 27 years of experience in the classroom, Master Practitioner Level Certification in Evolved Neuro Linguistic Programming, Quantum Time Release(^{TM}), Hypnosis, Trauma Aware Coaching & Quantum Change Process(^{TM}). Kim's life purpose is for all people to B Seen. Embracing who they were, who they are now & who they are becoming.*

45

TRACEY BOWDEN - Finding Your Inner Creative Flow Through Nature and Art

This is the story of finding my way and reframing who I am. We all carry baggage from our life experiences. Growing up with criticism was the norm and self-love did not exist in my world. Self-love is learning to unpack the baggage, what is useful to keep, disregard, and transform to lighten our load and find a new story. It's finding self-forgiveness through connecting with nature, meditation, mandalas, and painting to connect to my inner creative flow.

Mostly I have subscribed to the busyness of life. Being the good daughter, wife, mother, sister, friend, and teacher; fulfilling others' expectations. In my forties, I had 2 part-time jobs, studied 2 courses part-time, and ran 3 children around. That's not to mention housework, etc. My health suffered at this point, and it was when the doctor said "Your body is trying to tell you something" that I had to take notice! The faster I moved, the more chaotic life became. The more my thoughts became chaotic as well.

What changed the chaos was Qi Gong and walking. Walking along the beach each day for me is my form of meditation and healing. I let my thoughts wander as they take on less significance when connecting to mother earth.

Observing the ebb and flow of the tides, seasons, moon, sun, wind, wildlife, and rain; the constant changes be they subtle or strong. This deep connection reinforces that we are not separate from nature but part of the web of life and the infinite creativity around us. Filling the lungs with fresh air and airing out the mind while seeing beauty and inspiration all around me. For me it's moving, getting the excess energy out of the head and body. Letting thoughts flow, and having inner dialogues with yourself, whether it is happy, sad, angry, or critical, leads to self-reflection and self-forgiveness. The power is in letting go of judgment.

As a human, we need connection, a sense of belonging, and a sense of security. Walking in nature fulfills those needs for me. Smiling at passersby or stopping for a chat. Gathering inspiration to take back for my artwork. It is strengthening my new identity that honors my creativity. Finding my sense of place and me.

Here is how you can connect through walking, collecting, and mandalas, to create space for inner peace, slowing down, and finding your inner light. Are you ready to let go and slow down? The first step is to decide are you going barefoot for grounding or putting on your walking shoe?. As well, set up a quiet space to create your mandala and gather your materials such as found objects, notebook or sketchpad, paper, pencils, pens – whatever you wish to play with.

Step by step

Walking: I like to walk early in the morning as it sets me up for the day – you may prefer to walk later in the day to clear away the day's clutter from your mind. Choose what fits in with your day. Your walk may be around the block, in a park, in bushland, on the beach, or in your own backyard. The important thing is to take time for yourself.

On your walk, notice the thoughts and feelings that come up. Does your mood match the environment? We use our eyes to see the world around us. What we perceive to see is the interaction between our eyes and our brain. It is the recognition of shape, color, movement, and how bright or clear an object is. But it may not necessarily be reality. It is the same with our visceral emotions and how we perceive ourselves, and events. I see many changing environments on my walk, just as some days it is sunny, crystal-clear water and calming energy, and yet on other days, it's rainy, or windy and wild – different sensations and moods.

Our thoughts are how we create our own reality. When negative thoughts appear, notice and accept them with no judgment; smile and thank the thought, and let it blow away. Think of a feature that you love about yourself.

Collect objects that appeal to you. It may be leaves, flowers, shells, pebbles, driftwood, etc. While looking and being in the moment, subconscious thoughts will appear. Reflect on what appears. (Another way to collect is to take photos on your phone. Have it on flight mode so you are not disturbed.)

Mandala: Now find a quiet space to create your mandala. A mandala is geometric in shape, generally a pattern that is created within a circle. You don't need to be an artist to create a mandala – it is a form of meditation and creativity from your heart.

Play with the layout. Dividing a circle in half horizontally and in half vertically with your found objects e.g., the first division may be shells. At the center, it will intersect, and it is from here that you can draw a pattern with your found objects. Arrange around the circle as you find pleasing.

You may simply like to draw a mandala with a stick in the sand on the beach. In this space it is ephemeral. On a beach, it will either be washed back into the sea or blown away with the wind. Photograph your design if you like. Or in the bush or park, you can create one using flowers, sticks, or leaves – anything that you have collected. Again, impermanence.

Taking items home will depend on your beliefs and feelings about nature. You may like to stand still and ask the spirits of the land, water, air, and wind if it is ok for you to remove.

Alternatively in your own garden use items found in your yard only, and/or on your walk to create a mandala.

You may like to create a mandala for each week, month, or season. Sit with your mandala and note what feelings and thoughts came up as you were occupied with creating. Sketch your design, photograph, or reflect in your notebook. You can keep a record to observe how you change with the weeks, months, or seasons. Each season has its own character and reason. In autumn and spring for instance, the light is softer and more golden. It is a time to be softer with yourself. Did it make you smile? Appreciate your sense of place and connection to the land. Affirm your uniqueness and place in this world.

As I continue my journey of self-awareness, self-reflection, and self-acceptance the surprising thing is I now find myself on unexpected roads, as my inner creative flow is nurtured.

Try these simple practices that you can make your own starting point for change. Walking and meditating, creating artwork from nature. Breathing, sorting, letting go of unwanted baggage, and reframing you, leading to self-love and self-acceptance. Enjoy your journey while you build your connection to the land and to your inner flow, for you are unique and more than enough.

Tracey Bowden is a passionate multi-faceted artist who's colourful, vibrant works are inspired by her connection to nature, the energies seen and unseen. With a passion for transforming spaces, Tracey's art brings joy, harmony and uplifts any setting.

A love of teaching in Adult Education, studying a Diploma of Fine Arts mid-career and a desire for healthy and sustainable interiors led Tracey to study Feng Shui which ignited a new perspective of living in harmony with our environment. She believes how we connect to our environment both in our homes and in the natural world affects us deeply.

Tracey is beginning a new series of workshops, "Connection, Soul and Creativity through Art" for women, encouraging them to connect to their inner wisdom, weaving their own stories, peace, and freedom with a deep connection to place through art, no matter their art experience.

46

DIANA STELIN - Self-Love isn't Selfishness. It's a return to your inner child. SPARK Self-Love through Creativity.

The word 'selfish' carries a profound meaning for me. It stirs up deep emotions within me, reminding me of my childhood experiences. As a child, whenever I voiced my own desires, I was immediately labeled as selfish. Whether it was wanting to spend time with my friends, immerse myself in a book, or indulge in my passion for drawing instead of taking care of my younger siblings or doing household chores, my actions were deemed selfish. I now understand the origins of this perception. My mother, raised by survivors of World War II, was taught from a very young age to be selfless, to live for others, putting her needs last. I hold no resentment towards her for criticizing me, but it took me years to break free from this early conditioning and realize that sacrificing my own needs only breeds resentment. I discovered that I don't have to conform to anyone's worldview, and that neglecting my own happiness erodes the joy in spending time with my children, creating a beautiful home, or preparing delicious meals. When we lose touch with what brings us joy and what truly ignites our passion for life, we begin to lose ourselves.

In today's society, I see numerous women who believed they could do it all, and they are crumbling. I was one of them. We take on the world, juggling our children's emotional growth, managing the logistics of their education and extracurricular activities, holding executive positions at work, and maintaining household responsibilities such as cooking and cleaning. All the while, societal expectations place barriers on our self-care and self-love. It's almost as if our biological instinct to sacrifice and give as mothers conflicts with and shames the very idea of self-love. We fail to recognize our own worth and the contributions we make. We don't appreciate and acknowledge the achievements and abundance in our lives on a daily basis. We subscribe to the belief that we need to please others to deserve respect. Consequently, we struggle to establish clear boundaries and explicitly advocate for ourselves, all the while expecting implicit understanding, companionship, and equal distribution of responsibilities. We unwittingly embrace martyrdom.

As we approach our 40s, we often experience the desire to reconnect with our inner child. This mid-life crisis-like phase urges us to return to a sense of innocence and reclaim our true selves. However, maintaining this balance on a weekly basis becomes challenging, as we strive to prevent life's demands from overwhelming this delicate longing. Heaven forbid any sudden disruption to the status quo. Such disruptions force us to question everything, reassessing the boundaries between family and self, obligations and desires, and true intentions. We realize we don't know who we are anymore. The present moment becomes a time of reckoning—a time to decide who we truly want to be, despite all the external pressures. Who will we be once the children have grown and left? Who are we at our core? Are we primarily mothers or creators of our own lives? Are we followers or leaders? Innovators or mere drama queens?

It was only after going through a divorce and subsequent remarriage, coupled with multiple miscarriages, that I realized the immense toll my self-denial had taken on me. See, I studied to be an artist and didn't pick up by brush for many years. A huge part of me lay dormant, hiding behind masks and perceived responsibilities. It was during those trying times that I understood the futility of striving for societal perfection and the detrimental effects it had on my life. It was then that I embarked on a journey back to my neglected creative pursuits, and through that, a journey towards self-love. This revelation occurred eleven years ago: the simple revelation that ART HEALS.

Since then, I have shared my simple 5-step process, called SPARK, with hundreds of individuals. These steps have consistently guided people from all walks of life—doctors, lawyers, engineers, and countless others who have watched my TED Talk or attended my corporate workshops—into a state of creative flow. Try it with me?

1. Stay Present (S). This involves truly immersing yourself in the current moment and surroundings. Try any of these steps, or put them all together into a powerful morning routine. It can be done through an app, like Headspace, for instance. Take a 5-minute break. Begin with a body scan, closing your eyes and focusing on each part of your body from the top of the head to the jaw, down, and gradually relaxing each area. Following this, take 10 breaths, with complete focus on the act of counting. Finally, and this is especially important to me, visualize your future self—a version of you a year from now—and listen to the message your future self has for you today.

2. Pay Attention (P): When engaged in the act of creation, it is vital to pay attention not only to the four corners of the canvas or paper but also to our own emotions. When emotions overflow, or the need arises to escape the confines of our own thoughts, that is precisely the moment to create. It may not always result in something aesthetically pleasing, as emotions themselves may not be visually appealing. However, the process becomes raw, cathartic, and healing. It is the interplay of these conflicting emotions that adds depth and authenticity to our creations.

3. Allow Yourself to Play (A): Imagine yourself as a four-year-old, just learning how to make basic shapes while learning to draw. Embrace the ups and downs, knowing that mistakes are part of the creative journey. The scent of pencils and paint evokes a childlike delight, akin to the anticipation of a new revelation. When colors harmonize perfectly, a sense of exhilaration tingles in the back of our throats. Tears roll in. Something instantly softens within your soul.

4. Release the End Result (R): This entails letting go of the pressure to achieve perfection and silencing the critical voices of others. There are days when this becomes particularly challenging, especially when seeking external validation. We often give too much weight and authority to the opinions of others, questioning our intentions, steps, and playful outcomes. As shapes begin to take form, fear sets in. Is the composition too muddled? Is it unclear, oversaturated, or lacking precision? Our inner voice reassures us, urging us to take small steps and break the process down into manageable parts. We are encouraged to trust that the artwork will gradually emerge. With each small success, the bigger picture becomes clearer, allowing favorite areas to shine through. Our blood pumps with excitement, and we find ourselves falling in love with the creative process.

5. Be Kind to Yourself (K): There are days when nothing seems to align, and it becomes crucial to grant ourselves grace by stepping away and trusting that the energy will shift the next day. Perhaps stress has taken its toll, and rest is necessary. Maybe a particular idea requires time to incubate. However, it is an immensely blissful feeling when we return the following day, and everything falls into place effortlessly. This encapsulates the essence of self-love—self-empathy, self-compassion, self-gratitude, and ultimately, self-worth.

The most fulfilling experiences occur when we simultaneously work on multiple areas, and they seamlessly harmonize. By recognizing the interrelationships between various aspects of our lives, rather than being confined to singular identities, we realize that we are so much more. We possess an array of tools in our toolbox, and it is vital to break free from the labels, fabricated narratives, and insecurities that limit our potential. We have the capacity to contribute in numerous ways. We deserve fulfillment and happiness, through self-love.

Landscape artist, founder of the SPARK method, TEDx speaker, and recipient of the Best of Boston award, Diana Stelin is on a mission to reduce burnout through creativity.

Ms. Stelin published a highly acclaimed novel about the importance of art for our psyche. Through getting people of all ages out of their comfort zones, she helps them awaken to the beauty and fragility of our world while finding their inner child in the process. Her pieces are in corporate and private collections worldwide, and she uses her expertise in her proprietary SPARK processes as a consultant in creative corporate workshops and talks.

In recent years Ms. Stelin has exhibited her work at the 2022 Venice Biennale and presented a TEDx talk. She also appeared as a guest on dozens of podcasts and was featured on CBS Chronicle. In the midst of Covid, she founded a sustainable clothing line based on her art and released a children's book about her beloved Venice.

47

JESSICA HUGHES - Activating Creative Healing and Expression Through Intuitive Journaling and Painting

In a world where we often judge ourselves too harshly, finding a path towards radical self-love can feel like navigating a labyrinth in the dark. This is a story of how I found my way through, using a combination of intuitive journaling, abstract painting, and finger painting to re-ignite my inner light.

Stream of consciousness journaling is a unique form of writing, where you let your thoughts flow freely onto the paper, unfiltered and uninterrupted. This practice allowed me to lay bare my innermost thoughts, feelings, and fears. As I saw my thoughts manifest on paper, I gained a new perspective about my inner self.

Soon, I started to complement my journaling with abstract painting. I found that painting, particularly with my fingers, allowed me to express the emotions that words couldn't capture. The process of translating my thoughts and feelings into colors and shapes was liberating. As my fingers moved across the canvas, I felt a deeper connection with my inner self, embracing all its complexities and nuances.

The power of these combined practices lies in their ability to tap into the subconscious and give voice to our unexpressed emotions. Journaling allows for unfiltered thought flow, breaking down the walls we build around our vulnerabilities. Abstract painting and finger painting translate these uncovered emotions into a visible, tangible form, creating a mirror where we can view our inner selves without judgment. This synergy paves the way for understanding, acceptance, and ultimately, self-love.

Through this creative combination of journaling and painting, I was able to understand and accept myself better. It facilitated a kind of internal dialogue, which in turn led to greater self-awareness and self-appreciation.

The first step towards practicing this method is the willingness to confront your thoughts and emotions. Start by setting up a comfortable space where you can write and paint freely. Gather a journal, paints, brushes, and canvas. The rest of the journey is about letting your thoughts and emotions guide you.

Are you ready to embark on this journey? Here's how you can incorporate intuitive journaling and abstract painting into your routine:

Step-by-Step Instructions

- **Stream of Consciousness Journaling:** Begin by setting yourself in a quiet, comfortable space. Open your journal and choose a pen that feels right in your hand. Take a moment to center yourself, then let your thoughts flow onto the paper. Allow yourself the freedom to write whatever comes to mind without any self-censorship. Do not worry about grammar, punctuation, or making sense. Let your thoughts run wild, pouring onto the page without fear of judgement or scrutiny.

- **Identifying Emotions:** After you've filled a few pages, take a deep breath, and then read your entries. As you read, try to identify the emotions that surface. Do you sense anger, joy, fear, excitement, or sadness? Highlight or underline any phrases or sentences that feel particularly charged with emotion. Remember, this is not an exercise in judgment, but rather in observation and self-awareness.

- **Abstract Painting:** Now, turn your focus to your canvas. Reflect on the emotions you identified in your journaling. Consider how each emotion might translate into color, shape, or form. Start to paint, following your intuition. Allow the paintbrush (or your fingers) to dance on the canvas, guided by your feelings. You might choose bright, vibrant colors to depict joy, or perhaps darker shades for sadness. There are no rules—let your emotions guide your choices.

- **Finger Painting:** Incorporating finger painting can provide a more tactile and intimate connection to your art. This hands-on experience invites you to literally feel your way through your emotions. Try smudging, dabbing, or swirling the paint with your fingers. Feel the sensation of the paint, the movement of your hand, the connection to your emotions.

- **Reflection:** Once your painting is complete, step back and observe your creation. Spend a few moments in silence, just looking at the result of your emotional journey manifested in colors and shapes. Try to identify any patterns or themes. Do certain colors or shapes resonate with particular emotions? Reflect on how the process of painting made you feel, and what insights it may have revealed about your emotions. Note these reflections in your journal for further exploration.

Embarking on a journey of stream of consciousness journaling, abstract painting, and finger painting has allowed me to forge a path towards radical self-love. It has served as a mirror, reflecting my inner emotions and thoughts, providing a deeper understanding and acceptance of myself.

238

I encourage you to follow these steps and embark on your own transformative journey. With each thought you pen down and each color you stroke, you are creating a personal roadmap to self-love. It's a journey of exploration, acceptance, and love—a journey towards embracing the wonderful, unique person that you are.

Jessica Hughes is a visibility expert for creative entrepreneurs as well as an internationally collected fine artist, 3x #1 bestselling author, and mom of seven.

*She is founder of **Jess Hughes Media** and **Illuminated Press**, a boutique publishing company created to amplify the voices of thought leaders, artists, creatives, educators, and experts.*

*She is the visionary behind #1 International Bestselling **Creative Lifebook Series**. Her passion is supporting the audience growth of hidden gem entrepreneurs so they can step into the spotlight, lead with confidence, and illuminate our world.*

She offers educational programs, courses, and coaching to support values driven leaders with their mission to create true impact in the world. She teaches the mindset, skillset, and inspired action to be unstoppable.

Hughes has been a featured expert on ABC, NBC, FOX, TED, Forbes, Chopra, and more.

Sign up at the QR code to contribute to a future Creative Lifebook!

48

BONNIE McVEE - Soulful Living in Technicolor Grace

My life was indeed upside down and backwards for a long time. Between my two divorces and my daily struggle with drinking, it felt like I couldn't catch a break. Despite my best efforts to straighten things out, I always seemed to find myself right back where I started. However, I knew deep down that I couldn't continue living this way forever. I was unaware that there was another way to be in life.

I had grown so accustomed to my routine and surroundings that I failed to consider anything outside of my own experience. Throughout my life, I always thought that I needed alcohol to have a good time. I constantly found myself at bars or parties, sipping drinks and getting tipsy. However, after making a choice to be alcohol-free and some reflection and coaching, I discovered that there were other ways of being available.

As I reflected on my recent experiences, I couldn't help but notice a newfound sense of clarity that I had never experienced before. This clarity allowed me to become more aware of certain aspects of my life that had been holding me back and preventing personal growth.

In that moment of reflection, it became increasingly apparent that God had been with me all along, even when I had felt disconnected from his grace. This realization served as a catalyst for personal growth and transformation, and I am now eager to continue my soulful journey connected to the divine.

Life is full of transitions. Some are welcome and seamless, while others are jarring and shocking. Nevertheless, each and every one of them plays a role in shaping us into who we are today.

Jarring and shocking is exactly how I felt when I received my breast cancer diagnosis.

Receiving a cancer diagnosis was a life-changing experience. It felt like the ground had been pulled out from under my feet. However, I quickly realized that my attitude towards this journey was going to be key in determining the future course of my life. It was up to me to decide if I was going to be a victim of my illness or if I was going to choose **joy** in the face of adversity.

Living from our soul is something that many of us strive for. It is a way to connect with a higher power and truly live in the present moment. When we allow ourselves to be fully present and in touch with our own divinity, we can experience true radical self-love. It is a beautiful thing to be connected to the divine and to feel that we are a part of something greater than ourselves.

In my experience personally and in working with 100's of women, they too have made the choice to live soulfully in the unlimited unconditional love of the divine and his amazing grace.

Discovering one's soul is the key to living a fulfilling life. It enables the understanding of who we truly are. Suddenly life begins to flow, our intuition is heightened, and we have clarity for what is meant for us.

My husband and I decided to make a major change and leave our comfort zone by moving from Washington State to the sunny beaches of Florida. Our new home is just a short 5 miles from the beach, which has allowed us to live a more relaxed and adventurous lifestyle. To make this move possible, I created a business that let me work location-independently so that I could live my best life in both locations. Embracing change and pursuing passions has led me to a newfound sense of purpose and soul-fulfillment.

This is radical self-love.

Here are my 5 signature steps to creating your best life:

G.R.A.C.E

G- God, Grace, and Gratitude: As we embark on this journey of exploring the role of God's grace and gratitude in our lives, it's important to remember that we are never alone. Knowing that we are loved unconditionally and guided by a higher power helps us cultivate the strength and confidence we need to face any obstacle. With each passing day, I am increasingly grateful for the blessings in my life and the opportunities to grow and learn from my experiences. As we learn to trust in God's plan for us, we can move forward with courage and determination, secure in the knowledge that we are never truly alone.

R- Release-Receive: Releasing old beliefs and seeing new truths is the beginning of transforming ourselves. When we recognize that the beliefs that once served us are no longer serving us well, we can free ourselves from their limitations and step into a new reality. This process requires honesty, vulnerability, and a willingness to be open to change. Through this transformation, we can experience a renewed sense of our soul and our purpose.

A- Awareness: When we become aware of our old behaviors, it can be a shameful experience. It is the realization of seeing what we haven't seen before, and it can be quite confronting. This self-awareness allows us to reflect on our actions and decisions, evaluating whether they align with our values and goals. The discomfort that arises from this realization signifies growth and an opportunity for personal transformation.

C- Courage, Choice, Change: As humans, we often resist change, especially when it involves releasing old beliefs and embracing new ways of thinking. However, if we are to truly transform and grow in our spiritual journeys, we must choose to have the courage to change. It can be a difficult and scary process, but by stepping out in faith that God has us during these transformations, we can discover new strengths within ourselves and set new boundaries. By doing so, we open ourselves up to experience the fullness of life and all its blessings.

Girl, it's time to get your GRACE on!

E- Essence: Finally, after shedding our old beliefs and opening ourselves up to new truths, we can begin to live authentically and fully as the masterpieces we were created to be. By embracing our strengths and weaknesses, passions, and dreams, we can discover our true essence in life. We were fearfully and wonderfully made with a unique purpose and calling, and it is up to each of us to answer that call. When we acknowledge and honor our true selves, we can live fully in our essence, live life to the fullest, and make a positive impact with our friends, family and beyond.

Transformational Life Coach, Speaker, and founder of Technicolor Grace, Bonnie McVee has dedicated her life to empowering entrepreneurs and Leaders in their pursuit of a more vibrant, fulfilling existence. Through her creative soul discovery approach, she supports her clients in exploring their spiritual awareness and shifting their relationship with themselves as they create a life rooted in spirit, self-love, self-discovery, and soul fulfillment.

As a result, her clients are equipped with the tools and confidence necessary to manifest their dreams and live a life full of Technicolor Grace.

49

KAT BREEDLOVE - Create a Zine for Your Inner Child

If the journey to self-acceptance feels challenging, consider engaging in a light-hearted creative project that can gently open the door to inner healing. Crafting a zine inspired by your inner child offers a wonderful opportunity to reconnect with the sense of wonder and curiosity often overshadowed in life's chaos. Rather than striving to change yourself, embrace the younger version of you.

Not familiar with the term "zine"? It's a short, handmade magazine crafted to express your ideas in a book-like or pamphlet form. Typically self-published, zines provide a creative outlet for anyone looking to share their experiences and expressions with an audience. However, in this case, no audience is necessary; this project is designed to pave the way for a life with self-compassion.

Here's your roadmap to creating an inner child-inspired zine:

Suggested materials:
Collage materials; mod-podge, old magazines, childhood photos
crayons, colored pencils, markers, pens and pencils, craft paint, glitter,

stickers, washi tape, etc.

Optional: 8" x 11.5" paper, long-armed stapler, string, and access to a photocopier

Brainstorm:

What would you like to title your Inner Child Zine?

What types of spreads would you like to include?

Tap into your childhood memories and create a mindmap of ideas.

Prompts to consider:

1. What were your favorite colors growing up?
2. Incorporate these colors throughout the issue to make it cohesive
3. What themes, emotions, and experiences do you want to convey?
4. Did you believe in magic growing up?
5. Did you have an imaginary friend?
6. What was your dream job growing up?
7. Where was your safe place?
8. What did you do when you were feeling sad or alone?
9. Did you imagine any monsters under your bed – what did they look like?
10. Do you have any personal stories or narratives you would like to include?

Decide on the format:

I suggest putting your zine together traditionally, rather than on a design program. Listed below are two of the possible paper formats:

1. Booklet zine: Take as many pieces of paper as you want, fold each page in half, stack on top of each other, and bind the pages together at the fold either with three staples, or with string.
2. Folding mini zine: One 8" x 11.5" piece of paper folded into eight rectangles. Then, cut a horizontal slit in the center. Then, fold the

paper lengthwise and fold the sheet into itself to form the 8-page mini zine. Visual instructions can be found online with the key search words "How to fold an 8-page mini zine."

Create the Content:

- Look back to your brainstorm.
- What types of thoughts and feelings did the prompts evoke when you thought about your younger self?
- Add Visuals: sketches, painted pages, collaged images, mini-comics, photographs, etc.
- The purpose of this project is to honor your inner child – be unafraid to make a mess. Children have a sense of nonjudgement when it comes to their art, so harness that energy.
- Add writing: Recipes, playlists, childhood stories, poetry, etc.
- Use a variety of different fonts, markers, and pens to make the zine as playful as possible.
- Include an "about the author" page.
- What made you want to create this zine in the first place? Share where you came from, and what you are aspiring to become. What about your life lends itself to the type of art you filled your zine with?
- Design front and back cover
- Create the covers after you've filled out the rest of the pages. Decide on your final title and write it out on the front page.
- Add finishing touches: stickers, sparkles, scribbles, thought bubbles, etc.

Share your zines with others– or keep it for yourself

Since the Inner Child Zine is a personal project meant to heal, reproducing and distributing this zine is not a necessity.

However, if you do wish to duplicate your zine, go to your local library and photocopy the pages, print, and reassemble. Hit up your local bookstores and see if they would be interested in holding onto a few of your copies to sell or distribute. Even just handing your art out to people on the street is a way to share your passion for creating with others.

P.S. Here's a poem I wrote about my grandmother and me, included in my Inner Child Zine.

A Drive on The Pennsylvania Turnpike

The skies are blue, my surroundings are soft. The air from the car comforts me, my legs press against the car seat below me. I ride in the backseat of her car, taking in the love and comfort through the old newspapers beside me, the wrinkled books on the ground, and the melted cough-drop in the cupholder. Nonnie drives as her steady voice, filled with wisdom, tells stories of relatives I have never met. Words spill from her mouth, of fantastic stories, adventures, histories, and ancestors; a quiet craft honed through years of preaching. I think to myself: this is one of those moments... one of the moments I will treasure forever. I want to soak in her presence, this moment. Through her smudged glasses, she looks to the road before her, and I look to her. The car smoothly hums forwards, towards love, towards beauty, towards purpose. In the midst of these powerful conversations, of learning about my past, soaking up specific biblical verses and catching onto every single word she says, the bear appears. Six feet tall, with welcoming eyes, the bear invites us to dance. Time stills. We are powerful. We are safe. We dance with the bear. The bear dances with us. We dance together in various hues of purple, maroon and lavender, the same shade as Nonnie's voice. *The bear must be for us. The bear is for us. I know it is.*

Kat Breedlove is an emerging artist based in Pittsburgh, PA. Kat works full time as a Content Creator at Jessica Hughes Media, working with artists to develop their brand and propel their business' into the media. Utilizing painting as her primary medium, she aims to capture multiple themes of the human experience. Through the beautiful and painful process of creation, Kat learns to both explore and channel complex situations into a variety of creative mediums. She focuses primarily on turning the intangible tangible–capturing emotions through colors and lighting. Kat plays on the dichotomy of both the light and dark in an attempt to find harmony between contrasting feelings. During the process of creation, she grants herself permission to explore and process the external chaos and beauty of life. A few of her focal points include the exploration of sexuality, religion, and family, which she paints in an otherworldly fashion. Kat achieves this through a combination of figurative and abstract art. When she's not painting, she enjoys spending time in nature, designing tattoos, working as the creative director of self–published Rosary Magazine, and hanging with her lovely friends!

50

ANNETTE WALTERS - Finding Me In the Chaos

The call came in at 10 am. The EMT telling me my husband had been found on the floor of an Airbnb in central Colorado. By 4 pm, I landed in Colorado Springs and arrived at Swedish Medical Center an hour later. This was the day my world became very small, intensely focused, and without a solid place to stand.

Each day, I focused on learning about strokes, the hospital procedure, and how I could best take care of my husband. In a week, I was a shell of who I was just a week before. Exhausted, overwhelmed, and all my friends, family, and home were 700 miles away. I struggled.

I gave all I had, doing the right thing, pouring every ounce of energy, love, and attention into him and what he needed. The first of many walls shot up.

Friends said, "Take care of yourself so you don't hit the wall", but I had no idea what that meant until I left the hospital crying and uncontrollably screaming, "I can't do this. I just want to go home!"

The emotions waned and I stayed, listening, serving, and waiting because anything but this would be selfish...Right?

And like a good soldier, I continued selflessly until my back cramped up from sleeping on that green hospital couch. I couldn't ignore me anymore. My body screamed at me, "Do something! Take care of me!"

I was pouring from a bleeding cup.

I could not help my husband feeling like this physically or emotionally.

Needed Immediately

In the span of a week, I lost myself. I literally gave everything I had trying to will my husband to live and recover.

Without sleep and being unable to eat much, my body shook me painfully awake and forced me to think about what I required. If I wanted to continue, I needed to fill me up to have something to give.

I needed to pause, look around, and decide how to fill me up here, away from everything I knew. I needed the energy and wherewithal to figure this situation out, get him healed, and take both of us home.

Yes, this season was about him, but to walk it like I wanted to, I had to create a space in the midst of this...for me.

A Safe Space

For me, creating a safe space began with stepping away.

My back was a justifiable excuse to leave. I needed something like this to feel OK about leaving his side. This cracked open enough space for me to seek help. I found a chiropractor, like mine back home, who adjusted me and had my favorite protein powders and vitamins, which were now essential for my survival.

Out in Denver, I met several caring people willing to hear my story and help me to help myself. I got out of my head and I somewhat de-stressed my body so I could see what my body required.

Even though I was there to serve, I had to start with me...or there wouldn't be a me.

Cracked Open the Wall

I didn't know how much longer we would be in Denver - another week, or months for stroke rehab. I craved routine and consistency in an unknown place. As captain of this ship, I began by quieting me and the world around me. I listened, acknowledged, and decided to trust what I believed were the right decisions for both of us.

I neutralized everything, my thoughts, emotions, and negative judgments. Choosing to see everything as information to be sorted through, clarity came and the internal fight against our reality began to dissipate.

I cracked open the wall holding me in chaos.

This pause opened up a safe place where I could breathe and accept what was going on without distraction - a safe place of clarity and self-awareness.

The Power of THE PAUSE

I first used THE PAUSE to survive after my son left for college. Raising him provided such purpose and ongoing activity, especially during basketball season and senior year.

But when he left for college, I no longer had direction, activity, or expectations for my life. This lack of direction and purpose left me empty and struggling.

My Life Coach taught me THE PAUSE, to center myself and navigate this confusing time of loss, joy, hopefulness, and grief. I learned that they all exist at the same time and my experience was determined by which one I leaned into. She taught me to choose my experiences - both positive and negative.

As I walked into week two at my husband's side, I finally remembered to pause.

THE PAUSE created space for my emotions, the information, the situation and me to just be.

With a quieted mind and my heart opened I remembered...I did understand what was going on and truly trusted myself.

Ask yourself. *When can you truly trust yourself?* "The Pause" creates clarity, direction, and for me, a-ha's appear.

THE PAUSE
Recognize your cues to initiate THE PAUSE
(Frustration, Overwhelm, Sadness, Confusion, Apathy, Exhaustion, Lethargy, etc.)

1) Get Quiet
2) Write down everything that comes to mind
3) Observe as a researcher unemotionally

- There are no decisions to be made, no actions to take in this moment.

- See how things are, how they came to be, the actions taken, and their consequences. If emotions appear, ask them to step aside for a moment.

4) Look for your Clarity, your Knowing.

You are practicing "being" in the midst of everything, being present without activating the fight, flight, freeze, or fawn responses. Though they are normal human responses, when circumstances are mission-critical, these responses are no place to make good decisions from.

THE PAUSE and Radical Self-Love
Deciding to initiate THE PAUSE is a demonstration of Radical Self-Love. It demonstrates trust in ourselves to know we have the truth within us and that...

- Seeing ourselves in the moment, just as we are,
- Seeing the situation, just as it is,
- Seeing all our options, just as they are, and
- Believing we are enough, just as we are

...creates space to make good decisions and a solid place to step forward. Stand confidently in this place of knowing. You HAVE what you need within.

Seeing yourself, the circumstances, and what you truly need with clarity creates a genuinely loving place that fills your cup so high, pouring into anyone or anything else comes from an *overflowing cup.* ~ Thank you, Jessica Hughes, for this imagery. I work on this every day.

Full circle story: My husband continues to make great strides. The stroke ignited new insights, abilities, and passions that may have never come without it. He and I are evolving along this journey, like all of us, into the new version of who we are destined to be, better taking care of ourselves along the way.

Annette Walters is the go-to Empty Nest expert for the 95% of Moms who experience a sense of loss as they prepare for, or walk through, "My kids moved out...now what?".

Through her "Now What?" program, clients create clarity and confidence while embracing their new freedoms and navigating the emotional waters of an Empty Nest.

Annette founded Connected Life Coaching in 2020. She is a podcaster, columnist, conference speaker, 3rd generation Toastmaster, and mother to one amazing son who left the nest and sent her on this journey to an unexpected life of joy, opportunity, and community she never dreamed was possible.

She is a co-author of the upcoming book The Creative Lifebook: Radical Self-Love, an annual "Be Bold, Be Badass, Be You" conference speaker, and Vice President of DFW Women's Club - a non-profit for encouraging, educating, and empowering women as well as being a certified life coach through The Life Coach School.

If you or someone you know is facing an "Empty Nest" share the link to my FREE program above.

51

MICHAELENE SHANNON - Yes to Love

Through the ages, the virtues of Love have been expressed through writing, singing, speaking, painting, etching, and in a myriad of other ways. It can be challenging to fully describe the feelings and embodied sense that all sentient beings experience with Love. It is the beginning, the middle, and the end of a fully expressed life. Radical Self-Love is an invocation, a declaration, and an evolutionary spark of divinity that is sensed by all who come into contact with Love.

Elements of the human condition can induce a degree of forgetfulness or an awake amnesia in folks as they become focused on habitual daily activities, trudging through them like robotic automatons. This can be further reinforced by thoughts that are stuck in an endless feedback loop rather than filtered through a lens of love and creativity.

From my perspective, Love is the clearest, purest, and highest vibration that a human being can feel or express and many sages, philosophers, and other folks agree. Just think about the times when Love was a strong force in your life and how that impacted you mentally, emotionally, physically, and spiritually. For me, some of the descriptors that come to mind are: uplifting, joyous, in the zone, and timeless. Intention, kindness, and self-compassion are some of the characteristics of Self-love that all humans benefit from.

Creativity is an expression of Love.

"Yes" Creative Activity Series

Most of us have heard of personal boundaries and the important role they have in our lives. Let me clarify by acknowledging that there are appropriate times to say "no"; however, saying no can be a habit. Saying yes has a different, more vibrant energy and this is what empowers transformation. Retraining oneself to say yes more often means you are saying yes to yourself. In a manner of speaking, saying "yes" to something is an expression of "no" to something else – the idea is to stay in the expansive "yes" frequency while still honoring the need for declining certain things. One might object to this suggestion and say "This is mere word semantics", to which I respond "Perhaps" and "What of it?" In my experience, yes promotes positivity and it expands into the realm of potentiality. Creativity and Love have no limits.

I decided to experiment and engage in a creative activity to deepen further into Love by embracing the word "yes." I devoted time to painting "yes" on canvases to explore the expansive qualities that are available to each and every one of us. While I painted "yes" in different sizes, colors, directions, and fonts, I discovered that my heart filled with an incredible energy – both within myself and in my environment.

Very quickly, "Yes" became a code word for embracing myself and all things that filled me with Love. For me, painting "yes" was a permission slip that began on the canvas and expanded into everyday situations. I chose to say "yes" instead of "not right now" or "I don't feel like it" or "I can't do that." My creative expressions of "yes" started to ripple into other areas of my life and the energies of yes, creativity and love increasingly came back to me from others and from the universe in beautiful and unexpected ways. The jewel here, is that the canvas makes the process, the venture, and the changes visible. Self-love is boundary-less. Join us and say yes to love on the "Yes" Revolution Train.

ALL ABOARD

Here are 7 of The Many Ways You Can Claim Your Ticket on the "Yes" Revolution Train:

1. Experiment by speaking the word yes more often than the word no. For those of you who are evidence seekers, notice differences in the tone, intonation of your voice, and your body posture. Does it feel different emotionally, physically, or spiritually when you paint or say yes? Notice if those around you respond more positively.

2. Explore by painting, writing, or drawing "yes." Choose any method or creative tool that feels right for you. Create a series of 3 or 4 and note similarities and differences in the process and the outcome. What feelings do each of your creations evoke in you?

3. Use a variety of surfaces for your "yes." How about paper, canvas, pottery, rocks, feathers, leaves, empty teabags, or sand? Just imagine your child's delight when they see the word yes in their sandbox tomorrow. Or, laminate your personalized teabags, shuffle them as you would a deck of cards, then choose one for a daily dose of inspiration.

4. Impermanence has as much value as longer-lasting "yeses." For example, the decay of a leaf is one of the most natural cycles on Earth and we are a part of Earth's cycles. Best not to get too attached. You can always re-create as you have an abundance of love and creativity.

5. Write mini "yes" manifestos and place them in your shoe, wallet, purse, or pocket.

6. Gaze at your "yes" creations at random times throughout the day – notice whether you feel a smile arise, a surge of energy, or a mini mood boost. Love rises from your heart, and just like a boomerang, it returns right back to you.

259

7. Sing or chant "yes" to your heart's content. This is a beautiful form of self-love in action.

♥

These are gifts that keep on giving

♥

Say "yes" to this revolutionary call to action

♥

Be a champion of Love, self-love, and Love for All

♥

Michaelene is committed to conscious creativity as a regular life practice, which includes painting, writing, dancing, and photography. A connection to Nature informs her daily living and is a guiding force in her creative adventures. Engaging in a self-curated learning process has fueled her curiosity, exploration, and expression. Her poems have been published in an e-chapbook titled Water, and another was shortlisted in the 2023 Scugog Arts Literary Contest. She is a co-author of the best-selling anthology Reflections on The Art of Living a Fully Expressed Life. A photo of her Tara painting was included in the book Tara Paintings - An Offering to Inspire Your Journey to Personal Freedom. She shares her passion with others and offers coaching to those who wish to tap into their

own creative source. Allowing yourself to be intentionally creative will help you live your best life!

52

EMILY ROSE - What Does Radical Self-Love Mean?

At first glance this seems like the hardest question in the world to answer, you feel stumped, what does it mean? Well, let me tell you what it means to me and maybe that will help you figure out what it means for you.

To me, Radical Self-Love means a total self-care regimen, including: taking prescribed medications and necessary supplements on a regularly scheduled basis, and keeping track of it with an app on my smartphone; getting regular exercise, including physical therapy stretching, light weights and resistance bands; eating a well balanced diet that agrees with my body, mind and spirit, which means actively avoiding certain foods and at the same time making sure my diet is rich in healthy foods that nourish me; getting enough sleep at night and if needed taking full on naps or shorter catnaps during the day to stay well rested; another important part of my radical self-love is taking time every day to read, whether it be fiction or nonfiction, they are both satisfying. And lastly for me, the most important thing I do for myself is prioritizing time for creativity every day, sometimes I do multiple types of creative activities, sometimes it's as simple as photographing a flower, other times it's painting for an hour or writing.

Can you name some Radical Self-Love priorities that you have for yourself?

What Nurtures Your Soul?

When it comes to nurturing my own soul I take a two pronged approach. First, I spend time nourishing my spirit with direct communication with the Divine (God), the Universe, I do this primarily through writing, stream of consciousness, I share whatever comes to me until I have nothing left to say, I used to write it with a pencil in notebooks, now I use a program called Evernote to store my thoughts. Second, I "listen" for Divine inspiration, sometimes it's a thought that pops into my head, other times it's an image or a feeling, then there are those times I feel strong urges to follow a certain path, I may not know where the path leads, it may involve spending money I'm not sure I'll recover, but I leap into the unknown anyway and follow my bliss, I feel my bliss comes from the Divine Source that's both within and around me, and when I follow it, instead of butting heads with it trying to tell it what I "think" should be happening, amazing and wonderful things manifest.

Becoming a manifesting magnet

"How do you become a manifesting magnet?" you ask. This is a journey I am currently experiencing first hand, so let me tell you how it's happening for me now. I've completely poured my heart and soul into learning how to manifest the reality I want to be living and I can already see and feel the life altering shifts happening around and within me. First, it might help you to cleanse your mind with some deep, slow breaths, focusing on the air coming into your lungs through your nose and exiting softly through your nose or mouth. Next, take a pencil or pen and paper, or computer or tablet and open whatever text based software you have available to you and start writing what I call a "Mind Dump," begin with the date at the top, I also like to add the time and then just write whatever comes out of your brain, don't worry about getting stuck or not having anything to say, when your brain feels emptied, it means your done. Try this practice every day, at the same time of day if you can manage it, it helps to build a routine around your practice.

Second, practice "listening," it helps to sit or lay down in a quiet space and just relax and become open to the Divine that is within and around you. It helps to keep a notebook handy if you become inspired so you can jot down your ideas. I call this concept your "Idea Garden." This Idea Garden is where you take the seeds of your ideas and plant them, leave room to add more notes around them or doodles, maybe you just put down one idea per page and leave the rest of the page available to flesh your ideas out further along the line. You may also use an app like Evernote for your Idea Garden. Be sure to include the date of your original idea as a reminder of when it came to you, and perhaps when your ideas have been fulfilled you add a completion date at the bottom of the page. As you fill your Idea Garden you're letting the Divine know what you desire and by writing it down it becomes more a part of your reality. Take time to look over your ideas regularly and jot down notes about progress and remember to date them. It'll help you see just how fast you are manifesting your new reality.

Third, write down your goals, keep a goal journal or a document on your computer or Evernote. Keep track of when you set your goals, and when you complete them you can cross them off and/or you can add a completion date. If it helps to keep track of goals, find an accountability partner and meet regularly, set goals during your meetings and talk about what you've been able to accomplish and cheer each other on. Keep a shared document of your goals that you're working on and talking about together (don't worry you can keep separate goals if you like also). During your meetings you can discuss what goals you've each accomplished and the new goals or continuing goals you have until your next meetup then write down what you intend to do before your next meeting. Keep your goals organized by the dates of your meetups and cross off what you've completed since your last meetup. It's a great way to keep track of how much you've been able to accomplish and having that accountability partner is someone you can count on through thick or thin.

Radical Self-Love means all these things; self care, nourishing your soul, communicating with the Divine (God), creating your "Idea Garden", becoming a Manifesting Magnet, writing your daily "Mind Dump," keeping track of your goals, and getting an accountability partner (If it helps you). Is there anything else that Radical Self-Love means for you?

Emily Rose has been an artist her whole life; she is a creative entrepreneur, delving into the multimedia worlds of fine art and photography, she is also a writer and poet. Her passion is macro photography of nature, primarily insects, flowers, and fungi; she loves to buck the conventional and uses her smartphone in much of her photographic work. When it comes to her passion for painting and drawing she's more of an abstract artist – she paints with her feelings and the music she's listening to. When she writes, it's from her soul – the words flow naturally; she experiments a lot with her writing, especially her poetry. She has her own gallery website and is one of the featured artists in a gallery in Northern Kentucky. Emily also loves to give, gift, and sell note cards with her art and photography on them; she believes in hand-writing notes – that there is a certain kind of beautiful connection with them that you don't get from all our digital means of communication.

Emily has her BA in Business Administration with a concentration in En-

trepreneurship from APUS (American Public University System). She is a member of the Golden Key Honour Society and Delta Mu Delta. She graduated from the Perpich Center for Arts Education (High School) in Minnesota where she learned college-level visual arts. Emily plans to self-publish a book of her poetry, so keep an eye out for it.

53

AMBER PRICE - Finding Focus and Self-Compassion Through Mandala Painting and Mindfulness

Amidst the fast pace and busyness of life, it can be challenging to slow down and focus, much less take care of our heart and mind. Even as a mental health therapist, I have gotten lost in the hustle culture, felt a lack of direction and purpose, and felt like there wasn't enough time to care of myself after trying to take care of my never-ending to-do list. It took rediscovering my creative spark and prioritizing my time spent in creative activities to feel more centered in who I am. This is a story about how I found focus and self-compassion through a practice of mandala painting and mindfulness.

Mandalas are circular patterns that have been created for centuries within many different cultures as a symbol for meditation, focus, and connection to oneself and the universe. Mandalas can be created in many different ways, and I chose to create my mandalas using painted dots. Painting mandalas using dots of paint is a unique style of painting that allows the artist to slow down and focus on creating one dot at a time. This practice has allowed me to enjoy a slower pace of creating art and taught me how to focus on loving each moment, which also extends to loving myself and loving life more fully.

I intentionally pair mindfulness practices with the painted dot technique of creating my mandalas for an experience that offers more depth than simply just painting. By starting with a mindfulness exercise and focusing on my breath, I feel more centered before starting my mandala painting, which also starts at the center with a large dot of paint. I embrace the symbolism that echoes between my actions and the painting process.

Next, I remind myself to be gentle. I use gentle pressure when I place the dots of paint onto my canvas. Also, I use a gentleness in my thoughts to be kind and loving during the painting process rather than expecting or demanding a hurried perfection. I allow for mistakes to happen because I know they are a part of life that I can learn from and I always have a small jar of "oops paint" nearby to help easily take care of mistakes as they happen.

The painting takes time, practice, and patience to complete. It doesn't have to be big. I have painted dotted mandalas on canvases as small as 1.5 inches all the way up to 24 inches, and the process is the same for all of them. I love the experience of mandala painting and mindfulness and I hope you love it too.

The first step toward painting a dotted mandala is a willingness to let go of the never-ending to-do list and take time to try something creative and new. Start by setting up a comfortable workspace and minimize distractions and interruptions. Gather up your materials which will include: a square canvas, pencil, ruler, compass, paints, and mandala dotting tools.

I have simplified the experience of painting dotted mandalas into four steps: center, breathe, gentleness, and radiate. Are you ready to learn a fun, new painting and mindfulness practice that can become a healthy habit for your heart and mind?

Step-by-Step Instructions:

- **Center:** Prepare your canvas by finding the center using a ruler and a pencil. Once you find the center of your canvas, mark the horizontal, vertical, and diagonal lines all the way to the edge of the canvas. Next, use a compass to draw concentric circles every half inch from the center to the edge of the canvas. After the technical stress of marking the center and lines on your canvas, take a moment to center yourself before painting. Notice your surroundings through your five senses: what do you hear, what do you see around you, what do you smell, what do you taste, and what do you feel? Notice without judgment and notice how you are at the center of all of these sensations.

- **Breathe:** Notice your breath as it touches the edges of your nostrils with each inhale and exhale. At any time you feel stressed or frustrated during the painting process, come back to your breath. As you place dots on the canvas, you can also sync your breath with painting by exhaling when you paint a dot.

- **Gentleness:** Practice making painted dots with your dotting tools on a scrap piece of paper before starting on your canvas. Mindfully notice the tool in your hand as you dip it into the paint and gently press it against your scrap paper. You will be transferring a drip of paint to a raised dot onto the paper. When you are ready, go ahead and gently place a large dot at the center of the canvas. You did it. You've made your first mark! Why is it important to celebrate that first dot? It nourishes our creative heart to be encouraging and gentle with yourself. Throughout the painting process, come back to this reminder to practice gentle kindness toward yourself, allow yourself to play and make mistakes, and let go of the need for hurried perfection.

- **Radiate:** After creating the painted center dot, find the smallest mandala dotting tool and place small dots in a ring around the center. Use gentle pressure and hug the dots around the center dot without touching it. Go slow. The trick I like to use is imagining a clock and placing the first four dots at 12, 3, 6, and 9 o'clock. Then, I fill in two dots between the original four to create a ring of twelve dots, just like the twelve hours on a clock. Next, I use the next largest sized mandala dotting tool to create another ring of dots around the first ring, staggering the dots. I continue this process of increasing the tool size and creating concentric rings of dots until I reach the edge of the canvas or until I want to get creative and make different patterns of small and large dots.

Remember to breathe and be gentle with yourself through the doubts and mistakes. Allowing it to be a slow gradual expansion of dots radiating out from the center. There is no rush to get to the end and this mandala painting process can be built over several painting sessions. At various points along the way, I encourage you to stand up and look away and look back at the canvas from further away. Invite the gentleness back. We can be so critical when we are so close to the tiny details of our painting, but seeing the mandala from a different and more distant perspective helps us see the overall pattern more than the mistakes. Notice how far you've come by just painting dots.

This experience of mindfully painting mandalas has allowed me to find a beautiful path towards centering my mind in self-compassion. The process has served as a metaphor for how I approach my day-to-day life when I feel overwhelmed or lost in the hustle. I offer this to you with love and with the hope that we can all make more time for our creative spark to shine.

Amber Price is a multi-passionate creative, therapist, and entrepreneur that believes change IS possible. She supports others in connecting to more mindfulness, hope, and clarity in their lives. Amber has gone from struggling with burnout and an extreme lack of focus at her 9-5 corporate job to rediscovering a healthier mind and a more balanced life through a practice of mindfulness and creativity.

With professional training as a Licensed Professional Counselor, Art Therapist, Certified Coach, and Certified Yoga Teacher, Amber has both the experience and education to support others in their journey to reignite more hope and healthy balance in their lives. She offers clients a unique approach to change that incorporates mindfulness, creativity, and solution-focused conversation.

Also, Amber is the owner of Mindful Yoga and Art STL and offers community yoga classes and art classes in the St. Louis area. In the Fall of 2023, Amber will proudly release her new book called, "Gateway to Creative Possibilities," and will be a co-author within another book entitled, "Radical Self-Love + Creativity."

271

54

PHYLLIS ABBOT - Radical Self Love By Giving Your Body Your Full Attention

Everything good in life happens in your body. Joy, a good laugh, a good cry, a beloved in your arms, a swim in warm water. Our body is how we experience all the sweetness of life. Even sorrow and grief have a sweetness, an aliveness about them because they are real and raw and they are physical sensations in the now. The shortcut to more sweetness and more aliveness in life is to feel more of the sensations in your body. And the simplest method is paying more attention to your body.

I don't mean to say this is easy, but it is simple. After 50 years of self-development and self-realization work, I'm kind of lazy about self-love. I want the most fabulous results for the least amount of effort. And I've taken the best of all I've learned in 50 years and condensed it down to its simplest. It all boils down to your attention, where you put your attention, and how to focus your attention. Your attention is your most powerful force and your most precious resource.

Since most of the aliveness in life is experienced in sensations in your body, putting your attention on the body yields the greatest result with the smallest effort. And I suggest focusing your attention on your body in a new way. In an easy, lazy way. I suggest you focus your attention in a curious way. Use curiosity more than effort. What will happen when I simply feel my belly? Just let my attention wander around my belly in a curious way, feeling any sensation I feel. First, the skin of my belly. Then let my attention explore the muscles under the skin on my belly. Then let my attention wander around noticing anything I feel in the fat on my belly. Oh, yes, I said give your fat your full attention. Try it. It will transform the way you feel about your body. When you do this, you'll likely find a deliciousness in this effortless way of focusing your attention.

Here are 3 ways to focus your attention on your body in an easy, delicious way:

- Close your eyes and put your attention on your tongue. Just feel what your tongue feels like. Slowly rub your tongue over your teeth, so your tongue feels your teeth and your teeth feel your tongue. There's no point, no goal. Just explore the physical sensation in a curious way. Do it until you don't feel curious anymore. The magic is giving the sensation your full attention.

- Put some music on and arrange the speaker so you can lie down with your feet close to and facing the speaker. If you're using a laptop to play music, put it on the couch at your feet. Close your eyes and feel the music with your feet, with your body. Feel whatever you feel. Turn it up if you like. There's nothing that's supposed to happen. Whatever happens, you are feeling your body.

- Stand facing a wall with your toes 1 inch from the wall, feet bare if possible. Arrange your body so it's close to the wall without touching any part of the wall. Close your eyes. Notice if you sense the wall. Notice if any part of your body senses the wall more. Stay with this for a minute if you can. There's no right or wrong. Just be curious about any sensation. Then notice any movement in your body. What movement happens naturally? The focus is curious and soft. Do it until you lose focus. This simple to-do exercise tunes into many layers of subtle ways to sense your body.

Emotions are physical sensations. When we are in our head, and we think "I'm so happy" or "I'm angry" it can seem like a thought. But emotions are physical sensations. You feel emotions in your body. Imagine something that happened recently that made you happy. Or imagine something that would make you really happy and notice what you feel in your body. I notice my face forms a smile, my cheeks move upward, I get an expanded lifted feeling across my upper chest and my whole chest feels a little bigger. It's very pleasant. That's what happiness feels like in my body. You might feel happiness in a different part of your body, so notice what it feels like to you. Men and women tend to experience happiness differently in their bodies.

We receive information from our body and subconscious or our inner genius through physical sensations. When you stub your toe, the message is clear and simple. One big sensation in one small part of the body, and you know exactly what the message is. When you walk down a dark alley alone, the message you get from your body, and the physical sensations you feel, are more complex.

So how do we sort out which sensation is important and what do we do about all these sensations? All sensations are messages. The important thing to know is the entire message is in the sensation. When you give the sensation your full attention, you've done all that is required. Feeling messages from your body does not require thoughts.

Because we are human and we have busy minds, we feel a sensation, then we think about it, assign it a meaning, or think up a story about it. It's natural to think and to think about the sensations in our body, especially when we pay more attention to them. But, the thought, the story, or the interpretation of the sensation is not the message. The sensation is the message. By simply feeling the sensation and giving it your attention, you have received the message. This is a different way to experience life – a richer, more alive way.

So where to begin? By reading this, you began. If you spent time feeling into any of the suggestions in this chapter, you're making progress. There are lots of ancient practices with instructions teaching myriads of ways to tune into your body. You can study any of them. They will work, but it's likely they will be a lot of work. But paying attention can be simple. Using an easy lazy way of paying attention makes it easier. And using curiosity more than effort makes it simpler still.

Start where you are. You can pay attention to the sensations in your body while sitting in silence or while taking a walk, or eating your breakfast. You'll find your style. Once you begin giving your body your undivided attention, don't be surprised if you find your body will help you in finding more and more creative ways to tune into it.

Phyllis Abbott is the developer of the Microbiome Sessions, a bio-hack applying mindfulness and somatics to the microbiome. She's celebrating 50 years of a diverse spiritual practice ranging from Tibetan Buddhism to 12 steps, and leading a life of following her intuition. She teaches folks to communicate and cooperate with their microbiomes to reach genius-level intuition, feel the wisdom in desires, and love their bodies. Phyllis' next project is teaching groups to consciously

communicate with each other's microbes. You can tune into the magic in your gut feelings and experience a free video session right now at the link above.

55

MISTY FULGENCIO - Transformation Through Forgiveness of Self and Others

I looked at myself in the mirror that morning with disgust. What had I done? How did I end up here?

I was always the kid that my parents knew would do the right thing. I never got into trouble. I always pushed myself harder and harder to achieve and to be the best at everything I touched. I still do. But this time was different. At 19 years old I had failed all my college classes because I was too busy partying when I was not working. I drank and drank. Before going off to college I never touched alcohol. I feared it because my mom is an alcoholic. What I had gone through with her, and my family had left many scars on my heart.

My parents came and picked me up from college after I reached out and told them what I was going through. They were disappointed but nothing could top the disappointment they were about to have after I told them I got pregnant a few months later. How could I have let this happen? The words, "I am so disappointed in YOU" were probably the worst words that I could have heard. Those words were like daggers to me. I ruminate on those words for most of my life.

Those words impacted every area and aspect of my life. I was not the mother I should have been with my daughter. I was harsh, overly critical, and domineering, much like my parents were to me. I had failed relationship after failed relationship. I realized I was creating those problems. I was the one that hated myself and thought I was never enough.

Until I entered my forties. My forties have been the most transformative because it is where I found forgiveness. I forgave my parents for saying those things to me and most importantly, I forgave myself for what I perceived I was judged for so many years as "ruining my life". I didn't ruin my life, I created life. I created one of the most beautiful people on the face of this planet. I want to tell you about forgiveness and how it changed me and everything around me.

Forgiveness is a transformative act that can lead to profound healing and personal growth. It encompasses both forgiving yourself and extending forgiveness to others. When I truly embraced forgiveness, I embarked on a journey of radical self-love. By understanding the importance of myself and others, I learned to let go of resentment, pain, and self-judgment, paving the way for inner peace, happiness, and a renewed sense of well-being. My story explores the concept of forgiveness as an act of radical self-love, highlighting its benefits and providing practical strategies for cultivating forgiveness in our lives.

Self-forgiveness is an essential component of radical self-love. Many of us carry the burden of past mistakes, regrets, and self-condemnation, creating a constant cycle of negative self-talk and self-sabotaging behaviors. However, by embracing self-forgiveness, we break free from this harmful pattern and create space for self-acceptance and personal growth.

Self-forgiveness acknowledges our imperfections and recognizes that we are deserving of compassion and understanding. It involves acknowledging the mistake, taking responsibility, and making amends if necessary. By accepting our past actions with kindness rather than judgment, we open ourselves up to learning and growth, allowing us to move forward with a renewed sense of purpose. I want you to have the same. This is why I am including the steps I practice for self-forgiveness.

Steps to practice self-forgiveness.

1. Cultivate self-compassion. This involves treating ourselves with the same kindness and understanding we would offer a close friend facing a similar situation. By acknowledging that everyone makes mistakes and that it is a part of the human experience, we can release ourselves from the shackles of guilt and shame. Engaging in self-reflection and learning from our mistakes enables personal growth and empowers us to make better choices in the future.

2. Extend forgiveness. Extending forgiveness to others is equally transformative and is an act of radical self-love. Holding onto grudges and resentments not only damages our relationships but also harms our mental and emotional well-being. When we forgive others, we free ourselves from the burden of negative emotions, reclaim our power, and create space for healing and growth.

3. Forgiving is not condoning. Forgiving others does not mean condoning their actions or forgetting the harm caused. It is a choice to release ourselves from the grip of anger and resentment, allowing us to move forward with a lighter heart. Forgiveness is not an easy process; it requires courage, vulnerability, and empathy. However, it grants us the opportunity to break free from the cycle of pain and victimhood, enabling us to reclaim our personal power.

4. Extend empathy. One effective way to cultivate forgiveness towards others is through empathy. By trying to understand the perspectives, motivations, and struggles of those who have hurt us, we can develop

a broader outlook and find compassion within ourselves. Additionally, practicing gratitude can help shift our focus from negative experiences to positive aspects of our lives, fostering forgiveness and appreciation for the lessons learned from difficult situations.

Embracing forgiveness as an act of radical self-love offers numerous benefits for our overall well-being. Firstly, it promotes emotional healing by freeing us from the negative emotions associated with past hurts and mistakes. By letting go of resentment and anger, we create space for joy, inner peace, and emotional balance.

Forgiveness also improves our relationships, both with ourselves and with others. When we forgive ourselves, we develop a healthier self-image, build self-esteem, and cultivate self-compassion. You can make that choice today to no longer be the victim. The choice to love yourself radically.

Misty K. Fulgencio, CHLC and RMT, is a Certified Holistic Life Coach, Public Speaker, and Reiki Master Teacher. She is the Founder and Executive Director of the nonprofit organization DFW Women's Club with over 10,000 active members. Through her workshops and courses, she teaches women how to manifest their best lives. She is known for bringing love, high-vibe energy, education, and connection to people in her diverse community and worldwide.

Misty resides just outside of Fort Worth, Texas with her husband and four children.

56

DIANA KNEZEVICI - What Happened When I Meditated For 365 Days

I activated my higher self. It changed my life.

In our fast paced always ON culture, I had a hard time being physically still. I was hyperactive and always on the go. My yoga practice was solely for the physical asana. Here for the "workout," I was disconnected from my emotional, mental and spiritual bodies. During final resting pose (shavasana), I found that even when I was able to quiet my mind, my body remained restless.

Always fidgety and uneasy, it wouldn't slow down.

Several times I rolled up my mat and walked out of class before shavasana started to avoid the awkward moment when I would knock over my neighbor's water bottle with my foot because I knew I couldn't relax or find stillness.

Can you relate?

I began to research the distressed feeling I was experiencing during shavasana in an effort to calm my body down. Reading through possible causes for being on edge, many of my symptoms pointed to an unregulated nervous system. Our bodies thrive when there is a balance between the sympathetic and parasympathetic nervous systems. I was living in a sympathetic freeze state, the "fight or flight" that triggers the body of potential danger and perceived threats. It was chronic stress that kept me stuck in survival mode and completely numb.

Our society tells us we need everything outside of us to feel good, happy, and complete. Success, power, achievement, partner, family, substances, we need, we need, we need. We try not to prioritize how we feel, what to think and what you want. So for my whole life I had an underlying fear of missing out, the need to be involved in everything I was invited to even if I had no immediate desire.

My soul was exhausted.

As I explored my ongoing restlessness further, I knew something needed to change. Off my mat, I was experiencing major digestive issues and excessive thirst; physical signs indicating that it was time to slow down.

After ignoring myself for years, I decided to try a daily meditation practice. I knew I could start small and be consistent as I was committed to bring my body back to safety.

I started with a couple minutes of stillness first thing in the morning. A simple practice focused on my breath worked best as I built up comfort in being motionless. Minute by minute I would find my center, spending more time in my parasympathetic, "rest and digest" nervous system. I was finally beginning to embody a feeling of safety and calmness in my physical self.

Conscious breathing improves both your physical and mental health, yet it is such an underrated and underused tool we ALWAYS have available. For instance, deep belly breathing increases the supply of oxygen to your brain and stimulates the parasympathetic nervous system, which promotes a state of calmness that helps regulate the nervous system.

Your breath is the quickest way to bring you into the present moment. Fully allow yourself to be in the now, not in the past or the future.

Do you want to try?

read first and then practice

Softly close down your eyes.

Take a slow deep breath in through your nose. Expand your ribs out and up as you fill up with a big juicy breath all the way to the crown of your head. Pause for a moment. Open your mouth and sigh it out until you're empty of breath. Seal back up your lips.

Repeat as many times as you want. Continue by breathing at your normal pace.

Congratulations! You meditated!

There's no right or wrong way to meditate despite the nagging voice in your head asking "am I doing it right?" The answer is always: do you have a heightened sense of awareness? Are you more aware of your surroundings, of your own thoughts and feelings? Do you just feel better? A little lighter? Then yes, my friend, you are doing it right.

There were days when I would sit down to meditate and ping, ping, ping!

My mind would be firing off like a pinball machine. Our thoughts are like little pinballs whizzing all over the place setting off bells, flashing lights, and spinning things. We get distracted and follow them around the mind, unsure where we'll land but completely caught up in their journey that we forget we were on our own to heighten awareness.

Welcome to your thinking mind, the crazy pinball machine.

The good news is: **You are not your mind**.

Don't play the game. Let the mind do its pinball thing while you observe, 'sit back,' and surrender.

I would remind myself every day that my logical mind was trying to keep me safe, and meditation is a practice. Meditation made it a bit easier to filter the mental chatter that often gets in the way of appreciating ourselves.

Several months passed and I continued to practice for only a few minutes a day. I felt ready to increase the length of time I was meditating. In this newfound stillness, I discovered a white space.

A blank canvas where I was able to connect to my inner knowing.

Intentionally creating space in my mind empowered me to hear the soul whispers. Those heart pings I was closed off to for so long that were nudging me in the direction of a higher self.

It became louder than the familiarity and the fear of the unknown that had been keeping me safe. Your logical mind will convince you to stay in your current state since it knows the survival rate. Better to be safe than sorry is the mind's mantra. Good thing your higher self is persistent. As I released the fears and healed the wounds, I saw beyond the stagnation and feeling unfulfilled. I took action by trusting my intuition.

The freedom I feel within no longer needs distractions to feel safe. I opened my heart to receive as I continue to uncover who I am.

A year later my breath is light, even and flowing.

My body is open and at peace.

And perhaps one of the greatest rewards of meditation is the sense of be-longing that comes to us. We are no longer lost, frightened and purposeless. We learn to belong and thrive within ourselves.

I set out on a journey seeking to relax in shavasana to experience a state of bliss and I got so much more; it changed my life. I found radical self-love. Creating space to slow down, reflect and heal allowed me to step into the highest version of myself that radiates love and basks in inner peace.

I invite you to join The Power of Stillness, a FREE mini-series I created to bring this magic to you. Use the QR code below for a daily dose of feel-good energy as you embark on your own journey to connect to your higher self.

Diana Knezevici is a magnetic and passionate entrepreneur who specializes in women's leadership and mindfulness. Diana is the founder of Samadhi Gardens, a conscious organization created to inspire, transform and empower the lives of women both professionally and personally.

Her expertise lies in mentoring women through uncovering the invisible barriers that often block their ability to connect with their authentic self. Diana's heart-centered mission is to help them navigate bold action, aligned with their true self to cultivate a deeper sense of fulfillment and joy in their life.

Diana is an honored listee in the 2023 Marquis Who's Who publication for her notable professional achievements.

57

CAROL ARSCOTT - Living Your Purpose

To me, radical self-love is about discovering your purpose and giving yourself the permission to pursue it with your whole being. We are often blinded to our gifts and our purpose – too busy focusing on what we "think" we should be doing. Mindlessly trudging through our days, unaware of the passing of time and how truly precious it is. For me, radical self-love means connecting with my passion and discovering how that can make a difference in the world.

Signs are all around us if we are willing to slow down to notice them. The universe will give you clues. In my case, I ignored the pebbles of wisdom being tossed at me. It took a giant boulder to reawaken my creativity and set me on the path to radical self-love and fulfilling my purpose.

I never felt particularly creative or artistic or inspired. As an only child, I spent many, many hours with my dog - multiple dogs over the years. I felt a deep connection with them but never realized there was a deeper meaning there. I also loved photography, but after a negative experience in my college years, I did not pursue it.

Over the years, there were signs that I should return to photography but I ignored them, as I believed I lacked talent and creativity. Then one day, I fell ill – sicker than I had ever been. I later learned that I came closer to death than I had realized. Luckily, a conscientious doctor stepped in at just the right moment. He put the wheels in motion that would lead to my diagnosis of an autoimmune disease.

I was so sick that I could no longer walk the two blocks from the parking garage to my office. I had to be dropped off and picked up at the door each day by a dear friend/coworker. I was told that I must exercise regularly to manage this disease. My brain said, "That's not going to happen." While shopping with assistance one day, I found an entry-level point-and-shoot camera on clearance and purchased it. I then began taking short walks around the city at lunchtime, taking pictures of flowers, tourists, and buildings. Eventually, I outgrew that camera and upgraded. And then upgraded again, as my skills blossomed.

I truly believe that without that diagnosis, I wouldn't have picked up the camera. I am filled with gratitude every day. And when I have a flare, I remember how it shaped my life and my future, and I am grateful.

In addition to a debilitating autoimmune disease, I was diagnosed with ADHD. That answered so many questions about my perceived shortcomings – why I couldn't pay attention, but why I could hyperfocus on things I loved. Why I was messy and disorganized. Why I was able to think outside the box (I never saw that as creativity). Why I work extremely well under pressure, and why I do not perform well in a structured environment.

All of these things, though seemingly unrelated, were leading me to my purpose. As I continued my photography journey, I began photographing dogs and volunteering with local rescues. That's where the passion really kicked in. I could see that my photos actually had value. They led to adoptions and were a vehicle to raise money for shelters. And then the spark ignited within me to turn it into a business – a business doing what I love while helping animals and rescues. It started as a part-time thing until it was all

I could think about. I realized this was what my soul longed for. I did not want to come to the end of my life and think back on the endless 40-hour weeks of working on spreadsheets and charts. There was certainly purpose to that work, but it was not MY purpose.

I set the intention to quit my job and go full-time in my business. I had no idea how I would do it. And it didn't matter. The important thing was the thought and the belief. Because when you find your purpose and you focus your positive thoughts and attention on it, there is no other option but success.

I am now a full-time pet photographer. In the last year, I have worked with over a dozen rescues and raised over $25,000 for them. Rescue is the cornerstone of my business. I use my gifts to create beautiful artwork for my clients through projects that also benefit rescues. I mentor other photographers to help them create the business of their dreams through one-on-one and group coaching, courses, and in-person workshops. A year ago, I could not have imagined being where I am now. But the miracles continue to unfold as I follow my purpose. Every day is filled with magic and joy and I have received opportunities beyond my wildest dreams.

You, too, have the power to determine and create your life. No one else has the ability to shape your reality. It is ultimately in your hands.

So how can you jump into the pool of radical self-love?

- Identify the thing that makes you the most joyful
- If money were no object, what is the one thing you would love to do every day?
- What brings you the most joy?
- What can you do for hours on end, where you lose track of time?
- Pursue that thing in earnest, with all of your being

- Find ways to develop the skills associated with that thing
- Immerse yourself in it daily, practicing and enjoying being in the moment
- Stop comparing yourself to others. You don't have to be the best, you just need to have the best intentions
- See what benefit that thing brings to the world
- How can it help others?
- Who can benefit from it?

Radical self-love can feel selfish when you are focused on living a life according to society's expectations. But a healing occurs when you find your dharma. When you focus on it, you bring about powerful changes in your life. Opportunities and synergies begin to manifest, showing you the path to the life of your dreams.

Radical self-love is living without regret. The goal at the end of your earthly life is to know that you lived your purpose.

Identify the thing that makes you most joyful. Pursue that thing with your entire being. See how it can benefit others. Our loving Creator wants us to be happy and to use our gifts.

Carol Arscott is an award-winning, internationally recognized pet photographer in the Philadelphia area. She creates custom artwork for her private and commercial clients while raising money for rescues.

Carol mentors other pet photographers through group coaching, online courses, and in-person workshops and also helps individuals in all industries identify their purpose and manifest the life of their dreams!

Carol has appeared on many photography and animal-related podcasts, received the Best of Delco and Best of Main Line awards, and was named a Hometown Hero by 6 ABC for her rescue photography work. She published a book entitled The Heart of DVGRR, benefitting Delaware Valley Golden Retriever Rescue. Her second coffee table book, which benefits Providence Animal Center, will be released in 2024.

Carol and her four boys share their home with dogs, a cat, a bird, a lizard, and an undetermined number of fish.

58

JOAN FULLERTON - Radical Self-Discovery

Our personalities have many sub-personalities, as a symphony orchestra has various instruments, each contributing a different quality. Are you aware of the variations of you? How well do you know yourself?

What could be more helpful than identifying that critical voice and gaining control over the negativity that limits your fantastic potential? And how great would it be to identify and embrace your most creative self for painting, dancing, writing, or other forms of expression?

You will be amazed at how simple, fun, and fascinating it is to name the individual parts of your personality (your sub-personalities). While describing them in detail, you'll discover how they influence and impact your life. This process changed my life overnight for the better.

In my early 40s, I was a single parent with two teenage daughters at home, teaching art in a new role at the local college. I was very overwhelmed professionally. The harder I tried to do my best, the less I felt like I was. Learning and utilizing the theory of "sub-personalities" gave me helpful insight to change my mindset and, ultimately, my experience as a teacher.

Learn how this helped me.

The Process:

1. Recognize and name the voices in your head, their attitudes, and beliefs. Take some time to find and describe six or more versions of yourself. Give them names, genders, ages, and physical descriptions, and explain how they think and act. You may think it weird, but this identification process is valuable!

2. Notice when and how each sub-personality affects your behavior. Consider how you act differently with your mother than with your best friend, differently with your boss than with your children. Sometimes you might be a victim, sometimes a clown, sometimes a mentor—notice who presents themselves and when.

3. Accept, honor, and utilize these sub-personalities where they can best serve your highest potential. Is your most appropriate "self" doing the task they are best suited for? (Journaling or working with a friend or therapist is helpful.)

Get to know my sub-personalities:

Sol, 75, is gregarious and adventurous, curious about the world. He loves getting out of the house; he paints sun-filled watercolors while on location and enjoys cocktail parties, telling stories, and meeting new people.

Sadie, also in her 70's, is married to Sol. She is unassuming and reserved; she delights in homemaking, her children and takes pride in all things domestic. She and Sol often want different things!

Merry is eight years old. She wears fun and colorful clothing and a straw hat with flowers on the brim. Always playful, she giggles at inappropriate times.

Merry creates vibrant, whimsical paintings and brightly painted found object sculptures.

Violet is in her 30s and wears black clothing and lots of silver jewelry. She studies Sacred Geometry, Quantum Physics, and Psychology. Violet is not much for socializing. She prefers solitude, paints intuitively, and revels in mysterious compositions.

Wilma is 50 with red hair and freckles and is menopausal and generally pretty pissed off. She learned to fear life and dislike bad weather, spiders, snakes, loud people, aging, and the unpredictability of life; she's angry. Wilma paints images of her worries to purge her fears, including self-portraits about her physical aging.

Madge, also 50, seems much older. She has over-permed hair, tight lips, and squinty eyes. Madge is a hard worker, a perfectionist who desires control. She knows the "right" way to do everything and how everyone should behave.

Little Joanie is four and very shy. She shrinks from difficulties, is a people pleaser, and listens to Madge. Madge tells her she must be "perfect" and a "good girl."

With my sub-personalities identified, I addressed my dissatisfaction and frustration in the classroom.

Which of my sub-personalities had been teaching my classes? That was easy, Madge! Who would do a better job? Merry, Violet, Sol, anyone but Madge. With this realization, I planned to return to school but NOT take Madge. I would only take the fun-loving, engaging, playful, and imaginative parts of me.

Monday morning (without the voice of Madge in my head insisting everyone pay attention and be impressed by me), I "played at being a professor." I presented an informative, humorous lecture and a creative art assignment, then I "let go" of expectations regarding what my students "should" produce.

When I gave up Madge's narrow expectations, what happened was miraculous. I enjoyed the students; they appreciated the class, and we all became more imaginative artists.

The change in my approach was monumental! I could no longer tolerate Madge's nagging, worried, controlling voice when teaching. I let Madge go. I thought Madge was just a bitch. I didn't like her. As the wisdom of psychology informs us, you should not attempt to eliminate a significant part of yourself. Even a negative archetype has positive attributes. To her credit, Madge is punctual, pays bills and taxes, and is steadfastly responsible. She is needed. However, Madge should refrain from instructing art classes or being the artist painting in the art studio!

As a single parent, I could often become conflicted and insecure about decisions. Should I let my kids go to that party? Once acquainted with my sub-personalities, I imagined them around a table and polled them about situations like a party. Sol said YES, let them go; parties are fun social experiences! Sadie worried about not knowing the hosting parents; Merry voted yes, but Madge was a strict no. It became apparent why I was indecisive. Seeing the conflicting dialogue objectively, I found a compromise.

When I wanted to expand my career, I realized I didn't have a strong warrior persona to go out in the world with my art and teaching. So, I asked myself if I did have one, who would that be? I heard a voice say, Richard.

Richard (the Lion-Hearted) is brave, courageous, and daring. He pushes the boundaries of fear to expand his influence. He is a warrior who wants to make a difference in the world.

295

I did collages of Richard; I did art by Richard. Strong, self-assured, and unapologetic Richard has helped propel me toward larger audiences and greater confidence. I often asked, what would Richard do?

When I was 60, I was going through a second divorce. I felt vulnerable, small, and incapable of starting over again. To help me navigate the uncertainty ahead, I made a collage of "Little Joanie," acknowledging and celebrating her. I focused on Richard, the artist/teacher who had won awards and changed people's lives. I validated my vulnerability and remembered my strength to create a fantastic new chapter for myself!

Discover YOUR sub-personalities for greater self-awareness, or just for fun! I tell my students, "You have to love the one you're with, and YOU are the one you're with." Attention to the different aspects of yourself is a form of self-love.

1. **Make a list. Trust your hunches when identifying your sub-personalities.**
2. **Write about these personalities. Is one of them dominating a situation?**
3. **Are any of them underutilized?**
4. **Do you want to invent a new one?**
5. **Share your insights with friends. Host a dinner party where everyone identifies their sub-personalities and creates collages or paintings.**

Joan Fullerton is an acclaimed international Artist Educator devoted to uplifting others with Art. She is an expert creativity coach who inspires uninhibited humor, the ability to trust your impulses, and to play like a child. Her non-judgmental approach to artmaking expands students' confidence enabling genuine, expressive paintings. Her fine-art career of 50+ years has produced hundreds of poetic images that hang in museums and private collections worldwide.

Fullerton used her MFA painting degree to become an award-winning college art instructor. After 13 years of gaining valuable teaching experience in the classroom, she lived, painted, and exhibited full-time in Taos, NM. When divorce created a need for more income, Fullerton evolved her unique teaching methods to a workshop format and moved to the Denver area. As her reputation grew, she widened her reach well beyond the studio. Now Fullerton inspires audiences internationally.

Featured in several television interviews, painting blogs, magazine articles, and books, Joan Fullerton is most proud of her online art experience, "Paint Yourself Free."

59

JENNIFER WATSON - Radical Self Love For Your Heart

As a long-time cardiac nurse, I find the heart the most fascinating organ -significantly more than just a pump in our chest. It is the powerhouse and the engine of our bodies. The heart is also our essence- intermingling our being with our mind and spirit. It is where we feel, where we love and give and exist. It is where radical self-love thrives.

The heart is the light that shines from within, where we feel most deeply, and the one thing we can honestly share with others. It can break, tear apart, and be the source of healing, blessings, and joy. Our hearts are never so complete as when we truly feel love; our hearts never hurt so deeply as when we lose that love. Our heart's journey is our own. From self-blaming to guilt to a permanent sense of loss, a wounded heart takes us on a journey. We must cultivate the ability to guide and nurture ourselves back from tragedy and loss. Caring for a broken heart that has been torn apart takes time and patience, but there is hope for healing. If you feel a deep sense of loss or heartache, I hope my story can encourage you.

None of our lives turn out how we think they will- it is just a fact. In March 2021- my world changed forever, and my heart was torn and broken. While at work, my 16-year-old son called me to say that his 19-year-old brother was not breathing. He had called 911 and performed CPR; now, the paramedics were working on him. Toxicology reports confirmed that it was accidental fentanyl poisoning from a tainted Xanax. My son did not want to die; the fentanyl epidemic killed him. My life has never been the same, but I have found joy again and a way to count my blessings daily because my heart has learned to gravitate toward radical self-love.

How do you survive the worst day of your life? It starts with a desire to come out on the other end of grief as an even stronger and happier person. It is radical thinking to demand early in your grief journey that you will be happy and fulfilled again while still maintaining the memory of and cherishing a love lost. Such radical self-love happens one heartbeat at a time, one breath at a time, one day at a time. I started by accepting that I could not change what happened. I decided that my sorrow and heartache would not define me for the rest of my life. Instead, I have used grief as a tool in my toolbox to help me rediscover a path to joy, continue counting my blessings, and look for hope and the good around me.

So as your friendly neighborhood "heart nurse", I offer a care plan for Radical Self Love and a journey towards heart health: Here are a few things I have found to be heart healthy.

Find your tribe: Find a tribe of those who hear, support, love, see you, and encourage you to be the best version of yourself. While this is a challenging task if you do not already have a tribe, let me encourage you to find one-seek diligently as if your life depended on it until you find the people who can hold and love you.

Prayer and meditation: Reaching in, reaching out, and reaching up are all part of the journey. I know God is always with me, loves me, and cares for me. Sometimes the quiet times are the most difficult, but it is in those quiet times that we can find peace and learn to feel. Do not be afraid to talk to God-he is always listening.

Leaning in- digging in: Sometimes in the dirt (literally), connecting and grounding yourself to feel and learn to listen to your heart. Leaning in can be awkward initially and only happens after some time; just like a seed, we must find ourselves buried in the dirt and push through the soil to see the light and blossom. It may take years—be patient and give yourself grace and mercy.

Reaching out: When your heart is breaking and hurting so much that you cannot breathe, sometimes the best medicine is to look around. We can always find those who are worse off than we are. Reach out, and by giving to others, we receive joy.

Look for moments that feed our soul: A sunrise, sunset, the moon, a flower, clouds, whatever it is- seek opportunities to connect to beauty and feel alive. In these times of connectedness, we can feel and love more deeply.

Spread sunshine: It is more difficult to feel "down" when lifting others up. It can be awkward at first, but when you give yourself to others, the blessings you receive are medicine to the soul and healing.

Remember your pump (your myocardium or your heart): Seek to do something daily to benefit your cardiovascular system. Taking a short walk, doing a little stretching, getting out, and having a little fitness will help to heal your heart and help keep your pump healthy. As a cardiac nurse, I must insert here that cardiovascular health is essential, and moving–even if just a little every day- is so important to heart health, as is taking care of your mind, body, and soul.

Tend your Temple: Take care of your skin, wear sunscreen, buy age-appropriate skin care products, and learn to enjoy a bubble bath and mani-pedi. These things don't have to be expensive to count.

Seek happiness and peace: Do not let drama steal your joy or let crazy people sabotage your peace and cause you to worry or fret needlessly. Instead, seek like-minded people. Life is far too short to worry about what others think.

Choose happiness: When faced with a choice, choose the path that leads to happiness. Note: (this is not medical advice) Sometimes, chemical imbalance calls for medical intervention that may require medication to help us find our desired happiness. Do not hesitate to contact your PCP (Primary Care Physician) and ask for help. This advice applies to participating in Therapy as well!!!

Make a habit of gratitude: When we count our blessings, it is more challenging to wallow and feel down. If you find this impossible, re-read the previous paragraph and seek chemical assistance as a path to gratitude.

Radical self-love is within our grasp. It can be challenging work, but worth the effort. Evaluate where you are, where you want to be, and then make an action plan. Caring for our minds, bodies, and souls is worth it! If I could tell my younger self a few things, it would be to love fiercely, fight for what you know is right, and stick up for the little guy- sometimes that little guy is you. Remember, you are not alone; you are loved and deserve to feel all the love and happiness. This is Radical Self Love.

Jennifer Watson is a Registered Cardiac Nurse of over 30 years. She was chosen as one of Dallas/Fort Worth Texas's top 100 nurses in 2002 and has since received numerous awards for excellence, holding a national certification as a Nurse Executive and a Master's Degree in Nursing. As a mother to two adopted boys, she is passionate about the plight of orphans and those in foster care (human and otherwise), as well as women's heart health, women's issues, spreading sunshine, and seeking truth.

After losing her 19-year-old son to an accidental fentanyl overdose in 2021, she has become an inspiration, an advocate, and an educator of the fentanyl crisis. Finding healing through prayer and meditation while searching for joy, she believes that there is a purpose in all things and that our journey consists of finding and sharing that purpose with others.

60

WENDY COOPER - Re-Parenting Your Child Self

THREE GUESTS by Jessica Nelson North, 1912
I had a little tea party this afternoon at three
'Twas very small, three guests in all, just I, myself and me.
Myself ate up the sandwiches while I drank up the tea.
'Twas also I who ate the pie, and passed the cake to me.

Imagine turning on your computer in the kitchen of a house you just moved into, and on your screen are multiple pages of text messages between your husband and a woman, the woman who sent them to you anonymously because she saw red flags and wanted to warn you.

Within 24 hours, my husband asked for a divorce and I was told to leave our new home. "Wait a minute! Weren't you the one caught cheating?" In hindsight, I was grateful for the truth. It saved me from wasting my life trying to love someone who devalued me and slowly eroded my self-esteem and well-being. It also explained the red lace panties I found beside my bed the week before and dismissed as our dog sitters'.

Despair and anguish set in immediately. Like someone pouring hot metal into my chest, I let out unfamiliar sounding screams for days until there was no voice left. I couldn't eat, sleep, work, or socialize for *months*. Alone and afraid, suicidal thoughts haunted me. The end of my life as I knew it felt like the end of my life, period.

Sadly, this is not an uncommon occurrence, but if you aren't emotionally centered by nature, or you haven't adequately addressed (with a professional) past traumas in your own life, there will be no moving on. These past traumas may manifest with repeated unhealthy choices or bad behavior. Healing is intentional. It requires out-of-the-box compassion for yourself. It requires rigorous self-reflection to understand your unique behavioral patterns and to change what isn't working in your life.

As a fourth-generation creative in a family of musicians and artists, I'm a free thinker, a non-conformist, a highly sensitive empath, and a successful creative entrepreneur. However, I've also lived through a spectrum of traumas, which slowly morphed into unhealthy relationships and inappropriate behaviors over decades. Being discarded was the emotional and mental final straw, and the impetus for bravely navigating an agonizing crucible of self-reflection to be re-born and find joy. Pain has a purpose. With courage, it is what motivates change.

My own Radical Self-Love happened intuitively. For those of you who do not experience intuitive creativity, what it takes is a willingness to adjust your attitude around self-love... it's not being selfish. It can feel weird, wrong and uncomfortable. People don't normally stop everything to create a bubble of time and space for themselves. Do it anyway. As a wise woman once told me: "You can't change by staying the same." It took me over a year, but I have found my power and purpose and it is awe inspiring.

The following mental exercise is particularly powerful for people who look externally for validation and love. The only person who can take care of the neglected, abused or misunderstood child you is YOU. **No one is going to**

save you. Therefore, you need to re-parent yourself.

Start by closing your eyes in a relaxed setting. Imagine you see yourself as a small child and standing next to you is the adult version of you. You are walking side by side, holding hands. Your wiser adult self tells your innocent child self "I am here for you. I feel your pain. I'm sorry you had to endure _____. I will always love you, accept you and be there for you, no matter what. Tell me your troubles. You did the best you could. You're a wonderful, loving person and I will help you navigate a joyful life." While saying this, look into each other's eyes. Hug. Repeat as many times as necessary for as long as it takes to feel comforted by yourself! It moved me to love and respect myself and I was free to engage in child's play.

- As a child, in upstate New York, I loved the wonder and mystery of the woods. I regularly made forts from large branches, and forest debris that I could think and be still in.

- As a child, I collected many dolls and stuffed animals to play with. I couldn't sleep at night if even one of them looked uncomfortable on the shelf in my room. I had to make all of them comfortable.

- As a child, I loved making houses out of shoe boxes, experimenting with the design of each space, function and flair.

These early pastimes have one thing in common: I was creating intimate spaces, from my imagination or surroundings where my loved ones and I could feel safe, happy and understood. It was precisely those childhood pastimes that emerged as radical self-love while I was vulnerable, frightened and feeling intense despair.

- I made shelters in the trees in my backyard, because I felt troubled and misunderstood. It is a terrifically mindful activity to be one with nature, physically moving in creative play, and it served my need to heal.

- I was compelled to 'play with dolls' (I learned later this is a method of rehabilitation known as Drama Therapy). With a stuffed animal, a vintage troll, a turtle, and the turtle's tiny stuffed lion, I positioned the figures so that whatever emotion or feeling I had any given day would be played out in my choreographed scenes of tension, fear, power, suffering or joy. After 6-8 months, I added two vintage dancing girls because I was finally experiencing light, hope and for me, that meant dancing.

- I do not like to ask for help, especially during periods of depression or anxiety. It took radical self-love to reach out to my people, admitting I needed serious help. I was immensely grateful for the unwavering support and loyalty my friends showed me. To practice my appreciation, I started buying houseplants and naming them after each friend who radically supported me during my crisis. I wanted to nurture them, too.

If you are wondering how you can achieve your peace, here is what I believe: *Make more time for yourself than you feel comfortable having.* I am lucky that I could delegate a lot of my work to an employee, I lived alone, so I didn't have to apologize or ask permission for taking so much time to heal. I gave myself permission, without judgment, to do what I needed to feel better, including nothing.

Whether you consider yourself intuitively creative or not, look back at your own childhood and remember what you loved to do that captivated your soul before life started jading you. Reading? Building things? Exploring? Games with friends? Sports? Nature? Whatever gave you wonder and awe, the natural attributes of a child, can bring you back to wonder and awe and foster a life of abundance, joy, and happiness.

For over four decades, Wendy Cooper has been educating the public about, and selling Fine Art and Oriental Rugs, enhancing people's living spaces with creativity and intimacy.

Wendy Cooper is a respected figure, and expert in the business of exhibiting, promoting and appraising contemporary fine art throughout the US. Disarming, authentic and knowledgeable, she is a stealth risk taker and a career entrepreneur. Her mission: Introducing a curious public to the fascinating odyssey where art and culture meet, which also includes her passion for tribal Oriental rugs. Cooper has vitalized multiple cities in the US with her eponymous galleries and volunteerism for local museums.

With a uniquely gifted ability for observing and understanding patterns of behavior, Cooper's depth of intuition and empathy is an important aspect of serving her clients when engaging in the intimate process of placing art and rugs in their homes, which requires mutual trust and vulnerability.

The Wendy Cooper Gallery and the artists represented were written about in: New York Times, Wall Street Journal, Artforum, Art in America, Artnews, Art on Paper, Modern Painter, New Art Examiner, Business Inc., Chicago Reader, Chicago Tribune, Chicago Sun Times...to name a few.

61

ANNE ALMEIDA - 8 Ways to Love Yourself More

Love. Love always wins. Love is light. Love feels good. Love is in all the songs we sing in a crowd of thousands at a live show. Love brings us together. Love is in all the Disney movies of our childhood. Love is what we crave. Love is what we seek in others.

So why the f*ck does self-love feel so hard? How is it this elusive thing that we give away to everyone else besides ourselves?

I used to equate self-love with arrogance. Believing I was better than someone else was the last thing I ever wanted to feel. We all put our pants on in the morning one leg at a time, how am I better than anyone else? I used to believe self-love was selfish – putting my oxygen mask on before my children's was a joke to me. It was my job as a mother to take care of them first, to put their needs before my own.

I've learned a thing or two in my healing journey. Truth be told, I've learned a million things and more. I had self-love all wrong.

Self-love is not hard. Self-love is not arrogance. Self-love is not selfish.

Self-love is essential. Self-love is radical because so many of us do not feel it.

Self-love is paramount to all things that you want to cultivate in this life.

Because you, my friend, you are the key. You are what you have been waiting for. The world wants you to show up as you. This world needs you. With all of your quirks, weird habits, likes and dislikes, your perceived shortcomings and flaws ... all of the things that make you the beautiful f'ing mosaic of a human being that you are. We need you to be you. There is literally no one else on this planet of 8 billion people that can be you!!

Just as no one else can be you, no one else knows your journey in this life but you. And that can feel crippling if you have your mind constantly telling you all the things you've done wrong. Thankfully, we live in a world of duality. Where there is dark, there is light. Where our mind tells us all the things we've done wrong, our mind can also tell us all the things we've done right. We just need a little help, guidance, and redirection to get us there.

Here are my favorite 8 tips and tools, rooted in energetic principles and supported by science and the laws of the Universe, to get you started on loving yourself more today:

#1. The 1% rule.

The likelihood that you wake up tomorrow shouting from the rooftops "I love me!" may not feel possible at this point in your journey. That is okay! We want to shoot for a 1% change every day. Think about it – 1% every day for a week is 7%. 1% every day for a month is 30%. 1% every day for a year is 365%! It adds up. Every little bit adds up to be something even bigger than you can fathom right now.

#2: Make a list of what you like about yourself.

Go ahead. Make the list. No one is watching or reading it over your shoulder. List all the things that you like about yourself on a piece of paper. Read this list every day to remind yourself who you are.

Now if you find yourself staring at a blank piece of paper and cringing at the thought of even writing one thing down, welcome to my world. It took me five life coaching and healer certifications before I could wrap my mind around this one. I had to approach it a little differently. I made a list of all the things I like in other people – friends, family, mentors. Only then did I realize all the things I like about people in my world are also my own personal attributes.

#3: How do you talk to yourself?

We all talk to ourselves, and yet we all tell ourselves we're weird for doing it. What I want to address is how you talk to yourself.

Do you remind yourself of your intelligence by casually calling yourself an idiot? Or saying how stupid you were to say this or that? Or do you tell yourself how bad you are because you ate a third brownie last night?

Start to notice what you're noticing on a daily basis. I used to be an asshole to myself. This was a habit built over time and no, it didn't go away overnight. But it started to chip away with the 1% change every day. I gave myself the same affectionate name I give people I care about, "lovey". I call people I care about "lovey". And because I care about myself, I also call myself lovey. I call myself lovey in the notes I leave for myself, the alarms on my phone – even in my calendar appointments.

#4: The weight you give something matters AND you have a choice as to how much weight you give something. Where attention goes, energy flows.

When you find yourself on the never-ending loop of a record that won't seem to stop playing – pattern-interrupt the conversation in your head. Pattern interrupts can be physical or verbal, it is whatever works for you. When your mind starts to go down the rabbit hole of belaboring over past conversations or circumstances, try doing 10 jumping jacks or jumping up and down saying "I am a star!". Or give yourself a code word or phrase that means something to you, like "goddess" or "not today lovey" – whatever will help remind you you're teetering on a rabbit hole and choosing not to go down it today.

#5: Hold your own hand. Give yourself a hug.

This is one that you just have to trust me on and try. I used to get so frustrated because I am single. I don't have a partner. I don't have someone to hold my hand and give me a hug. And as it turns out, I don't need someone else to do these things. I needed to do these things for me.

#6: Walk barefoot in the grass.

If you have a dog, clean up after your dog before you do this.

#7: Take a salt bath.

Every grocery store and major shopping center sells salt. If you feel like you don't have time, or baths give you the heebie-jeebies, soak your feet in salt water.

#8: Discover how your body loves to move.

It's no secret that physical activity and movement is good for your body. But what so many of us do is move our bodies in ways that don't feel good to us. We force ourselves to run when we really hate running. The no pain, no gain philosophy is bullshit. Go outside for a walk. Dance in your living room like nobody is watching. Move your body in a way that feels good to you.

There is only one you in a sea of 8 billion other beautiful souls. I do not know your journey personally, but I do know that you are not alone. Give any or all of these things a try for a few days, a week, a month, or a year. I promise you this - your life will change as you start to love yourself more.

As a devoted mother of five children, Anne has always been caring and compas-sionate, but her own journey of healing was ignited by a powerful inner calling.

Having spent 25 years in public accounting with a successful computer science career, Anne seemingly had it all. However, beneath the surface, she felt an increasing sense of discontent and a yearning for a more purposeful existence. This feeling culminated in a deeply transformative dark night of the soul experience that would change the course of her life forever.

During this soul-searching period, Anne confronted past traumas and limiting beliefs that had held her back for far too long. She delved into the depths of her emotions, mind, and energy, seeking answers to profound questions about life, authenticity, and inner healing. Through this challenging journey, she discovered a hidden passion for emotional well-being and a strong desire to help others find their own path to healing.

Fueled by her own transformative experience, Anne embarked on a quest to serve and support others on their healing journeys. She became a certified Love & Authenticity Practitioner, a Whole Healer, an Emotions, Mind and Energy Integration Practitioner and a Geo Love I & II Energy Healer. With her unique background in both computer science and emotional healing, Anne skillfully integrates energy work and solution-oriented approaches to create new neural pathways in the mind, allowing her clients to heal from past traumas and life experiences.

Determined to follow her heart's calling, Anne also embraces her love for movement and wellness. She is a Pilates, Yoga and Dance instructor, using intentions and movement as tools to further support her clients' emotional and physical well-being.

Anne's courageous decision to embrace her own dark night of the soul experience as a catalyst for positive change has transformed her life and the lives of countless others. Her journey from a successful career in accounting to a compassionate and gifted healer reflects the depth of her dedication to guiding others towards self-discovery, healing and authentic living. Through her own personal experiences, Anne has become an inspiring beacon of hope and transformation for all those seeking to find inner peace and genuine fulfillment.

About the Author

Jessica Hughes is a visibility expert for creative entrepreneurs as well as an internationally collected fine artist, 2x #1 bestselling author, and mom of seven.

*She is founder of **Jess Hughes Media** and **Illuminated Press**, a boutique publishing company created to amplify the voices of thought leaders, artists, creatives, educators, and experts.*

*She is the visionary behind #1 International Bestselling **Creative Lifebook Series**. Her passion is supporting the audience growth of hidden gem entrepreneurs so they can step into the spotlight, lead with confidence, and illuminate our world. She offers educational programs, courses, and coaching to support values driven leaders with their mission to create true impact in the world. She teaches the mindset, skillset, and inspired action to be unstoppable.*

Hughes has been a featured expert on ABC, NBC, FOX, TED, Forbes, Chopra, and more.

Interested in contributing to The Creative Lifebook Series?

We want to spread YOUR single creativity hack/tip/strategy to the world so everyone can benefit from your creative genius to live a more creative life. Send an email to hello@jess-hughes.com.

You can connect with me on:

- http://www.jesshughes.com
- http://www.creativelifebook.com
- http://www.facebook.com/jessicahughesfineart

Subscribe to my newsletter:

- http://gowritethatbook.com

Also by Jessica Hughes and Contributors

The Creative Lifebook: Reflections On The Art Of Living A Fully Expressed Life

"Try something with me. Open this book anywhere. Go ahead. Do it right now. What did you find? Do it again. Open the book anywhere. What did you find this time? Pretty cool, right?

You can open this book anywhere, at any time, no matter who you are or what you do, and you will find a useful tip—a shortcut, a hack, an insight, a method, a tool—to help unlock and unblock your creative juices.

And believe me, *we all need this.*"

-Dr. Joe Vitale, foreword author, co-star of The Secret and 80+ bestselling books.